YALE AGRARIAN STUDIES SERIES
James C. Scott, series editor

James C. Scott, *Seeing Like a State: How Certain Schemes to Improve the Human Condition Have Failed*

Steve Striffler, *Chicken: The Dangerous Transformation of America's Favorite Food*

James C. Scott, *The Art of Not Being Governed: An Anarchist History of Upland Southeast Asia*

Michael R. Dove, *The Banana Tree at the Gate: A History of Marginal Peoples and Global Markets in Borneo*

Edwin C. Hagenstein, Sara M. Gregg, and Brian Donahue, eds., *American Georgics: Writings on Farming, Culture, and the Land*

Timothy Pachirat, *Every Twelve Seconds: Industrialized Slaughter and the Politics of Sight*

Brian Gareau, *From Precaution to Profit: Contemporary Challenges to Environmental Protection in the Montreal Protocol*

Kuntala Lahiri-Dutt and Gopa Samanta, *Dancing with the River: People and Life on the Chars of South Asia*

Alon Tal, *All the Trees of the Forest: Israel's Woodlands from the Bible to the Present*

Felix Wemheuer, *Famine Politics in Maoist China and the Soviet Union*

Jenny Leigh Smith, *Works in Progress: Plans and Realities on Soviet Farms, 1930–1963*

Graeme Auld, *Constructing Private Governance: The Rise and Evolution of Forest, Coffee, and Fisheries Certification*

Jess Gilbert, *Planning Democracy: Agrarian Intellectuals and the Intended New Deal*

Jessica Barnes and Michael R. Dove, eds., *Climate Cultures: Anthropological Perspectives on Climate Change*

Shafqat Hussain, *Remoteness and Modernity: Transformation and Continuity in Northern Pakistan*

Edward Dallam Melillo, *Strangers on Familiar Soil: Rediscovering the Chile-California Connection*

Devra I. Jarvis, Toby Hodgkin, Anthony H. D. Brown, John Tuxill, Isabel López Noriega, Melinda Smale, and Bhuwon Sthapit, *Crop Genetic Diversity in the Field and on the Farm: Principles and Applications in Research Practices*

Nancy J. Jacobs, *Birders of Africa: History of a Network*

Catherine A. Corson, *Corridors of Power: The Politics of U.S. Environmental Aid to Madagascar*

Kathryn M. de Luna, *Collecting Food, Cultivating People: Subsistence and Society in Central Africa through the Seventeenth Century*

Carl Death, *The Green State in Africa*

James C. Scott, *Against the Grain: A Deep History of the First Civilizations*

Loka Ashwood, *For-Profit Democracy: Why the Government Is Losing the Trust of Rural America*

Jonah Steinberg, *A Garland of Bones: Child Runaways in India*

Hannah Holleman, *Dust Bowls of Empire: Imperialism, Environmental Politics, and the Injustice of "Green" Capitalism*

Johnhenry Gonzalez, *Maroon Nation: A History of Revolutionary Haiti*

Christian C. Lentz, *Contested Territory: Điện Biên Phủ and the Making of Northwest Vietnam*

Dan Allosso, *Peppermint Kings: A Rural American History*

Jamie Kreiner, *Legions of Pigs in the Early Medieval West*

For a complete list of titles in the Yale Agrarian Studies Series, visit yalebooks.com/agrarian.

Peppermint Kings

Kings

A Rural American History

DAN ALLOSSO

Yale UNIVERSITY PRESS/NEW HAVEN & LONDON

Published with assistance from the foundation established in
memory of Philip Hamilton McMillan of the Class of 1894,
Yale College.

Yale University Press books may be purchased in quantity for
educational, business, or promotional use. For information,
please e-mail sales.press@yale.edu (U.S. office) or sales@yaleup.
co.uk (U.K. office).

Printed in the United States of America.

Library of Congress Control Number: 2019952507
ISBN 978-0-300-23682-8 (hardcover : alk. paper)

A catalogue record for this book is available from the British
Library.

This paper meets the requirements of ANSI/NISO Z39.48-1992
(Permanence of Paper).

10 9 8 7 6 5 4 3 2 1

For my family

Contents

Preface

Peppermint Kings explores often-hidden aspects of rural American history by looking at the stories of the people most responsible for the growing, distilling, and selling of peppermint oil in the long nineteenth century. Although only some of these people self-consciously described themselves as peppermint kings, the group includes Samuel H. Ranney, who introduced peppermint to Ashfield, Massachusetts, the first major center of domestic peppermint oil production; Henry Ranney, who continued working as a merchant and supplier of peppermint oil to essence peddlers in Ashfield when his uncle Samuel and his own immediate family moved to Phelps, New York; Hiram and Leman Hotchkiss, brothers who operated sometimes cooperative but mostly competing peppermint oil businesses in Phelps and Lyons in western New York; and Albert M. Todd, who built a business in Kalamazoo, Michigan, that dominated the world peppermint oil market into the twenty-first century. These peppermint kings all knew or knew of each other, and some even occasionally communicated, since the peppermint oil business in the nineteenth century existed simultaneously in Massachusetts, western New York, and southwestern Michigan. Each region, however, took its turn as the center of the peppermint oil business. Although each region and each peppermint king are considered separately, the ongoing interaction between these regions is an essential element of the story that is readily apparent. The influence of each of the kings on his home region is also apparent, as are those regions' influences on them.

Perhaps the first thing that needs to be said about this book is that it is not about peppermint oil. Although I consider peppermint oil a very interesting commodity, which I enjoy using in its raw form and as an element of many products, this is not a study of ways that peppermint oil has influenced events or changed history. Many historians have focused on the changes produced by commodities, such as the influence on a region like the Caribbean of a commodity like sugar. Others have examined the commodity as a cultural object and explored its symbolic nature and its potential role in art, literature, and public imagination. A recent cultural history of the pumpkin argued that examining Americans' interest in the rarely eaten vegetable informs our understanding of American attitudes toward art, nature, and cultural traditions. There may be a valuable book detailing an interesting story of peppermint oil as a commodity or as a cultural artifact. This is not it.

Nor do I think the peppermint plant or the oil distilled from it has agency. Peppermint oil afforded people an opportunity to accumulate power in their rural settings, but had they not found peppermint I believe they would have kept looking. The people who grew, distilled, sold, marketed, experimented on, and consumed peppermint oil all had agency. This book focuses particularly on the people who, for better or worse, became peppermint kings. The Ranneys and their friends, for example, wanted to change America by eliminating slavery. Ashfield-based peddlers carried abolitionist tracts, despite the distrust and resentment this caused in some communities. Peppermint oil producers who supplied the peddlers took time away from business to organize political action, speak at political rallies, and represent their region in the legislature as "Liberty Men." The Hotchkisses of western New York pioneered modern branding, including the counterintuitive reality that their brands were not that objectively different from other peppermint oils, except that they said so. And they responded to changes in the American financial system and to changing mores in business in ways that illustrate the agency of rural entrepreneurs. Albert M. Todd in Michigan prized education. He sought to educate himself and then his customers on the properties of peppermint oils and objective measures

of purity and quality. And as a politician and social activist, he attempted to educate his fellow congressmen on the corruption of plutocracy,
established a national Public Ownership League to advocate for change,
and supported schools of social science that would teach young people
about social justice. I think the stories of the peppermint kings this book
uncovers each illustrate elements of rural life in nineteenth-century
America that should be more present in our understanding of American
history. Taken together, these stories suggest that nineteenth-century
rural America was a much more interesting place than it is generally
understood to be.

Acknowledgments

Peppermint Kings has been about a decade in the making, although I wouldn't claim it was a decade of solid effort! I came to the history game later in life, so thanks are due first to the people who encouraged me to follow my interests and build a new career after my retirement from high tech. J. B. Shank at the University of Minnesota began an elective on the Enlightenment with a rousing "Welcome!" that I took personally. At Mankato State University, Charles Piehl, Erwin Grieshaber, and Christopher Corley all encouraged my interests and challenged my assumptions. Chris later helped me get my current job, so I am quite in his debt! At the University of Massachusetts Amherst, David Glassberg and Marla Miller helped develop my focus on environmental history and on biography. Christopher Clark at the University of Connecticut graciously agreed to help guide my research, always radiating interest and support. Edward Melillo at Amherst College exposed me to a global version of environmental history and its extensive historiography, and has become a good friend as well as a mentor.

Nancy Gray Garvin and Grace Lesure at the Ashfield Historical Society encouraged my interest in their town and its residents and were always interested in my findings. Ian Blair and Winship Todd welcomed me to the A. M. Todd Company and told interesting tales of their experiences in the peppermint oil business. "Peppermint Patty" Alena opened the H. G. Hotchkiss building in Lyons and gave me a personal tour. And since this history would have been impossible without a *lot* of primary documents, I'm very grateful to the historians and archival staff members at Cornell, the Phelps Historical Society, the Kalamazoo Valley Museum, Western Michigan University, Harvard Business School's Baker Library, and the Records and Archives Department of Ontario County, New York, who were all very welcoming and helpful. Very late in the writing of this book, Cathy Moran Hajo kindly sent me correspondence between my subject, Albert Todd, and heirs, Jane Addams, that added confirmation of a relationship I had only suspected.

Chris Fobare was a generous colleague, who provided valuable insights and offered much-appreciated support and encouragement. Terry Davis at Mankato State University encouraged me to write as I was beginning my serious study of history. Jean Thomson Black at Yale University Press has been a consistently encouraging advocate. My father, Salvatore F. Allosso, has helped me improve my writing over many years and remove a lot of commas. Last but not least, I'm very grateful for the support and encouragement of my family to develop and write this book. When obstacles or other interests threw me off course, they gave me the nudge I needed.

Introduction

According to traditional histories of early American agriculture, frontier agrarian communities were nearly always based on subsistence farming, because the roads were poor.[1] Farm products could not be easily transported to seaport markets, so farmers were unable to sell their surpluses and buy urban manufactures or imports. Rural culture languished until better roads and the growth of local industrial centers caused a farm-products boom.[2] Seeking potential profits, urban capitalists invested in transportation infrastructure like the Erie Canal and early railroads, which spurred agriculture in, and migration to, the Middle West.[3] Backward, somewhat ignorant New England farmers were caught unaware by rapid economic changes and were unable to compete with rich western farmlands. The abandoned farms of the eastern states were quickly overrun with second-growth forests.[4] This vision of early America is considered out-of-date by historians such as Brian Donahue, who observed that, contrary to previous portrayals, commercial farming continued in many New England towns until the end of the nineteenth century, and that, when agriculture did decline, the reduction in planting was balanced by substantial appreciation in the value of farmland being abandoned. Also relevant is William Gilmore-Lehne's discovery that the reading habits of rural New Englanders were much wider and more varied than had previously been suspected.[5] Some of the

specific errors of American agrarian history are less well known, however. *Peppermint Kings*, which begins in a very remote backcountry hill
town that did not even get a telegraph until the 1890s and follows the
rapid adoption and spread of commercial production, addresses some of
these errors.

Since Frederick Jackson Turner's famous speech at the 1893 Columbian Exhibition, westward migration and the frontier have been a
major focus in our understanding of the nineteenth century.[6] Every history that covers territory west of the original coastal republic must in
some way address Turner's frontier thesis.[7] Taking cues from agricultural and economic historians, an earlier generation of historians of
westward migration considered some combination of population pressure, improving transportation networks, and expanding markets for
farm products as the primary enablers of expansion.[8] Initially, many of
these histories repeated Turner's narrative of a frontier experience so
powerful that it even stripped eastern culture and patterns of thought
from the settlers. Migrants in these histories were thought to have returned to an earlier, less civilized state of mind, and social evolution to
have recapitulated at each new outpost on the frontier.[9] *Peppermint
Kings* shows that people moving to the nineteenth-century agricultural
frontier remained deeply embedded in family networks that shared information, retained ties of affection and obligation, and even did business across the miles.

Later historians abandoned Turner's romantic notions of social
evolution and focused on the peculiar eastern traditions settlers took
with them.[10] Some historians of migration focused mainly on immigrants from Europe or on domestic migrants who moved from city to
city.[11] Others explored the cultures of the old, rural New Englanders who
stayed behind.[12] In most cases, these populations of urban migrants or
rural stay-at-homes were treated as individual groups, embedded in distinct cultures little affected by interaction with other groups or indeed
the rest of American society. *Peppermint Kings* suggests that a more accurate depiction would focus on families rather than locations. A mul-
tigenerational look at families shows dynamic, fluid movement of
people, information, and capital between old eastern and new western
communities.

In addition to migration, historians of the early republic have debated the character of economic change. At the turn of the twentieth century, progressive historians such as Charles Beard proposed that economic interests influenced social and political life from the nation's founding. Following Beard, Richard Hofstadter located the roots of the Populists' nostalgia in Jefferson's agrarian myth, and Louis Hartz declared that capitalism had come to America with the Pilgrims. But in the 1970s, social historians began to question the details, timing, and even existence of a transition from pre-commercial agrarian society to a market economy.[13] America's New Social Historians drew both on British social history and on earlier agricultural historians who, following Adam Smith, had argued that commerce could not develop where goods could not reach markets. They suggested that before inexpensive transportation linked producing areas with consumers in American cities, Europe, and the West Indies, many American farmers enjoyed a period of relative isolation, during which they engaged in a "subsistence-surplus" style of agriculture.[14] Farmers produced first for their own family use; only after they had provided for their families did they sell their surpluses in the market. The need to provide a secure, consistent food supply for the family dictated the types and quantities of field crops and livestock farmers chose to raise. And because they only rarely sold commodities for cash, these remote farm communities relied on personal relationships and traded work among themselves, forming elaborate webs of interdependence and mutual obligation.[15] *Peppermint Kings* shows that these remote frontier outposts were not as isolated from markets and consumer culture as they had seemed to be.

As soon as the New Social Historians had articulated this vision of precommercial rural life, factions formed to their political left and right. On the left, historians argued that the rapid expansion of the frontier was due in part to people fleeing as far as possible from the market-driven Atlantic economy. The agrarian frontier, these scholars argued, was a commerce-free haven for Europeans and Americans seeking a life outside the capitalist market.[16] On the right, another group of historians argued that early farmers were keenly interested in getting to market with their surpluses as early and as often as possible, and that even Jeffersonian agrarians were commercial. Farmers did not object to capitalism, these historians insisted; they objected only to aristocratic urban merchants.[17] The argument over the transition to capitalism became heated, the passion frequently reflecting contemporary political divisions rather than irreconcilable historical claims.[18] It is most useful to read this debate, which continues into the twenty-first century, as strong evidence of the variability of nineteenth-century conditions.[19] *Peppermint Kings* suggests that both sides in the debate were right: commerce began early and extended to the remotest frontiers, but rural people imagined their relationship with markets quite differently from the depictions in many histories.

Business and banking histories, like many of the more commerce-friendly histories of the market transition, are usually written by economic historians.[20] In contrast to the industrial orientation and celebratory nature of most business history, a few social historians have focused on frontier manufacturing, on the processing of rural commodities, and on the growth of western cities as intermediaries between eastern markets and western producers.[21] Other historians have chronicled the growth of transportation and communication networks that enabled trade and rural consumerism.[22] And environmental historians have followed the flow of resources from hinterlands to manufacturing centers, the return flow of consumer products to the periphery, and the financial mechanisms that facilitated these transfers.[23] *Peppermint Kings* uncovers a commercial network that existed before the advent of advanced transportation networks, bringing not only consumer products and market sensibilities but also news, information, and even political controversy to the remotest farmsteads of the frontier.

The historiography of banking may actually extend farther back into the nineteenth century than that of manufacturing because accounts of the history of banking were operative in debates about its future.[24] Banking has been socially and politically contested throughout American history, and historians of both nineteenth- and twentieth-century America have entered the fray.[25] Recently, a new generation of business historians has begun to chronicle the histories of state banks before the national banking acts of the Civil War era.[26] But reflecting the traditions of their predecessors, these historians have retained a centralist approach to issues such as credit and capital formation, even while they have extended their view to the varied regional banking regimes of antebellum America. The primary sources explored in *Peppermint Kings* suggest that rural businessmen had very sophisticated ideas about finance and credit, which are not adequately accounted for in center-focused banking histories.

These are some of the main historiographical issues explored in *Peppermint Kings*. By following the stories of three families of leaders in the peppermint oil business, some of whom actually referred to themselves as peppermint kings, I hope to deepen the depiction of rural America in the nineteenth century and to complicate histories of the settling of American frontier, the growth of commerce, and the integration of rural economies in the world market. The peppermint kings were agricultural entrepreneurs. They moved easily between rural and urban settings and were effective in both. They built enterprises that helped expand frontiers of western expansion. They refused to conform to religious, political, and social norms prevalent in the times and places they occupied. And they had a much more complex understanding of their identities and their roles in American society than historians have usually attributed to country people. Not every complication improves a story, but I believe the complications introduced in *Peppermint Kings* add interesting and important insights that deepen our understanding of rural American history.

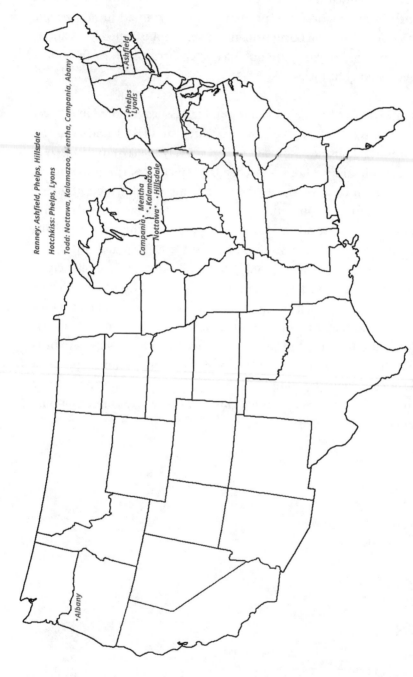

Ranney: Ashfield, Phelps, Hillsdale

Hotchkiss: Phelps, Lyons

Todd: Nottawa, Kalamazoo, Mentha, Campania, Albany

Ashfield

Phelps
Lyons

Campania Mentha
Kalamazoo
Nottawa Hillsdale

Albany

Map of the areas mentioned and the peppermint kings active in them. By the author.

Peppermint in America

Peppermint probably arrived in Connecticut when Samuel Ran-ney, the first peppermint king, was growing up in Middletown. Samuel was born in 1772, while commerce in peppermint makes its first appearance in colonial America in the early 1760s with advertisements for peppermint essence in the *New York Mercury* and the *New York Gazette* in 1763 and 1764.[1] By 1770, advertisements for "Essence of Peppermint . . . an highly useful family medicine" were appearing in other New York newspapers, three Boston papers, and as far away as Pennsylvania and Georgia.[2]

Peppermint essence, made by mixing peppermint oil with alcohol, was first manufactured in the London suburb of Mitcham, where hybrid peppermint plants were first commercially cultivated around 1750. *Mentha piperita*, a hybrid of spearmint and watermint, is a sterile hybrid that can only be propagated via root cuttings called stolons. Peppermint had been discovered growing by the side of streams and millponds in rural Essex in England around 1690.[3] Physicians and apothecaries had quickly recognized peppermint's superior effectiveness in treating all the ailments for which more common mint varieties had been pre-scribed, and for a while they had attempted to keep peppermint secret to create a monopoly. Finally, "a tiny crumb" was smuggled by a rival apothecary and sprouted.[4] By the end of the eighteenth century about a hundred acres of peppermint was grown in Mitcham and three thousand pounds of essential oil distilled annually.[5]

The first advertisement for imported peppermint essence in 1763 described its "very great ... cordial and stomachick effects," claiming peppermint essence "speedily relieves cholick, and gouty pains in the stomach and bowels, and all disorders arising from wind." Most early advertisements specifically offered imported peppermint essence, sometimes "by His Majesty's Royal Letters Patent." Although it is unclear exactly when enterprising merchants first imported British peppermint roots to the colonies for cultivation there, Americans were growing and distilling their own peppermint well before the Revolution. In May 1768, a druggist named Robert Harris placed a notice in the *Pennsylvania Chronicle and Universal Advertiser,* looking to buy "Mint and Peppermint, fresh and in their season—of which any quantity will be purchased."[6]

With the outbreak of the Revolutionary War, distinguishing between British and American peppermint products gained a new urgency for advertisers eager to capitalize on either the newfound patriotism of the rebellious colonists or the loyalty of royalists. Although London peppermint was still considered superior, only royalists carried British products. New York City, occupied by British forces until 1783, was a battlefield for imported and domestic peppermint products. In September 1778, New York's *Royal American Gazette* carried an advertisement for, "By the KING'S PATENT. The Genuine Essence of PEPPER-MINT, SOLD WHOLESALE and RETAIL, BY RICHARD SPEAIGHT, Chymist."[7] A few months later, Atwood's Medicinal Store on Water Street offered readers of the *New York Gazette and Weekly Mercury* "some of the most approved Patent Medicines, such as ... Essence of Peppermint." The domestic nature of Atwood's peppermint essence is confirmed by its offer in the same advertisement of "two commodius, elegant, and compleat chests adapted, with braces, for a Regimental Surgeon to be sold cheap."[8]

The American Revolution was a repudiation of British rule, but not of commerce with Britain. London peppermint was still in demand in America. In the summer of 1784, Boston's *Independent Chronicle and Universal Advertiser* announced, "Just imported, in the Ship UNITED STATES, *A large Assortment of* Drugs and Medicines, Which will be sold

on the lowest terms for Cash or Credit . . . Essence of Peppermint."⁹ Although imported on a ship whose name celebrated the new nation, the
cargo of London peppermint essence and other drugs shows there was
still a ready market for British medicines in the newly united states. Nor
was the perception that premium quality London peppermint commanded higher prices restricted to East Coast cities. In 1784, a western
Massachusetts druggist advertised "Essence of Peppermint. . . . Just imported from London, And to be sold by Ebenezer Hunt jun. At his
Apothecary Store, opposite the Meeting-House, in Northampton."¹⁰
Hunt's advertisements appeared regularly in the *Hampshire Gazette* into
the early 1800s.

By the last decade of the eighteenth century, markets for both English and American peppermint-based medicines were well established
and growing quickly. In Salem, Massachusetts, the apothecary Jonathon
Waldo sold vials of English essence of peppermint for eighteen shillings
and his own domestic essence of peppermint for ten shillings sixpence a
dozen. In 1799, Beverly druggist Robert Rantoul placed an order in London for a variety of English patent medicines and also for "empty vials
in which to put British Oil and Essence of Peppermint." Whether Rantoul actually intended to fill the vials with English peppermint is unknown, but according to historians of patent medicines, "for decades
thereafter the catalogs of wholesale drug firms continued to specify two
grades of various patent medicines for sale, termed 'English' and 'American,' 'true' and 'common,' or 'genuine' and 'imitation.' "¹¹ A druggist's
1797 advertisement in the Providence *United States Chronicle*, for example, announced "MEDICINES, genuine and fresh from EUROPE, which
he will sell wholesale and retail, on as liberal Terms as may be had in
New-England. . . . *True* Essence of Peppermint."¹²

As time passed, domestic peppermint-based medicines gained
ground. In the first decade of the 1800s, growing tensions between the
new republic and Britain led to an American boycott of British products
formalized in the Embargo Act of 1807. American leaders preached self-
sufficiency and domestic manufacture, which gave local peppermint producers a valuable opportunity to expand their markets. In 1806, for
example, the *Eastern Argus* of Portland, Maine, carried a notice for "NEW-
TON'S HIGHLY APPROVED ESSENCE OF PEPPERMINT, Having four times the

strength of the Essence which is in common use, and is eight times as strong as some which is sold for good Essence, and will be always of equal strength. Prices 2/, 3/6 & 6/6."[13] The advertisement made a claim about quality that was no longer tied to the origin of the product, implying that users should be able to distinguish quality peppermint essence without resorting to a simple distinction based on the source nation. In 1811, Dr. Hayward of Norwich, Vermont, advertised "Genuine Essence of Peppermint, Tansy, Gum-Hemlock, and Checkerberry."[14] By this time, the term "genuine" was losing its connotation of British and was beginning to suggest quality and to affirm that the products were really what they claimed to be and were not adulterated with other substances.

The early history of American medicine is tied to the history of plant essences and patent medicines.[15] The term "patent medicine" is inexact. English medicines were first marketed in the eighteenth century by royal patent, but chemical patents did not come into use in the United States until the twentieth. Nostrums that claimed "patent" pedigrees eventually lost their proprietary associations and were manufactured and sold generally. A characteristic of these generic patent medicines was usually a distinctive container that made a medicine easily recognizable to consumers and a recipe often known to all merchants but not to consumers. Essence of peppermint was usually sold in special vials alongside patent preparations such as opodeldoc, balsam of life, and hot drops. As a result, historians sometimes inaccurately refer to peppermint essence as a patent medicine.

In the first half of the nineteenth century, physicians acquired their credentials by training as apprentices with practicing doctors or by attending three- to four-month-long medical lectures loosely affiliated with colleges such as Harvard, Yale, and Dartmouth.[16] In either case, the students became acquainted with a *materia medica* that had its roots in antiquity and wound its way tortuously through the writings of medieval alchemists and early modern natural philosophers. A germ theory of medicine was not firmly established until the final quarter of the nineteenth century, although scientifically minded physicians like Charles Knowlton of Ashfield, Massachusetts, and Oliver Wendell Holmes of Boston began publishing their observations and theories of contagion as early as the 1840s.[17]

The materia medica of the early nineteenth century contained a wild variety of substances, among which peppermint oil and essence were not only benign but also relatively efficacious. Before 1850, physicians routinely prescribed substances like calomel (mercury chloride), antimony, and cantharides (Spanish fly), despite mounting evidence of their toxicity. Debate over medicines gradually expanded from specialist venues such as the *Boston Medical and Surgical Journal* into a public backlash against dangerous and ineffective prescriptions and other heroic treatments such as bloodletting. Frustrated with their physicians, many patients turned to Thomsonian herbalists, hydrotherapists, homeopathists, electerizers, and a tradition of do-it-yourself medicine that was as old as the republic.[18] Peppermint was one of the few medicines upon which orthodox physicians and their critics agreed.

Edinburgh physician William Buchan's *Domestic Medicine*, first published around 1772, spread rapidly through the English-speaking world and was the model for many home health manuals. Buchan mentioned peppermint several times and suggested peppermint water was preferable to brandy for colic and other stomach ailments.[19] Peppermint products became not only key ingredients in many medicines prescribed by physicians but also components of every family's home medical shelf.

In 1798, physician William Currie wrote a pamphlet on cholera in which he offered a dozen prescriptions for the various symptoms of the disease. Peppermint oil ("Minth Piper") was a component of all.[20] The 1788 edition of *The Pennsylvania, Delaware, Maryland, and Virginia Almanack and Ephemeris* cited peppermint essence as a "Recipe for the Cure of the most excruciating Pain in the Region of the Stomach, attended with severe Griping."[21] Edinburgh medical professor William Cullen's two-volume *Treatise of the Materia Medica*, 1789, described "*Mentha Piperita*" as containing "more essential oil than any other species of mint." There was no doubt, Cullen said, "of its answering the purposes of any other species of mint; and the water distilled from it is manifestly more immediately antispasmodic and carminative."[22] In 1793, Isaiah Thomas's Worcester edition of *The Family Female Physician* included dosage instructions for essence of peppermint and the recommendation that Peruvian Bark (quinine) should be administered in a glass of peppermint water.[23]

During the yellow fever outbreak in Philadelphia, William Currie's *Treatise on the synochus icteroides* recommended: "Small doses of a cordial mixture composed of the oil of peppermint and compound spirits of lavender, may be taken until the sickness abates."[24] Dr. Benjamin Rush's *Account of the Bilious Remitting Yellow Fever* copied Currie's peppermint prescription word for word.[25] In 1796, Samuel Hemenway's *Medicine Chests, with Suitable Directions* described essence of peppermint as "good in pains of the stomach, colicky pains, attended with wind, in trembling and nervous complaints, and in sea sickness" and prescribed "20 or 30 drops" taken on sugar or in a cup of warm water.[26] In 1801, Samuel Stearns's *American Herbal; or Materia Medica*, which many historians consider America's first original herbal, listed peppermint as "a stimulant [that] restores the functions of the stomach, promotes digestion, stops vomiting, cures the hiccups, flatulent colic, hysterical depressions, and other like complaines."[27] And in 1802, the *Bee* in Hudson, New York, carried an advertisement for "*A few articles necessary for country life—such as,* Rawson's Bitters, Stoughton's do. Essence of Lemon, Bergamot, Lavender, and Peppermint—Oil of Peppermint."[28]

Physicians considered peppermint not only a valuable remedy in its own right but also an important additive to many medicines whose properties would complement those of the other active ingredients while making the overall mixture more palatable and digestible. In 1807, *Oram's New York Almanac* reminded its readers in its recipe for a "Cure for Dysentery" that "if a considerable portion of the essence of peppermint be added, it will be a valuable improvement of the medicine."[29] In 1814, Connecticut publisher T. M. Skinner printed Howell Rogers's fifty-eight-page manual *On Essences and Their Use*, which advised its readers on the uses and also the preparation of "a variety of tinctures and syrups." Rogers described peppermint essence as a remedy that might be taken regularly "and repeated with safety."[30] Practitioners and patients appreciated the fact that peppermint oil was safe at the dilutions used in essences. Many other remedies of the day, such as calomel and antimony, were highly toxic and unsafe even in the hands of doctors. Peppermint's combination of effectiveness and relative safety made it a valuable addition to both the doctor's bag and the farm family's medicine shelf.

One of the most feared and hated adversaries of professional medicine in the early nineteenth century was Samuel Thomson, a self-taught herbalist from Alstead, New Hampshire. Although today Thomson's treatments seem to have little basis in medical science, at the time they appeared effective. At the very least, unlike the doctors' so-called heroic treatments, Thomson's herbal preparations had the virtue of not damaging the patient further, thereby allowing for natural healing. Thomson's philosophy of medicine revolved around heat, based like some of the ideas of his contemporary physicians on Galen's four humors. Thomson's favorite herb for warming the patient's inner system was lobelia (*Lobelia inflata*). His second line of defense consisted of "Cayenne, Peppermint, Pennyroyal, or any warm article to assist in raising the inward heat."[31] Both mainstream physicians and their Thomsonian opponents had vials of peppermint essence on their shelves of favorite remedies.

Samuel Ranney, who would become the first peppermint king, grew up in Middletown while peppermint was becoming established as an important element of American medicine. The Ranney family, begun by a Scottish immigrant named Thomas Ranney, who was among the original proprietors of the Connecticut town, prospered as Middletown became the most important port between Boston and New York City. Middletown was the northernmost port on the Connecticut River open to ocean shipping, and its population in the year of Samuel's birth exceeded that of New Haven and Hartford. Shipbuilding, the West India trade, and coastal trading had made Middletown wealthy, and steadily increasing property values made it possible for enterprising immigrants who arrived at the right time to leave the city with money in their pockets.

The euphemism "West India trade" refers to the sugar economy of Caribbean islands such as Barbados, based on the forced labor of enslaved Africans. Sugar was a native of Europe introduced to the Americas as part of the Columbian exchange. Although an ancient luxury, sugar became an item of mass consumption when the West Indies enabled "the links between colony and metropolis, fashioned by capital," described by Sidney W. Mintz in his seminal commodity history, *Sweetness and Power*.[32] Repeated grinding and boiling of sugar cane produces table sugar, with the first boiling of the cane creating brown sugar and a by-product, molasses. A second boiling of this raw sugar (which in the seventeenth and eighteenth centuries was often done in Europe) produces white table sugar and a by-product called syrup. West Indian distillers turned molasses into rum, and Europeans distilled syrup with juniper berries to make gin.

But not all West Indian colonies produced rum. Saint Dominique, the French colony on the east side of Hispaniola that became Haiti, threw away its molasses or sold it to smugglers. The French government, in an attempt to protect its domestic wine industry, had outlawed the distilling of anything not made from grapes. And even on the English sugar islands there was enough molasses available to support an export market. Middletown became a center of rum distilling from Caribbean molasses.

According to historian William J. Rorabaugh, during the Revolutionary Era, British North Americans drank four gallons of rum annually per capita. That total is twice as much as all the alcohol modern Americans consume, and it does not count gin, hard cider, beer, ale, wine, brandy, and whiskey, all of which the colonists also consumed in substantial quantities.[33] Before the Revolution, the mainland colonies contained twenty-five sugar refineries and 140 rum distilleries. After the war, these numbers increased. Among the new suppliers was a distillery opened in Middletown that produced six hundred sixty-three-gallon hogsheads of rum per year through the early 1820s.[34]

Thomas Ranney's great-great-grandson George (whose father and grandfather were also named George) was born in the summer of 1746. "In early life," a Ranney family genealogy reluctantly admits, "he was in the West India trade."[35] The experience of George Ranney with Middletown's triangle trade in molasses, rum, and slaves probably began in his youth, well before the American Revolution. It is not known whether he ever went to sea, but by his early thirties George had left the business and quit Middletown altogether. In 1771, he married Esther Hall, daughter of another Middletown founding family. The couple had eight children in the next nine years. The last child, also named George, was born in 1780, the year the family moved to Ashfield, Massachusetts. The senior George bought "a 100-acre farm, most of which was a forest, and built a log house." Remembered as a short, stout man "of industry and perseverance," George senior cleared the parcel with the help of his four sons, and in 1798 he built a two-story frame house that still stands today. George senior's oldest son, Samuel Hall Ranney, was born in 1772 in Middletown. Samuel moved to Ashfield with this family as a young boy in 1780, but he seems to have returned to Middletown frequently. Samuel's uncle Thomas Ranney and his cousin Roswell Ranney had remained in Middletown, but they moved to Ashfield when Samuel was twenty, in 1792. Two years later, Samuel returned to Middletown to marry Polly Stewart, a sea captain's daughter from nearby Branford, Connecticut. Samuel's younger brother Joseph also returned to Middletown in 1801, married a local girl, and remained in Connecticut, working in local quarries until 1818.

Returning regularly to Connecticut in the late 1780s and early 1790s, Samuel Ranney was probably exposed to the distiller's craft there. Middletown's rum distillery was owned by a relative on Samuel's mother's side, the merchant William C. Hall. In 1793, the general store of Ranney's neighbor Selah Norton in Ashfield advertised "Old Jamaican Spirits" as well as "New England Rum" in the *Hampshire Gazette*.[36] It's not difficult to imagine Ranney transporting Hall's Middletown rum and barrels of Caribbean spirits to Ashfield and learning a bit about distilling in the process.

Samuel Raney was unorthodox from a young age: a freethinker of sorts. The bride he returned to Connecticut to marry, Polly Stewart, was the illegitimate daughter of a privateer named William Stewart and a Middletown resident named Lucretia Braddock. Although reputedly descended from the *Mayflower* Braddocks, Lucretia never married William Stewart. When Stewart died in 1779 "in an engagement with the British at sea," he left his estate to a different woman and family. But apparently Polly's ancestry did not concern the sixth-generation descendant of one of Middletown's founders. Samuel married Polly in 1794, and Lucretia's legacy must have been a powerful one. Polly and Samuel's first two children were named Lucretia and Braddock. Their second son was named William.[37]

Traveling between western Massachusetts and central Connecticut with cargoes of rum, Samuel Ranney would hardly have been able to avoid coming into contact with people growing and distilling peppermint. According to an undated western Massachusetts newspaper clipping held at the Ashfield Historical Society, "In 1934, when the former Richard Pritchard house in Lanesboro, almost 150 years old, was being repaired, several documents were discovered. One was a receipt dated Oct. 4, 1811, for 88 pounds, 14 ounces of peppermint oil valued at $440."[38] This is consistent with local stories and with other documents, such as a December 1800 *Pittsfield Sun* advertisement placed by the Lanesboro brewer John Hart for a "Distillery & Brewery, One mile east of the Meeting House in Lanesborough, Where may be had, Beer of the best quality by the Hogshead, Barrel, or less quantity as may suit the purchaser. Also, Essence of Pepper Mint, American and English, warranted genuine, in patent vials, by the single, dozen, gross or thousand. Mint Cordial by the Gallon."[39] Similarly, according to an 1885 history, around 1790 "at the Kitchen [a village in Lanesboro], Nathan Wood had a grist and a saw-mill, and a little later a distillery on the old Lanesborough road near the town line. . . . Peppermint was grown quite extensively and the essence manufactured."[40]

Coming from Middletown, returning there regularly as a young man, and traveling in western Massachusetts gave Samuel Ranney all the exposure he needed to peppermint and distilling. Samuel and Polly established a farm adjacent to George Ranney's land to the south, and in 1821 Samuel built a brick house that still stands beside Route 116 in Ashfield. Samuel began growing and distilling peppermint around 1812, and his brother George, who inherited their father's house and land 1822, quickly turned his fields over to peppermint as well. It is likely that George and Samuel's brother Jesse (who had the farm just north of George's land) also planted peppermint.[41]

The town of Ashfield sits in the Berkshire foothills about twelve miles west of Deerfield. The 1879 *History of the Connecticut Valley* described Ashfield's location as "well watered, though possessing no great waterpower. . . . The surface of the town is broken into hills and valleys, and contains but a comparatively small portion of arable land. Indian corn succeeds well, but English grain is of secondary quality. Wheat is seldom sowed."[42] Ashfield's farmers were unable to grow staple grains in commercial quantities and had no gristmill to grind them. They turned instead to peppermint, distilling, and commerce.

The town was difficult to reach, and its elevation extended and intensified the winters (and still does). When it was incorporated in 1765, it could be reached only by foot or on horseback over rough woodland trails. The first regular stage route, a private weekly mail service from Northampton via Whately, did not begin until 1789. In 1893, lifetime resident Henry Ranney noted that in its early years the town was "peculiar in its extremely isolated condition, for none of the towns adjoining it, on the north, south, east, or west, had received its name or even its first inhabitant."[43] But its isolation did not result in its residents feeling remote from the outside world and its concerns. From their earliest days, Ashfielders were intimately engaged in political and religious struggles often characterized as being more central to urban areas. By the time Samuel Ranney arrived in Ashfield, the seemingly isolated town was rife with religious and economic conflicts of national importance. These conflicts would help shape the development of the Ranney family and the peppermint oil business the Ranneys built in Ashfield and later expanded to western New York and Michigan.

Early in the town's history the first Ashfield settlers were joined by Chileab Smith and his family. Smith was a poor man from Hadley on the Connecticut River who had distinguished himself by siding with revivalist theologian Jonathan Edwards against Solomon Stoddard and his elite supporters, known as the River Gods. Smith settled his family in Ashfield in 1751, and he and his son Ebenezer quickly became notable Massachusetts Baptists. Religious differences exacerbated the wealth inequality among the settlers, driving a wedge between Ashfield residents. This social division was aggravated with the arrival of Israel Williams, the son of William "Hatfield" Williams, a wealthy, Harvard-educated River God and a relative of the Stoddard clan.[44]

Ashfield's town history describes Williams as a man who "seemed unable to resist asserting himself from time to time." In 1762 Williams and his fellow River Gods, many of whom were nonresident proprietors of Ashfield, called a Yale-educated "orthodox" minister to establish a Congregational Church in the town. The minister, Jacob Sherwin, was known for his "virulent opposition to [Baptist] separatists, [and] once ordained he busied himself preaching against the Baptists, and once even barged into one of their meetings and ordered them to disperse."[45]

The college in New Haven would provide several ministers over the years to support the conservative Congregationalists. Against them, the Baptists would appeal to eastern religious leaders, and ultimately to the king himself.

The town's religious controversy was more than merely a contest of words. Until 1753, Massachusetts colonial law had exempted Baptists from attending or supporting the established church, which was Congregational. After his arrival in Ashfield, Israel Williams used his influence in Boston to get the law changed, allowing the new Congregational Church in Ashfield to tax *all* the town's inhabitants. Chileab Smith went to Boston in 1769 to protest the "Ashfield Law," carrying with him not only a petition from the town's Baptist residents but also a "companion petition from a group of Ashfield Congregationalists suggesting, in Smith's words, that 'it is not all the other Society that would thus Oppress us.'" The second petition stated that most of the community had "no objection a Gainst the anabaptest societys Being set free from paying to the maintenances of the other worship which they Do not Belong unto." Historian Mark Williams has suggested that the support Smith and the Baptists received from their Congregationalist neighbors "was a dangerous development for Israel Williams, for it set the non-resident proprietors apart from the majority of inhabitants in whose best interest they were supposedly acting."[46]

The Ashfield Baptists called attention to the irony of the River Gods' position, in town meetings, in Boston, and beyond. Following the Boston Massacre in March 1770, Smith and his supporters sent a "biting petition" to the Massachusetts legislature. Invoking the principles of the rebellious Sons of Liberty, the Ashfielders wrote: "No Taxation can be equitable where such Restraint is laid upon the Taxed as takes from him the Liberty of GIVING his *Own Money Freely*." The conflict began to attract regional attention and was even noticed in Philadelphia. Ezra Stiles, Connecticut's delegate to the Continental Congress and later president of Yale, noted in 1774 a degree of "coolness" in Congress toward the Massachusetts delegation "because of the persecution of the Baptists."[47]

The leaders of the Congregational Church were undeterred, in spite of acting without the enthusiastic support they had claimed from most of the parish. The churchmen seized four hundred acres belonging to the Baptists and sold the land at public auction. The properties consisted of "mowing lands, winter grain, orcharding, one dwelling house of a poor man's, and [the Baptists'] burying place," and they were disposed of "for a very small part of their value."[48] When early America's leading Baptist minister, Isaac Backus, described the events in Ashfield in his *Church History of New England*, he concluded, "This plainly discovers what wickedness is the consequence of supporting religious ministers by force."[49] In addition to his high-handed treatment of his neighbors, the selection by Israel Williams of Jacob Sherwin as pastor of the new Congregational Church was also problematic. The new pastor turned out to be an autocrat, and the church was "constantly distracted by disciplinary issues that drove a wedge between Sherwin and many of his parishioners." To make matters worse, in a town where several of the original settlers were formerly enslaved blacks and poor whites who had endured indenture, Sherwin was a slave owner.[50]

Thomas Hutchinson, the royalist governor of the Bay Colony, forwarded the Ashfield Baptists' petition to London, perhaps thinking it would discredit the revolutionary cause. King George III's Privy Council ruled in favor of the Baptists, and the king decreed their property should be restored to them. This action of the Crown caused Ashfielders to ask some pointed questions when Boston's Committees of Correspondence began soliciting support for their rebellion against the monarchy that became the American Revolution. Chileab Smith called the Sons of Liberty "Sons of Violence," and his son Ebenezer denounced them from the pulpit and said "they were calling themselves sons of liberty and were erecting their liberty poles about the country, but they did not deserve the name, for it was evident that all they wanted was liberty from oppression that they might have the liberty to oppress."[51]

During and after the Revolution, Ashfielders remained jealously protective of the freedoms for which they had fought. In October 1776, a town meeting rejected the idea that the state legislature should be permitted to rewrite Massachusetts's Constitution without popular supervision and resolved "to Oppose the Least Apearanc of them Old Tiranical Laws taking place again." The majority of Ashfielders continued to push for an interpretation of liberty that was much more egalitarian than the society envisioned by the River Gods and their elite allies in Boston. In October 1774 the town voted "to Give Liberty for all men to vote in this meeting that are town Inhabitence that are twenty one years old and upward," at a time when 40 percent of Ashfield's taxpayers did not meet the property limits required for voters. And in October 1779 the Ashfield town meeting instructed the town's delegates in Boston to advocate a "Legislative Court" to govern the state. Its members would be chosen by "ye Several Towns & . . . every Man being 21 years of Age who has not by his own Act forfeited his Freedom Shall be accounted free and have a Right to Vote." Finally, beginning a long tradition of abolitionism, Ashfielders declared that even slaves should vote. And they stated that the legislature's "Business shall be to protect all Persons in ye free Enjoyment of their religious Sentiments So far as they are good and peacibul Inhabitants."[52]

When the Ranney family relocated from Connecticut to Ashfield in 1780, they discovered a town that held fast to its vision of liberty in spite of worsening economic conditions. At a 1783 town meeting, residents denounced taxation without representation and resolved: "We will not pay the five & twenty shilling State Tax on the pole Nor no other State Nor County Tax or Taxes is or may be Assessed upon the Town of Ashfield until we are informed by Genl Cort or Some other Authority the perticular use the said Money is Designed for." To prevent militia officers being called to use their authority to enforce the taxes, the meeting called on the town's officers to "resine their Commissions." Although it has been traditional to characterize the "regulators" of Shays' Rebellion as debtors, peasants, and poor Revolutionary War veterans angry over scrip speculation, Mark Williams has observed that the regulators of Ashfield were the town's 1776 militiamen, acting as "the executive arm of a whole town in rebellion." The townspeople's continuing "stream of objections to the republicanism of the eastern elite," Williams concludes, "contain a bold foray into a radical political culture that was neither traditional nor peasant-minded."[53] Ashfield residents, far from feeling cut off from the religious and political controversies of their day, thrust themselves into the forefront of national and even international issues.

Among Ashfield's regulators in Shays' Rebellion were brothers Samuel and Lamberton Allen. Cousins of Vermont's heroes and leaders of the Green Mountain Boys, Ethan and Ira Allen, Samuel and Lamberton had arrived in Ashfield around 1770 from Deerfield. Samuel was a lieutenant in the Revolution who had reenlisted three times and captain of the company that marched from Ashfield to aid in Daniel Shays' harassment of foreclosure courts and attack on the Springfield armory. The Allen brothers appear often in town records, but they were disfranchised for refusing to accept official pardon, and their names are conspicuously absent from the list of those who took the oath of allegiance following Shays' Rebellion. Samuel was apparently a bit eccentric and was remembered by Ashfield residents who had known him as "Barefoot Allen." He and Lamberton moved to Grand Isle, Vermont, in 1780 after selling their mostly wooded hundred-acre "farm" to George Ranney.[54] Ranney took advantage of the opportunity to buy a flat, well-watered parcel when the Allens decided to move to a territory even more radical than Ashfield (Vermont did not become a state until 1791). Ranney's son Samuel continued the Allens' tradition of leadership and free-thinking when he introduced peppermint to Ashfield and later helped move the peppermint industry west.

In the next chapter, we examine the history of Ashfield's stills, the essence-peddling business run by the Ranneys and their friends, the development of a wholesale peppermint oil market, and the expansion of the Ranney family across the western frontier.

Essence and Peddlers

The remote Massachusetts hill town of Ashfield was not the most obvious base of operation for an essence-peddling business. The first road into the town was a woodland trail from Deerfield and the Connecticut River Valley. Weekly stage and post service from Northampton was not established until 1789, and there was no post office until 1814, when Levi Cook became postmaster and devoted a corner of his saddle shop to distributing the weekly mail. All of Ashfield celebrated in March 1824 when a daily mail stage from Greenfield to Albany, New York, began making early morning stops.[1] The stage started from Greenfield at three o'clock each morning and reached Ashfield via Conway between five and six. According to a resident who remembered the service, "It was a lively scene when in the early dawn, with the bugle blasts, the four horse coach rolled into the street from the east with its eight or ten passengers, pulled up at the hotel to change horses, while Esquire Cook hurried to change the mail; then on through Spruce Corner and Plainfield . . . to Bowker's in Savoy, to Adams, and on to Albany, where they arrived the next morning at three." The fare from Greenfield to Albany was three dollars.[2]

Peppermint oil had likely been carried through the Berkshires along what would become the mail route between Ashfield and Albany long before Samuel Ranney brought peppermint roots to Ashfield.

Lanesboro distillers had grown, distilled, and sold peppermint oil and essence since 1800, and Pittsfield and Lenox entered the business in the 1820s.[3] But the unprecedented scale of peppermint growing in Ashfield and the lucrative peddler trade Henry Ranney helped develop brought Ashfield the lion's share of the credit for propelling the peppermint oil industry through its first phase of development.

From the time that Samuel Ranney first planted peppermint roots in Ashfield, around 1812, the town's peppermint oil business grew rapidly. Many histories of agriculture and of the "market transition" in the early republic focus on the subsistence-first nature of farming, especially in remote rural communities.[4] Historians observe that commodities such as wheat, barley, and apples had primary uses as food products. Surpluses might be fermented and distilled for storage, home use, or sale, but these uses were secondary. In contrast, peppermint was not a food and had limited value as a perishable fresh herb. The only reason to plant fields of peppermint was to distill it and sell the oil. All the primary accounts of distilling in Ashfield agree that although the town's stills were occasionally used to produce other spirits, they were built to process peppermint and other essential oils. Counting Ashfield's stills in the 1820s and early 1830s thus shows the rapid growth of the peppermint business and its abrupt change around 1835.

Ashfield's tax records for 1826 show that Samuel Ranney's property consisted of "2 Houses 2 Barns & Sheds, 35 acres improved Land, 56 D[itt]o unimproved, 1 still & still house." Samuel built the sprawling house that still stands by the side of Route 116 in 1821. His brothers Jesse and George Jr. had similar improved acreages nearby and presumably distilled their peppermint using his still. Samuel's cousin Roswell Ranney owned "2 Houses 2 Barns & Sheds, 1 still, still house & Cider Mill & other buildings, 1 sawmill, gristmill, 117 acres improved land, 100 D[itt]o unimproved." Although a later arrival to Ashfield than his cousins, by the mid-1820s Roswell was already one of the town's most prosperous farmers.[5]

Roswell, the son of George Ranney Sr.'s younger brother Thomas, had arrived in Ashfield in 1792 at the age of ten. He was an energetic young man and in 1821 was one of only ten farmers in the town who managed to harvest as much as fifty bushels of corn annually. In 1803, Roswell married Irinda Bement, a cousin of the local merchant Jasper

Bement, who later mentored Henry Ranney in his mercantile business and entered the essence business. Roswell was active in local politics, leading town meetings and serving twice as militia captain and twice as representative to the legislature in Boston.[6]

In 1828, Ashfield's tax assessors found even more stills. Roswell's brother-in-law Samuel Bement owned a "Still & House." Jasper Bement had built a still and a still house and had a half-interest in a cider mill. A few more cider mills appeared over the years, and since peppermint distilling is seasonal work, Ashfield's stills were occasionally put to other uses in the off-season. But the fact that Ashfield never produced a surplus of grain supports the claim made in all the memoirs and histories that the main purpose of Ashfield's stills was distilling peppermint and other essential oils.[7] By 1830, the number of peppermint distillers in Ashfield had increased dramatically. Tax assessors listed ten stills in operation. In addition to Samuel and Roswell Ranney and Jasper Bement, five other Ashfield farmers had built stills and still houses. Even the namesake nephew of River God Israel Williams operated two stills. Although local distillers did not know it at the time, the 1830 assessment marked the peak of peppermint oil production in Ashfield.

Itinerant sales or peddling is probably as old as civilization. The practice was well established in Europe in the Middle Ages and seems to have begun in the Americas as soon as Europeans settled here.[8] Peddlers sold a surprisingly wide variety of goods in early America, ranging from small, inexpensive items such as pins, ribbons, and buttons to tinware, clocks, pottery, chairs, and even washing machines. Low population density and underdeveloped transportation networks made peddling a relatively efficient way to bring manufactured goods to rural markets, and the presence of a salesman in a remote farmyard or kitchen was a strong influence on rural people to consume goods produced beyond the bounds of home production or even their local market. Some historians have suggested that peddlers helped create a culture of consumption in early America.[9]

Most histories of peddling focus on two well-documented groups of peddlers: the Yankee peddlers of Connecticut and the Jewish peddlers of the second half of the nineteenth century.[10] An important group of early American peddlers has been all but forgotten. Although essence peddlers were ubiquitous enough in the first half of the nineteenth century to become the subjects of songs, jokes, cartoons, and the source of a slang term for skunk, a contemporary search for the term "essence peddler" in historical writing returns only a 1949 article entitled "The Social Significance of the Language of the American Frontier."[11] The fact that this article locates the origin of "essence peddler" on the American frontier in 1838, however, is telling. Young men from Ashfield were frequent enough visitors to remote frontier farmsteads that they were memorialized in language long after their disappearance from the American social scene.

Closer to home and to their own time, some nineteenth-century regional historians remembered the trunk- and basket-carrying foot peddlers of Ashfield in their histories of the region. An 1888 history of Ashfield remarked that it was "not far from truth to say that about the first and second generations in the present century of New England youths, when they attained to years approaching manhood, invariably supplied themselves with a pair of willow baskets or tin trunks, and with these well filled with oils, essences, pins, needles, thread, etc., suspended from their shoulders with a yoke, started out from the parental fireside to 'see the world' and prospect for a situation in life." The local historian recalled that "*many thousands* of these young men, full of life and energy, and Yankee sagacity, thus equipped, perambulated New York and the western States" (original emphasis). Young men from Ashfield visited "all the newer sections of the West," and many found themselves homes and careers in the territories they had explored as itinerant salesmen. Although a bit self-congratulatory, these accounts make the important point that Ashfield peddlers helped spread not only commerce into newly settled western regions but also some degree of the Yankee culture the historians regarded as "New England's best genius, independence and love of justice and liberty."[12]

A few historians have joined Ashfield's locals in recognizing essence peddlers. Richardson Wright, an early historian of peddling, wrote that peddlers covered the entire settled area of the United States and "played an unforgettable role in the romance of our early widening frontiers." Wright observed, "Even Horn's *Overland Guide to California*—the

Baedecker of the forty-niners—contains the advertisement of a Mr. Sypher in Fort Des Moines, who is willing to supply peddlers . . . at the lowest possible rates." "The essence peddler," continued Wright, "was quite a different sort" from the typical Yankee peddler. "Usually a free-lance, he managed to scrape together ten or twenty dollars [and] fill his tin trunk with peppermint, bergamot, and wintergreen extracts and bitters. In the backwoods these bitters were in great demand. They were mixed with the local brand of homemade liquor. . . . Other extracts were used as remedies and antidotes." Undoubtedly the use of essences to flavor unpalatable local alcohol, in addition to the medical uses discussed earlier, would have substantially expanded the market for peppermint and other strongly flavored essences.[13] An indication that Wright may have been correct about the popularity of essences as flavorings for alcohol can be seen in an 1802 advertisement by a Philadelphia distillery: "The Large Rum Distillery in New Street, No. 13. Is now taking in Molasses, returnable in good flavored Rum. . . . Where also, may constantly be had on exchange or otherwise Anniseed, Cinnamon, Peppermint, Caraway . . . and other Cordials in usual request."[14]

Some historians of the market transition have suggested that remote frontier settlements operated without commerce; a few have even claimed that settlers may have fled to the frontier to escape the "getting and spending" of eastern cities.[15] The story of peddling, in contrast, suggests that peddlers brought manufactured goods and market sensibilities to the remotest frontier outposts.[16] However much peddling may be implicated in the market transition, it is clear that peddlers helped people moving to the frontiers retain a connection with Atlantic commercial markets that had existed since Europeans began coming to the Americas. Peddling was a continuation of a type of commerce that had existed in Europe long before the colonial era. As American families moved westward, away from coastal cities, peddlers kept them connected with economies beyond their remote rural communities. Many historians have characterized rural people as producers of food and raw material for urban and export markets, suggesting that farmers in remote districts did not become consumers until merchants were able to ship urban goods to their stores via rivers, canals, or rail.[17] Yankee peddlers who visited farms and villages in remote areas of their own regions as well as on the frontier were of great cultural significance. They brought news, ideas, and an opportunity to be consumers as well as producers to people who might not otherwise have had these options.

In some cases, historical references to Ashfield's essence peddlers have been mistaken for accounts of their Yankee confederates in Connecticut. A passage from Nathaniel Hawthorne's diary that often finds its way into such comingled accounts actually mentions Ashfield by name. Hawthorne described a trip by coach from Worcester to Northampton in the mid-1830s. After riding outside for most of the day chatting with the driver, Hawthorne said the coach "took up an essence-vendor for a short distance. He was returning home, after having been out on a tour two or three weeks, and had nearly exhausted his stock. He was not exclusively an essence-pedlar, having a large tin box, which had been filled with dry goods, combs, jewelry, &c., now mostly sold out." The essences, Hawthorne discovered, "are concocted at Ashfield, and the pedlars are sent about with vast quantities."

Hawthorne wrote that the peddler was "good-natured and communicative, and spoke very frankly about his trade, which he seemed to like better than farming, though his experience of it [was] yet brief." The young Ashfielder "spoke of the trials of temper to which pedlars are subjected, but said that it was necessary to be forbearing, because the same road must be traveled again and again. The pedlars find satisfaction for all contumelies in making good bargains out of their customers," Hawthorne explained. The peddler was on a short circuit but was considering making a longer trip westward, "in which case he would send on quantities of his wares ahead to different stations." Sending resupply shipments to stops along a larger route helped peddlers avoid carrying too much inventory. Hawthorne concluded that the "driver was an acquaintance of the pedlar, and so gave him his drive for nothing, though the pedlar pretended to wish to force some silver into his hand; and afterwards he got down to water the horses, while the driver was busy with other matters."[18]

Hawthorne's observations highlight important details of Ashfield peddlers' work. Most were young men, and many peddled for just a short time to raise a stake and enter another venture. Most traveled on foot, carrying wicker baskets of essences and tin trunks of other goods, suspended by webbing and sometimes hung from a wooden yoke. Occasionally peddlers traveled in wagons, but this was much less prevalent with Ashfielders than with tinsmiths or the Connecticut vendors of bulky items like clocks. More often, a peddler traveling a lengthy route planned ahead and shipped resupplies to post offices along the route. Sometimes, when sales exceeded expectations, peddlers wrote to the Ashfield merchants who supplied them, to have additional stock forwarded to the next town on their way. These requests depended on the post, because the telegraph did not reach Ashfield until the 1890s.[19]

Hawthorne mentioned the "contumelies" experienced by peddlers. Anyone who has worked in sales can imagine the frustrations faced by door-to-door salesmen; but in many remote communities, peddlers were welcomed, or at least tolerated, because they carried needed products. Although peddlers like the young men of Ashfield became subjects of cartoons, jokes, and even popular songs, there was great demand for the products they carried.[20] And despite contemporary accounts like Thomas Hamilton's 1833 "Men and Manners in America," which claimed, "The whole race of Yankee peddlers in particular are proverbial for dishonesty," the numbers of New Englanders making their fortunes as salesmen increased throughout the first half of the century. Hamilton complained, "They go forth annually in the thousands to lie, cog, cheat, swindle, in short, to get possession of their neighbor's property in any manner it can be done with impunity. Their ingenuity in deception is confessedly very great."[21] He was right, at least with respect to the peddlers' numbers. In 1850 one account estimated there were 10,669 peddlers traveling America's roads. A decade later, the number had grown to 16,595.[22]

Although other itinerant salesmen offered lines of credit to their customers, and often priced products such as clocks and furniture to reflect carried interest and the risks and costs of collection, Ashfield peddlers did their business using cash.[23] They carried hard money, and as a result many traveled armed. In addition to essences, other wares, and the baskets and trunks used to carry them, Ashfield merchants like Jasper Bement and Henry Ranney occasionally sold pistols to the young men they sent out on the road. For example, when Ashfield essence peddler Sextus Lilly made his first peddling trip in July 1840, his bill in

Bement's ledger included ten dozen essences, a variety of patent medicines, thread, needles, ink, pencils, combs, a basket for carrying the
essences (67 cents), three yards of webbing (34 cents), a lock (12 cents),
and a brass pistol ($1.38).[24]

Most of the peddlers of Ashfield were supplied by Jasper Bement
and Henry Ranney. Other families, like the Beldings, were very active in
the production and sale of peppermint oil. But Jasper Bement, with his
son Joseph and their longtime friend and partner Henry Ranney, were
the focus of Ashfield's peddler business. Jasper Bement, whose cousin
Irinda had married Roswell Ranney in 1803, had been involved with
peppermint since at least the 1820s. Bement was among the owners of a
still and still house listed in the Ashfield tax records of the 1820s and
early 1830s. He opened a general store in Ashfield in the 1830s and either
originated or quickly took over the provisioning of peddlers with Yankee notions and essences. When the R. G. Dun Company's local credit
investigator reported on Bement in September 1841, he described the
business as "General Store. Jewelry. Patent Med, Yankee notions, &c."
and rated Bement's creditworthiness as "good." Two years later, the reporter added: "Good, consid prop, mtgs [mortgages], money at interest
&c. besides what he has in trade."[25]

Henry Sears Ranney (1817–1899) was the third son of George Ranney Jr. and grandson of the elder George Ranney who had moved to
Ashfield from Middletown in 1780. His uncle Samuel had introduced
peppermint to Ashfield five years before Henry was born. When his father moved the family to Phelps, New York, in August 1833, sixteen-year-
old Henry remained in Ashfield to pursue a career as a merchant. He
clerked for Jasper Bement and lived in Bement's household for a time,
preparing himself for life as a merchant in Ashfield and briefly in Boston. In 1893, Henry remembered Bement as "a successful merchant; a
public-spirited man of strong and sterling characteristics, the most pro-
nounced and active abolitionist & free-soiler of this region." Henry had
received his start in business working as a clerk in the store Bement
owned and "a member of his family for six years—during which time,"
Henry observed, "I failed to receive from him a cross or impatient
word."[26] In addition to their business association, Bement and Henry
were both committed to the cause of abolishing slavery in America.

The entire Ranney family objected to the institution of chattel slavery, as demonstrated in letters between Henry Ranney and his brothers that Henry collected throughout the nineteenth century. Henry's friends were also Free-Soilers, and many of those activists were peddlers. Although they helped rural people remain connected to the wider world through the products they carried and their interactions with customers, Yankee peddlers were not welcomed by everyone when they arrived in a new town. Local merchants often saw the itinerants as competitors, and as early as 1717 Connecticut peddlers (who, as mentioned, often traveled with wagonloads of big-ticket items) found themselves taxed twenty shillings for each hundred pounds of goods they carried into a particular town. By the middle of the eighteenth century, many states had enacted license fees for peddlers.[27] Historian Richardson Wright remarked, "We can trace the dislike of the town for the country through practically all phases of itinerant life." Despite the fact that "had there been no peddlers there would have been no countryside distribution, and . . . manufacturing, even of the humblest household sort, could never have survived, the peddler's foe was the established, settled, town merchant."[28] But commercial rivalry was not the only reason peddlers were unwelcome. Another cause, especially in the South, was that many peddlers were quite political. Henry Ranney's customer and good friend the Ashfield career peddler William Sanderson was an ardent abolitionist who mentioned "Liberty Party" and "Free-Soil" politics regularly in letters to Henry. Along with the essences and "Yankee notions" in his inventory, Sanderson regularly carried copies of *Slavery as It Is, Testimony of a Thousand Witnesses*, a 225-page jeremiad written by Theodore Dwight Weld for the Anti-Slavery Society in 1839.[29] Although Sanderson and peddlers like him probably found many appreciative customers for abolitionist tracts in the New England countryside, their frankly expressed politics also alienated many, especially in the South and the West. If profits were paramount, it would have been much more prudent for peddlers to leave their politics at home. Ashfield peddlers like Sanderson continued the town's long-standing tradition of political engagement, once again blurring the boundaries between local and national activism.

William Sanderson was one of Ashfield's busiest peddlers in the late 1830s. In a single season, Sanderson made twenty trips, buying supplies from Henry Ranney and Jasper Bement every two and a half weeks. Bement and Ranney often sent Sanderson resupply orders to points as far from Ashfield as Brattleboro, Vermont, and Pittsfield, Massachusetts. Sanderson's average order size for a trip was about fifty dollars. Sanderson paid forty cents for a dozen vials of Bement's premium peppermint essence, six cents for pencils, forty-five cents for razors, thirty-seven and a half cents for a gross of pearl buttons, and $1.88 for a box of a thousand needles. It's not difficult to imagine Sanderson at least doubling his money on each trip.[30]

Bement and Ranney supplied more than 120 peddlers annually. About half of them traveled at least once a month during the peddling season. Unlike Connecticut peddlers of tinware and clocks, who usually worked for wages, most of Ashfield's essence peddlers were self-employed. Bement's account books include only a couple of entries out of hundreds where the merchant seems to have paid a peddler to make a trip, and those entries could be interpreted in other ways. Bement had business relationships with people in many of the towns his peddlers visited, and peddlers often carried letters, goods, and cash for Ashfield businessmen. Nearly all the transactions with peddlers recorded in Bement's account books were inventories of goods, charged to the peddler. Bement outfitted most of his peddlers on credit, which is unsurprising, as most of the young peddlers came from local families that did regular business with Bement. All the records listed products charged at consistent wholesale prices, indicating that the peddler set the retail price of his wares and pocketed the profit.[31]

Like Ranney and Bement's other peddlers, William Sanderson took a wide variety of items, but by volume and by weight his most significant cargoes were always vials of essences, mostly peppermint. Peddlers regularly left Ashfield with baskets containing from twenty to a hundred dozen glass vials of essences, the most popular being peppermint. Essence vials were bulky, heavy, and fragile. They must have been uncomfortable to carry, but they were the Ashfield peddler's core product line. Bement didn't have to pay the young men to distribute his products: their popularity with the peddlers' customers and their profitability made essences the leading product of Ashfield's salesmen.

After several years of peddling, William Sanderson gained enough experience and made enough money to start his own general store in the nearby town of Whately. Still interested in politics, Sanderson corresponded with his friend Henry Ranney regularly. In the summer of 1845, Sanderson wrote: "The wind blows softly by my cottage, the cats fight nights, Whigs twist and turn to get into office and prevent slavery. Democrats brow beat them for so doing, but I can sit and read my *Heralds of Freedom* and enjoy the same which is listened to with profound silence. Not an abolitionist in the center of this town but my dear wife."[32] Two years later, Sanderson wrote again to congratulate Henry on his new baby daughter and then ranted for two additional pages about the slave power.[33] Sanderson's interest in abolition was by no means an isolated instance of Ashfield peddlers meddling in national politics. Southerners were right to be suspicious of Yankee peddlers—at least those from Ashfield. Jasper Bement and Henry Ranney were both active free-soil abolitionists and in the early 1840s formed the nucleus of a "Liberty Party" in Ashfeld. In 1843, Jasper Bement campaigned for state representative as a Liberty candidate and lost, but a year later he won.[34]

Although they were interested in their businesses, Bement and Ranney were passionate about abolition. In August 1844, Jasper Bement wrote to Henry Ranney from Syracuse, New York, where Bement had stopped on his way to Detroit. Bement touched briefly on business and then offered detailed descriptions of several conversations he had enjoyed with "Liberty men," and the reactions of strangers to whom he had offered abolitionist tracts at a political gathering. Bement said he was introduced to "Mr. Jackson the editor of the *Democratic Freeman of Liberty* paper. He began with 30 subscribers and has now got 700. We are gaining ground in this quarter if I can judge from what I see."[35] A few days later, Bement wrote again: "The country seems all alive with Whig and Loco mass meetings. By inquiring I find a respectable number of Liberty men in almost every place." Bement told Ranney a local Liberty man solicited him to give a lecture to a group of nearly two hundred people in Hannibal. In addition to the forty Liberty activists present, Bement said, "the Whigs present were rocked up. Asked questions and disputed. Some of our friends started for home in high spirits singing the Liberty Ball. Some of the Whigs were almost ready to vote for Liberty, but they think they must vote Clay in this time to keep Texas out."[36] In spite of being rural businessmen from a remote community in the hills of western Massachusetts, Bement and Ranney shared a lifelong involvement in national politics. They both represented Ashfield in the legislature in Boston, and they maintained a far-flung commercial network, as we will shortly see.

Peddlers were an ideal means to reach a widely distributed, rural retail market. But there were also concentrated urban markets, and each city and large town had its physicians, apothecaries, and patent medicine manufacturers. In 1802, for example, the *Philadelphia Directory* listed "Calvin Flora, peppermint maker, St. Tammany." In 1804, the directory included "Boyl Jonathan, peppermint maker near 27 Brewers alley."[37] Nor, as previously mentioned, was the only use of peppermint medicinal. In a society that drank at least four times the per capita volume of alcohol as modern America, the market for flavored cordials was substantial.[38] New York City distiller Michael Miller announced to readers of the 1803 *Daily Advertiser* supplies "at his CORDIAL DISTILLERY, No. 11 Barley street, three doors eastward of Broad-way, Anniseed, Mint, and Pepper-mint cordials."[39] And in 1804 the *American Distiller* included a section entitled "How to make peppermint essence."[40]

By 1805, production of peppermint essence was widespread enough that glass manufacturers did not need to await orders from merchants like Bement. A broker named William Little, of 49 State Street, Boston, advertised a diverse variety of surplus products, including "Window Glass [many sizes], . . . 40 groce essence of peppermint Phials, an assortment of warranted Anchors."[41] Perhaps Little's supplier had produced a large volume of vials imprinted with "Essence of Peppermint" for a specific customer and was selling a surplus quantity. But the fact that the broker expected to find a buyer simply by offering the vials within a list of disparate products suggests a fairly wide market.

An 1808 advertisement in Utica's *Columbian Gazette* announced, "Drugs and Medicine, at the Sign of the Good Samaritan. Solomon Wolcott, Has received an addition to his former stock. . . . 1000 Ess. Peppermint. . . . Instruments: Mortars, Scales and Shop Furniture . . . Peppermint Bottles, &c. &c."[42] And in 1809, an ad in the *New York Gazette and General Advertiser* advised of "Opium, &c. . . . 10 lb. Oil Peppermint, for sale by John Wade, 181 Water-street."[43] A four-ounce vial of peppermint essence contained less than an ounce of peppermint oil, so ten pounds was enough oil to make quite a bit of retail product.

Wholesalers cast a wide net. In April 1814, the *Washingtonian* in Windsor, Vermont, carried an advertisement for peppermint oil for sale in Boston. At the "Wholesale and Retail Chemical and Drug Warehouse, No. 1, Liberty Square—Boston. Paul Spear, Jr. Has for sale" a long list of bulk products, including "50 d[itt]o. [pounds] Oil of Peppermint."[44] City merchants advertised for distant buyers and also for suppliers of peppermint oil. In 1818, wholesalers "J. & T. L. Clark & Son, at 85 Maiden-lane," advertised a hundred pounds of peppermint oil in the *New York Gazette and General Advertiser*, and J. Bissell and Co. advertised in Pittsfield, "Will contract for 200 pounds of Oil Peppermint and 50 Oil Wintergreen, to be delivered the 1st October, and will pay cash on delivery."[45]

By the 1820s, when the peppermint oil business was reaching its maturity in Ashfield, the volume of oil that passed through the hands of urban wholesalers had also expanded rapidly. In May 1823, for example, Charles F. Kupfer, the superintendent of the Boston Glass Manufactory, ran an advertisement in the *Pittsfield Sun*. The Manufactory made essence vials like the ones used by Jasper Bement in Ashfield, but Kupfer was not above trying to fill the vials himself and take a bit of his clients' profits. Kupfer announced in the *Pittsfield Sun*, whose readers included Hudson River and Erie Canal shippers, "The subscriber will purchase from 2 to 3000 lb. of OIL OF PEPPERMINT, and pay CASH for the same, on delivery at *Boston* or *Albany*. Any person having part or the whole on hand, or desirous to make a contract for the delivery of that quantity, in part or whole, this fall, will please forward their proposals, which will meet immediate attention."[46]

Shipments of peppermint oil along the Erie Canal began in earnest, even before the canal was completed. Although construction continued to the west, the first 250 miles of canal between Brockport and the Hudson River opened in September 1823. This eastern section of the canal passed through Lyons, New York, which was directly north of the peppermint fields of Phelps, where many former Ashfielders had settled. In 1824, the Boston *Commercial Gazette* reran a notice from a newspaper in Geneva, New York, of a "*New article of Domestic Manufacture*": "Last week was obtained from the Bank in this village, on a check, between two and three thousand dollars, being the proceeds of sales of Oil of Peppermint, manufactured in the town of Phelps, by F. Vandemark & Co. The past season, and sold to a person in Massachusetts."[47] Frederick Vandermark was the brother-in-law of Archibald Burnett, the Ashfielder who first carried peppermint roots to western New York.

The success and prosperity of Ashfield's peppermint growers did not go unnoticed. In 1825, Northampton's *Hampshire Gazette* ran a feature story that was reprinted in newspapers all over the region, including the New Bedford *Mercury* and the *Rhode Island American*. The article described several hundred acres in Ashfield devoted to growing peppermint, with an average yield of between twenty-five and forty pounds of oil per acre. The article concluded, "The process of cultivation is said to be tedious and expensive, but we are inclined to think there are but few, if any crops raised in this part of the country that make greater returns for the money and labor expended on them."[48]

In spite of expanding awareness of peppermint's potential profitability and some large urban sales of wholesale peppermint oil, however, Ashfield continued to dominate the essential oil market through the 1820s. A letter about the products of Ashfield, written in 1824 and quoted in the *History of the Town of Ashfield*, "gives the value of peppermint oil made as over $40,000 yearly." This is a significant sum: in comparison, the total value of the land and buildings in Ashfield in the town's 1826 tax assessment was $9,812.38.[49] An 1833 report prepared by Andrew Jackson's secretary of the treasury, Louis McLane, noted that Ashfield "has been somewhat celebrated for its manufacture of essences of various kinds, such as peppermint, hemlock, winter green, tansy, &c. It is estimated that 700 groce of essence, at $6 per groce, have been manufactured yearly, for several years past." The report also declared that "the average amount of essential oils sold in New York, (exclusive of what has been used in the manufacture of essence in town) has been $3,000 worth, annually, for ten years past. It is considered fair business, when the oil will sell for $2 per pound; it is now worth $5 a pound."[50]

The report listed $4,200 in essences plus another $3,000 in peppermint oil sold in New York City, for a total of $7,200. Since the reported New York wholesale receipts of $3,000 annually were an average over the previous ten years, when peppermint oil averaged two dollars per pound, the report implies that in addition to supplying essence peddlers, Ashfielders supplied the wholesale market with about fifteen hundred pounds of peppermint oil per year. Based on frequent newspaper notices of large transactions and the large quantities offered and solicited in advertisements, this may be a substantial underestimation.

The $4,200 listed for essence sales must also be considered a wholesale price, since it corresponds with prices charged by suppliers of peddlers like Jasper Bement. The reporter gave a price of six dollars per gross; Bement sold his peppermint essence to peddlers at forty cents per dozen. It is impossible to determine what the hundreds of peddlers taking essence into the countryside from Ashfield would have made on their sales. Some were probably better negotiators than others. But if the peddlers averaged forty cents per vial, their earnings would be consistent with the forty thousand dollars that Ashfield was reported to have made on oil annually in 1824. The wholesale prices reported by the Treasury Department are more relevant to comparisons with other industries, but since Ashfield's economy relied much more heavily on retail peddler revenue than its neighbors, estimates of the income derived from peddling suggest the general prosperity of the town. It is also significant that, in keeping with Ashfield's long-standing egalitarian ideals, the widespread prosperity of self-employed peddlers seems much more democratic than the concentrated wealth of other industries.

The other manufacturing activities Ashfield reported in the Treasury Department document were forging axes and hoes, worth $2,729; splitting four hundred thousand shingles, worth six hundred dollars; turning seven hundred thousand broom handles, worth $7,700; and making thirty-three hundred pairs of boots and shoes, worth $4,950.[51] If peppermint oil had been an exclusively wholesale business, its significance to the town would have been merely equal to broom handles. The advantage Ashfield had over other regions involved in peppermint oil production was that the town's economy was able to realize the *retail* value of the essences sold by peddlers who were overwhelmingly from Ashfield and nearby communities, while products like broom handles were simply sold in bulk at prices determined by a competitive wholesale market to "Hadley, Hatfield, and other towns on the Conn. River" that manufactured brooms. While some products such as shingles might have been produced by local free-lance workers, many were probably produced by wageworkers employed by sawmill owners. Rural communities were not immune to the shift from artisanal labor to wage labor; Ashfield was lucky to have had an economy built around a model of entrepreneurship that spread its rewards more widely and evenly.[52]

Ashfield's $23,179 of wholesale manufacturing income in 1833 was similar to that of similar nearby towns. Conway reported manufactures worth $20,475, led by $13,600 in horn combs. New Salem manufactured ten thousand palm leaf hats, worth $27,500 when delivered to Boston and New York resellers, and had a leather and lumber business worth $9,550. The neighboring village of Buckland produced $9,750 in manufactures, including three hundred wooden clocks valued at $7.50 each. In the river valley were larger towns like Deerfield, which manufactured $58,600 in wholesale products, including 205,000 brooms and thirty thousand yards of wool satinet. But even when measured against these larger towns, Ashfield's widely distributed retail income was substantial.

Another factor supporting claims of very high profits for Ashfield's peppermint essence business is the extreme variability of peppermint oil prices. Demand for peppermint-based products was relatively constant and predictable, but supply varied widely from season to season. It was not uncommon for peppermint oil prices to double from one harvest to the next. In 1836, for example, a list of wholesale prices published in New York newspapers quoted "Oil of Peppermint" at $5.50 to $6.00. In comparison, imported opium was only $3.75 for Turkish and $3.95 for Egyptian.[53] In 1837, prices remained high. The *Pittsfield Sun* reported in December, in a notice reprinted as far away as Philadelphia: "Among the items received on the Hudson by the Erie Canal, we notice the singular one of 6,000 lbs. of oil of peppermint, valued at $30,000."[54] When costs of a product's key component, such as peppermint oil for peddlers' essence vials, fluctuated widely, prices tended to be maintained at levels where retail sales could remain profitable even at the highest ingredient costs. This worst-case approach to pricing would lead to windfall profits for the peddlers, and especially for suppliers like Jasper Bement and Henry Ranney, when costs decreased.

In 1835, Ashfield's tax assessors began recording the town's assets in much greater detail. In addition to buildings and machines, financial assets and farm animals began to be counted and taxed. But for the first time the assessors of 1835 found no stills. George Ranney had moved to Phelps, New York, in 1833, and Roswell Ranney was making final preparations to follow him. Roswell's taxable assets in Ashfield had dwindled by the summer of 1835 to a fractional interest in a sawmill worth a hundred dollars, a single horse and cow, and three thousand dollars "Money at interest." One of the last members of the family to move to Phelps, Samuel Ranney had not yet begun selling off his assets. His 1835 assessment included houses and barns, acreage, and animals. But even Samuel no longer distilled peppermint oil in Ashfield.

The Ashfield merchant Jasper Bement, whose assets included a "Factory" and a "Shop" valued at seven hundred dollars, still bottled essences but no longer distilled peppermint oil. Bement's other assets taxed in 1835 included four horses and a cow, "Stock in trade" worth $350, which probably consisted of the essences and wares he supplied to his peddlers, and two thousand dollars "Money at interest." Bement's relative by marriage Roswell Ranney seems to have been one of the early conduits of western New York peppermint oil to Ashfield. Jasper Bement's account books show the shift in Roswell's role, from local peppermint oil producer to broker of New York oil. In 1833 Bement's account books had recorded handling fees Bement had charged Roswell to process oil, when Roswell had owned his own still. In 1836, after Roswell moved to Phelps, Bement's accounts recorded transactions with Roswell involving bulk peppermint oil. And in 1838, after three years without a home of his own in Ashfield, Roswell Ranney was once again taxed for a small "House & Garden" in town, valued at a hundred dollars, as well as a cow and $3,020 "Money at interest." Apparently, Roswell's business connections with Ashfield remained substantial enough to justify a part-time residence on the town's main street.[55]

As families like the Burnetts, the Ranneys, the Beldings, and the Bements left Ashfield and expanded peppermint growing and distilling into western New York (discussed in the next chapter), the town's rocky, uneven fields were converted to pasture for the town's growing herds of sheep. By 1835, when peppermint stills had disappeared from Ashfield, the town was home to 7,748 sheep valued at $1.25 each.[56] Even Roswell Ranney, who no longer lived in Ashfield full-time, invested in the new venture. In 1838, he was assessed for $2,652.50 of "money at interest" and for 150 sheep.[57]

In December 1833, the *New England Farmer and Horticultural Journal* and the *Boston Courier* reprinted an article from Greenfield's *Franklin Mercury* that serves as a retrospective of the Ashfield peppermint venture. The article, entitled "Essence Peddling," began: "There is not a town in the east, nor a prairie in the west of the United States, where the essences and the essence-peddlers of Yankee-land have not been seen and heard of: nor do we believe there is any business which has been so much celebrated and whose origin is yet so little known. It commenced about twenty years ago in Ashfield, in this county." Although "a great many pretty properties were made there, while the place enjoyed a monopoly of the business[,] ... [v]ast supplies are now derived by the Ashfield merchants from Phelps," where many Ashfielders had recently moved. The article described peddlers who in "flocks of twenty or thirty have sometimes taken their departure from the place in a single day to the east, west, north and south, bearing '*Goods* from all nations lumbering at their back,' making money and driving bargains with invincible perseverance under the very noses of the stationary traders." The large number of full-time Ashfield peddlers, the article concluded, was increased by the "infinitely greater [number] of those who have made this business an apprenticeship to regular country trading, and an avenue to moderate wealth."[58]

In addition to the ready availability of western New York peppermint oil that could be purchased from family and trusted friends, another factor that may have encouraged Ashfield merchants like Jasper Bement to give up distilling was a growing temperance movement in the town. As an Ashfield clergyman recalled in a memorial address reprinted in the town history, "The inhabitants of this town ... have suffered much from the scourge of intemperance ... many of the distilleries, first set up for the distillation of mint, by a little additional expense could be employed for a part of the year in distilling cider." He described the movement he had led to discourage drinking, concluding that "although one or two distilleries, and a few retailing stores and some temperate drinkers stand in the way, yet the purifying process is in progress which will not stop until the whole town and region is reclaimed from the cruel grasp of this common enemy."[59]

Although Ashfield's "temperate drinkers" such as Bement and Henry Ranney seem to have thought the prohibition movement's goals were themselves a bit intemperate, everyone admitted there was some truth to their claims. In May 1827, a group of Ashfield residents, including a deacon of the church, his sons, and several others, were washing sheep in the town pond. Under the influence, six men loaded two sheep into a large canoe and took it out on the pond. About ten yards from shore, the canoe sank. The deacon's eighteen-year-old son, a twenty-eight-year-old neighbor, and two brothers, aged fifteen and thirteen, went under and did not resurface. The deacon, who had been watching from shore, jumped into the water and also disappeared. All five drowned.[60]

While Ashfield's famous essence business was not blamed for the 1827 tragedy, townsfolk regarded the stills with increasing suspicion. And many of the farmers who had done the difficult, time-consuming work of growing and distilling peppermint had moved to the area around Phelps in the early 1830s. Since the peppermint straw distilled into oil is bulky and perishable, distilling is always done as close to the fields as possible. When Ashfielders stopped growing their own peppermint, they no longer needed their stills. And the era of the Yankee essence peddlers persisted only as long as the single generation of merchants like Bement and Ranney who supplied them. Without peppermint and the widespread prosperity created by the peddler trade, Ashfield's prominence faded. The 1910 History of Ashfield remarks, "It seems hardly credible that the cultivation of a single crop should have anything to do with the lessening of the population of Ashfield, but facts go to show that the rise and fall of the peppermint industry here affected the population seriously."[61]

In the second half of the nineteenth century, many American farmers became enmeshed in commodity markets, sending their harvests and livestock to urban centers for processing into standardized food products. The details of this commercialization of agriculture vary from place to place and are key elements of the hotly debated market transition. Although the argument over the market transition often devolves into disagreements over the definitions of terms such as capitalism, the change in agency brought about by the rise of commodity agriculture and development of impersonal markets is a key to understanding the mentalities of rural people.[62] But too often historians have restricted their view to commodities such as wheat that were most suited to undifferentiated aggregation, shifting power from atomized producers to central processors.[63] In the most extreme examples of this reduction of agency, farmers lost their independence and became mere raw material suppliers for an industrialized food system.[64] But the well-documented history of this decline tends to obscure the fact that many early American farmers were innovators who worked hard to increase the diversity and value of the products they offered. As historian Martin Bruegel has observed, early American farmers "straddled two worlds that historians and ethnologists have often tended to construe as incompatible."[65] When we fail to recognize that many rural people understood the complexity of the systems within which they operated, we deny the agency that seems very apparent in the actions and documents of the Ranneys and their associates.

Because most American farmers today grow monocultures of ever-decreasing diversity, it is easy to forget that since the beginning of the Columbian exchange, Euro-Americans and others have been importing new plants and animals and spreading them across the Americas.[66] Early American farmers were always on the lookout for new opportunities both to feed their families more efficiently and to produce novel products for local and distant markets. John Rolfe's theft of high-quality tobacco from the Spanish Empire breathed new life into the Virginia colony at Jamestown. The reintroduction of potatoes, carried to Europe by the conquistadors after their discovery in the Andes, by Scots-Irish settlers in Maine created an industry that continues to this day. The American enthusiasm for chicken breeding that produced a "hen fever" in the early 1850s, the opening of Chinese ports after the Opium Wars, and the introduction of premium livestock breeds such as the Merino sheep that grazed on Ashfield's pastures suggest a mental flexibility and interest in innovation that we do not currently associate with American farmers in particular and rural people in general.[67]

It should not be surprising that farmers like the Ranneys and their neighbors quickly took advantage of the opportunity to diversify and add value once Samuel Ranney had brought peppermint roots to Ashfield. It is worth restating, too, that the Ashfield farmers who grew and distilled peppermint between 1812 and 1835 produced a well-differentiated commercial product for a direct consumer market. Although most Ashfield farmers continued growing staples for their families and hay for their animals, there was no local-first, subsistence-to-surplus trajectory; peppermint was a commercial commodity from the outset. The peppermint oil industry challenges the paradigm that the undifferentiated nature of commercial agricultural products inevitably leads to the concentration of power in the hands of urban processors, and it suggests that the traditional agrarian history of independent yeomen gradually drawn into urban-dominated commercial markets that eliminated their agency is incomplete.

The Ranneys were central to the growth of the peppermint oil industry in western New York and Michigan, but they were not the first family to carry peppermint to western New York. Peppermint roots were introduced to Phelps by the Ranneys' neighbor Archibald Burnett. It is fair to say, however, that the departure of most of the Ranneys from Ashfield caused the abrupt end of peppermint growing there.

The first Ranney family to sell off its stake in Ashfield and move to Phelps was that of George Jr., the youngest son of the senior George Ranney, who had first moved the family to Ashfield and was the inheritor of the original family farm. Youngest sons typically inherited in rural early America, because older sons usually had started their own families and farms long before their parents were prepared to retire. Youngest sons were still in the household when the parents became too old to work the farm, and they generally took over the work and cared for their parents in their declining years, in exchange for an inheritance.

George Ranney was well established in Ashfield when he decided to move. He had inherited the family farm in 1822, when his father George had died at the age of seventy-five. The younger George had married Achsah Sears in 1811, and they had eight sons and a daughter who lived to adulthood. In 1830, George's property consisted of a house and barn, forty-six acres of improved farmland, and sixty-six acres of unimproved land. Although George's property was valued at only about a third of his cousin Roswell's, he was a substantial landowner running a successful farm in Ashfield.[68]

George sold out and in August 1833 moved his entire family to Phelps, except his third son, Henry, who remained in Ashfield, living in Jasper Bement's household. Apparently pleased with the prospects of his new home,

George encouraged his relatives to join him. In February 1835, Roswell's son Horace Ranney bought a farm in Phelps, and in June 1837, Roswell made the first of several purchases in Phelps, buying a farm from peppermint farmer Frederick Vandermark. In February 1838, George bought a 105-acre farm on Flint Creek in Phelps, for five thousand dollars.[69] The substantial price Ranney paid shows that the region was already very well established by the time he arrived in western New York, and that the Ranneys were quite prosperous after their years in Ashfield.

Samuel Ranney's move to Phelps in 1835 was certainly influenced by George, Horace, and Roswell's success there. But Samuel's decision to leave Ashfield seems also to have been precipitated by a new wave of social turmoil, revolving once again around Ashfield's Congregational Church. In January 1834, Massachusetts finally disestablished the church, which had dominated the state since the days of the Puritans. Unlike New Hampshire to the north, which had separated church from state in 1790, and Connecticut to the south, which had banned government-supported religion in 1818, Massachusetts retained the Congregationalism of its colonial origins as the state's official religion until 1833. Facing the sudden loss of its ability to forcibly tax the residents of Ashfield and compel their attendance, the church's leaders looked for other ways to retain their authority.

The Ashfield church's solution came in the form of an evangelist named Mason Grosvenor, who was called to Ashfield in his first ministerial assignment after graduating from Yale's conservative divinity school. Grosvenor and the leaders of the Ashfield congregation immediately set to work combating what they characterized as extreme licentiousness in the town. Part of their program focused on prosecuting the town's physician, Dr. Charles Knowlton, for publishing America's first birth control manual. Another part involved admonishing residents whose attendance had lapsed and who had failed to pay their church tax. Grosvenor and the church leaders continued to use the word "tax" in spite of the fact they were no longer able to compel contributions with the force of law.[70]

One of the church's immediate targets was Samuel Ranney. The sixty-two-year-old farmer had neither attended services nor contributed to the congregation in years and may have seemed an easy target for a church leadership eager to set an example to intimidate the flock.

Grosvenor drew up a list of charges against Ranney, accusing him of "a transgression of the laws of Christ's kingdom by withholding his support both pecuniary and personal from the ministrations of the word to this church" and "a violation of his covenant vows, voluntarily solemnly and publicly made to this church and to god; consisting in almost entirely absenting himself for several years from the worship."[71] In addition to failing to contribute and attend church services, Grosvenor wrote in his notes on the case, Samuel Ranney had "denied the ~~existence~~ reality of a future state, and declared himself not in the least responsible to the laws of Christ's Kingdom," which the minister declared "manifested contempt to this church, its laws its peace and its fellowship."[72] The church wrote Ranney a letter of admonishment, insisting that he confess and repent his transgressions and immediately resume his attendance and financial support of the congregation. The alternative, church leaders warned, was excommunication.

Excommunication in a small, religious community such as Ashfield was not an idle threat. Like shunning in other traditional communities, excommunication split families and ruined lives. The church, under Grosvenor, had resorted to this punishment before, targeting another old Ashfield farmer, named Nathaniel Clark, who had been overheard in a tavern criticizing the congregation's ongoing persecution of the town's doctor, Knowlton. Clark had tried to protest the church's actions to the Congregational hierarchy and had endured hearings and church tribunals before finally giving in and humbling himself before the congregation. Samuel Ranney was familiar with Clark's case and did not take the threat lightly, but his reaction was not what the church expected. On May 20, at the conclusion of the four-week period the church had given him to consider its threat, Samuel Ranney delivered the following letter to Grosvenor:

> To Rev Mason Grovsenor [sic], Chairman of the Committee of Christ's Church in Ashfield,
>
> Sir I received your letter of the 22d ult containing charges against me as a member of the church of which you are pastor, which charges I am requested to take into serious consideration, and I have done so.

The first charge amounts to this: "A transgression of the laws of Christ's Kingdom" by not paying away my money to support preaching.

Now as Christ's Kingdom is not of this world, and as I have no knowledge of any other world, nor consequently of the laws of any other world, you should not be surprised that I should transgress the laws you speak of inasmuch as I know nothing about them. I once thought that I did, but that was when I took names for things, and supposed that immaterialities were realities. And as to pecuniary support, it cannot be expected I should give away my hard earning for what I consider of little or nothing worth.

The second charge is, "A violation of my Covenant Vows." To this I have only to say, that the same consistency—the same honesty which required me to make these vowes when I did make them, <u>now</u> require me to disregard them. As a man's opinions and feelings are not voluntary nor under the control of his will, but are governed by circumstances, it is the height of absurdity for me to promise what my opinions and feelings shall be at a future time. The most I can consistently do or be required to do is avow what they are at the time being.

I therefore this day excommunicate the Church of Christ in Ashfield for my further support and membership. And I do hearby request the chairman of the committee of said church to read this at the meeting appointed for acting upon my case.

Your fellow townsman,

Ashfield, May 20 1834   Samuel Ranney[73]

Samuel Ranney's letter is remarkable in several ways. First, of course, for Ranney's dramatic, preemptive excommunication of the church. But also for Ranney's discussion of names and things, immaterialities and realities. The language suggests Ranney was not a simple old farmer who had lost interest in supporting the church but rather was someone who entertained radical opinions about the role of religion in his life and in

Ashfield society. The specific terminology he used also suggests familiarity with the ideas of the local freethinker, Dr. Charles Knowlton, who
had published a book on the subject a few years earlier, entitled *Elements
of Modern Materialism*.[74] The fact that Knowlton was a country doctor
living in Ashfield and that Ranney was familiar with the argument of a
456-page atheist tome Knowlton had self-published suggests that in
spite of its remote, rural setting Ashfield was the scene of one of America's earliest philosophical challenges to organized religion. Knowlton
had been prosecuted for offering copies of *Elements of Modern Materialism* to students at Amherst College, and he had lectured to freethinking
audiences in Boston and New York City. Once again, rural Ashfielders
were at the forefront of an intellectual and cultural movement traditionally believed the exclusive interest of urban intellectuals.

The apparently deliberate misspelling by Ranney of the pastor's
name and his decision to sign his letter to the church "Your fellow
townsman" when the expected, customary closing would have been
"Your brother in Christ" also seems to stand as an accusation against
people Ranney believed had wrongly put religious orthodoxy before social solidarity and as an expression of his wider, more cosmopolitan
concept of citizenship. Ironically but unsurprisingly, the words "Your
fellow townsman" were true for only a few more months. Samuel sold
his farm and followed his brother and cousins to Phelps in 1835.

At the same time the Ranneys were settling into Phelps, they were
simultaneously setting the stage for the next phase of the family's expansion across America by purchasing land in Michigan. In spite of President
Andrew Jackson's 1836 Specie Circular, which had declared that western
lands had to be paid for at the Land Office with hard money rather than
paper notes, in 1837 Samuel Ranney, his son William, and many of their
Phelps neighbors traveled to the Detroit Land Office and bought land on
the frontier. Perhaps the elimination of speculation based on credit in the
form of paper banknotes had convinced the Ranneys and other New Yorkers that the opportunity presented by western land was legitimate. In any
case, on March 13, 1837, Samuel bought a farm in Phelps, and on April 15,
he and his son William purchased a 160-acre and a forty-acre parcel.[75]

Samuel's health deteriorated rapidly, perhaps exacerbated by the
controversy in Ashfield, the move to Phelps, and the trip to Michigan.

Years later, Henry Ranney described his uncle as "enterprising and successful, but . . . overtaken by some misfortunes as age drew on. . . . [H]e
made his abode in Phelps, but was broken in health, and died the following year."[76] Samuel wrote his will in April 1837, naming his wife, Polly, and
friend Russell Bement as his executors. He died on June 28, 1837, leaving
his recently purchased Michigan land to his minor son Frederick. His
estate inventory included notes for debts owed him by Russell Bement, by
Samuel's son-in-law, the Michigan merchant Nehemiah Hathaway, and
by the local peppermint oil producers Vandermark and Company.[77] Samuel's wife, Polly, and their four children all ultimately moved to Michigan,
where at least one son, Frederick, remained active in the peppermint oil
business. In 1847, Henry Ranney received a letter in Ashfield from his
cousin Frederick, then living in Centerville, Michigan. Frederick wrote,
"Dear Sir, I am obliged to call on you for the money on that peppermint
oil that was sent last fall. I have some money to make out in a few days or
sell property at a low price. Lucius nor Lewis [Henry's brothers living
near Frederick in Michigan] cannot help me to money this fall therefore
I shall expect it in a return letter. You must write on the receipt of this for
time is short with me. Let me know what you can do."[78]

    Although the first peppermint king had passed, the Ranneys
remained active in the peppermint oil business. Roswell Ranney continued to prosper in New York, where he built a large house, a barn, and
outbuildings, all of fieldstone. Roswell "dealt largely in peppermint and
other essential oils," acting as a conduit for New York peppermint oil
into Ashfield and other eastern markets.[79] Roswell kept between three
and four thousand dollars "at interest" in Ashfield for years after he
moved to Phelps and, as mentioned earlier, bought a small house on
Ashfield's main street in 1838. In 1845, one of New York's new peppermint merchants, Leman Hotchkiss, wrote to his brother Hiram to tell
him about peppermint oil "which old Ranney took to [the New York
City broker] David Dows and requested him to ascertain the most he
could obtain for it."[80] Roswell remained active in the peppermint oil
business well into the 1840s, when the Hotchkiss brothers are typically
believed to have controlled the market. Apparently Roswell was acquainted with the same people in New York City, and his opinion was
worth something even to his rivals, the Hotchkisses. A few days later,

Leman wrote Hiram again to say "Old Ranney" had returned from his trip to New York and Boston and Leman had met with him. "He told me that if he had an offer for 10 Thousand pounds of oil for 10/ he would not take it. At the same time he said he had contracted 200# with one of his old customers in Boston & he no doubt should be obliged to pay 12/ to fill his contract."[81] The "old customer" in Boston could well have been Roswell's nephew Henry, who had a business in the city in 1845 and 1846.

Roswell died in September 1848 at the age of sixty-six—apparently unexpectedly, because he had not prepared a will. He left a substantial estate of $44,215.43, consisting of real estate, bonds, mortgages, and notes, which was distributed equally among seven beneficiaries.[82] With Roswell's death, Henry Ranney in Ashfield became the principal member of the family involved in the peppermint oil business. But the business had expanded, and other families had taken the center stage. Our focus is on on Phelps and its peppermint kings in the next chapter, and then we revisit the Ranneys as they carry the first peppermint roots to Michigan, establishing a peppermint oil business that straddled the country from Boston and New York to the pioneer farms of the Yankee West.

Migration

The conclusion of the American Revolution with the Treaty of Paris in 1783 brought a rapid increase of Euro-American settlers into western New York. Indigenous peoples who had sided with Britain in the war lost their territories, and speculators took most of the eastern land forfeited by Loyalists. In 1790, when the United States government took its first national census, more than half of the Americans counted were under the age of sixteen. Rural families like the Ranneys had an average of six children. As this agrarian population came of age, sons of Yankee farmers seeking to begin their own farms found fewer parcels available close to home, containing less attractive land at higher prices. In 1783, after decades during which would-be settlers had been frustrated by the British Proclamation Line and been afraid of strong native nations to their west, only one-fourteenth of white Americans lived beyond the relative safety of the old colonial settlements. By 1800, the frontier population west of the Appalachian Mountains had expanded to 921,000, more than one-fifth of the country's white population.[1]

But even on the new frontier, speculators and land companies controlled vast swaths of unimproved western lands. Historian Allan Kulikoff recounts, "Starved for funds, New York sold 22,000 square miles, almost half of the state's land, to developers. Two land companies—Phelps and Gorham and the Holland Land Company—held 6.2 million acres, much of the western half of the state."[2] Histories of western migration describe Oliver Phelps and Nathaniel Gorham as "two Massachusetts speculators" who "for $100,000 . . . bought preemptive rights to a vast tract in the western part" of New York and began the "Genesee Fever."[3] Older histories of the early frontier also recall that the fever rose quickly after British and Indian incursions from Canada, Oswego, and Niagara, called the Border Wars, ended around 1779.[4]

At the conclusion of revolutionary hostilities, western New York was a land occupied by trappers, Indian traders, and small pockets of settlement such as the "one or two white families [who] had settled at Catharine's Town, at the head of Seneca Lake."[5] This pattern of sparse frontier settlement extended all the way to the French village and British garrison at Fort Detroit, which may help explain why migrants to western New York like the Ranneys so quickly looked farther west and bought parcels in Michigan even as they began making new farms in Phelps.[6]

Acquisition of western lands highlighted the competing agendas of rural settlers and urban speculators. Oliver Phelps and Nathaniel Gorham had acquired the six million acres that became known as the Phelps and Gorham Purchase in an elaborate series of negotiations with the native Haudenosaunee (Iroquois Confederacy). Phelps and Gorham paid the Indians five thousand dollars and promised a perpetual annuity of five hundred dollars. The Commonwealth of Massachusetts relinquished its western claims for a fee of a hundred thousand dollars that the speculators tried to pay in devalued Massachusetts scrip. When the federal government assumed the war debts of the states and rehabilitated Massachusetts currency, the speculators were nearly ruined.[7] The purchase was concluded by 1789, and the establishment of townships quickly followed.

The town of Phelps, located near a large stream called the Canandaigua Outlet, was one of the first settlements formed after the conclusion of the purchase. Two employees of the land company, John Decker Robinson and Nathaniel Sanborn, drove a herd of cattle into the area and distributed them to the Indians in exchange for signing land-sale documents. They operated a land office in a log cabin in return for grants of land. Robinson brought his family to the new town in 1789 and opened a tavern in 1793. By then, settlers from western Massachusetts had begun flooding into the new township.[8]

Many of Phelps's original settlers were from Conway, Massachusetts, Ashfield's neighbor to the east on the road to Deerfield that passed by the Ranney farms. Jonathan Oaks arrived in 1790 and settled at a crossroads on an old Indian trail that became known as Oaks Corners. The settlers told their families and friends in Massachusetts about their new farms, and a steady stream of migration began from Conway, including the families of Benjamin Wheat, Captain Lemuel Bannister, Osee Crittenden, and Augustus Dickinson, whose daughter Fanny married Thaddeus Oaks. Their daughter, Lucretia Oaks, would later marry Phelps's peppermint king, Leman Hotchkiss.[9]

Solomon Gates arrived in 1790 from Conway with Jonathan Oaks. Gates's sister, Esther, was married to the Ashfield merchant Selah Belding. Wells Whitmore of Conway also arrived with Oaks and became the town's first constable in 1793. Solomon Goodale, Phelps's first town clerk, was also from Conway. Since entire families from Conway often migrated together, the town's contribution to Phelps's early population growth was substantial. Jesse Warner left Conway with his five adult sons in 1796 to settle in Phelps.[10]

Historian Hal S. Barron attributed the generally declensionist view of migration's effects on rural New England to the "pervasive influence of Frederick Jackson Turner ... [and] the agrarian myth." Turner had believed that migration involved a cutting of ties with home that was extreme enough to cause a cultural break, resulting in civilization recapitulating itself on the frontier and creating a new American culture. In contrast with this traditional story of western settlement, in which young people left for the frontier and then had only sporadic contact with their families back home, traffic from Conway to Phelps was two-way.[11] In spite of the difficulty of traveling 250 miles over challenging terrain, many settlers regularly went back and forth between Conway and Phelps. John Salisbury first visited Phelps with Jonathan Oaks in 1790. He went home to Conway for a while and then returned to Phelps in 1796, when a local history records he "came alone and walked all the way." Salisbury visited Conway again, married Elizabeth Banister, and returned to Phelps with her and his brother Stephen's family (presumably not on foot).

When Elizabeth died in 1806, Salisbury returned to Conway once again and married Polly Wilder.[12]

Just up the road from Conway, near the South Ashfield plain where the Ranney brothers had their farms, lived the Burnett family (sometimes spelled Burnet). The first Burnetts to visit Phelps were the brothers named John and Patrick. They arrived in 1794, and Patrick moved on, but John remained. John's son William Burnett was a town magistrate and became a brigadier general of the militia after fighting on the Niagara frontier during the War of 1812.[13]

Joseph and Lodowick Vandermark (sometimes spelled Vandemark) also arrived in 1794, from Pennsylvania. Lodowick was a millwright who operated a successful sawmill on Flint Creek in Phelps. His children were Frederick (1785–1862), a farmer who later sold some farmland to Roswell Ranney, Experience (known as "Spiddy," 1793–1851), who married Archibald Burnett, and William, who also married a Burnett sibling and named his son Archibald, after the man who brought peppermint to Phelps.[14] Archibald Burnett was the son of Archibald and Eunice Burnett, who had settled in Ashfield just after the Revolutionary War. Of their nine children, the three youngest, Andrew, Nahum, and Archibald, moved to Phelps after 1813. They are the source of the first peppermint planted in Western New York.[15]

In the early 1810s, Archibald Burnett was a peddler working out of Ashfield, who like many others carried a trunk of wares and a basket of essences to the newly settled farms and villages of western New York. Archibald liked the area and decided to stay, finding employment and lodging on the four-hundred-acre farm of Lodowick Vandermark. Archibald married Vandermark's daughter, Spiddy, and bought a farm in the neighboring township of Junius on the nearby Canandaigua Outlet. At about this time, Archibald received an urgent letter from his brother Nahum, who was still living at the family home in Ashfield on the road to Conway, near the Ranneys. Nahum wrote that he had important news that was too sensitive to relate in a letter and urged his brother to come home quickly. Archibald rushed back to his childhood home and discovered the news was peppermint, which Samuel Ranney had recently brought to Ashfield. Archibald walked back home to Phelps, carrying a bundle of peppermint roots in his backpack. He planted them in mucky soil by the Canandaigua Outlet, and the plants thrived. Within a few years, peppermint fields could be seen on western New York farms throughout Ontario and Wayne Counties.

Archibald and Nahum Burnett's names began appearing on Ontario County Tax Assessments and Indentures (land sales) in 1820 and 1822, respectively. This may be due to the lack of complete records available for the 1810s. Or, rather than first planting peppermint on his own property, Archibald may have carried the roots he brought from Ashfield to Lodowick Vandermark's farm while he boarded there. The Vandermarks were also early adopters of peppermint in Phelps and remained prominent peppermint farmers for generations. Archibald's brother-in-law, Frederick, was the recipient of the check for two to three thousand dollars recorded in the newspaper notice mentioned earlier, in payment for an 1824 shipment of peppermint oil to Massachusetts. Peppermint was already becoming an important cash crop in western New York during the period when Ashfield was the center of the peddler trade. The Vandermarks later became major suppliers of peppermint oil to the Hotchkiss brothers, whose careers I follow next.

In contrast with a historical tradition that often depicts westward migration as a cutting of family ties and a financial and cultural declension for the region from which people migrated, the connection between the Ashfield area and western New York was so well established and fluid that people, information, and products traveled easily in both directions. As peppermint became economically important in Ashfield, it was almost simultaneously planted and distilled around Phelps. As the hub of the lucrative essence-peddling business, however, Ashfield remained the center of demand for peppermint oil and a principal destination for New York oil shipments for another thirty years. The town retained its preeminent position in the peppermint oil market until Western New Yorkers devised a new way to sell oil. The rise of wholesale and branded peppermint oil and the Hotchkiss brothers is the second phase of the peppermint oil story.

Although the New York peppermint oil business was later dominated by the Hotchkiss brothers (who both declared themselves peppermint kings), the Ranneys remained active in the business until the 1870s. And the Ranneys were responsible for introducing peppermint roots to southwestern Michigan, which became the third major growing region and the site of the final peppermint kingdom, of Albert May Todd. So before turning to the Hotchkisses and Todd, let us return for a while to the story of the Ranney migration.

On June 25, 1831, the *Genesee Farmer* reprinted a feature article from the *New York Sentinel* that discussed "the powerful influence, physical and moral, on our country" exerted by "locomotive engines [that] can be propelled at the amazing speed of from 30 to 50 miles an hour." This prophetic article appeared only a few months after the legendary demonstration of America's first locomotive, Peter Cooper's Tom Thumb, in August 1830. Cooper's engine had lost to a horse-drawn train due to a mechanical failure, but the Baltimore and Ohio Railroad's managers saw the future clearly. The newspaper article went on to predict that remote towns and villages would come to seem as if they were right next door and that this conquest of distance would have a profound effect on American society.[16] To put this in perspective, imagine traveling from New York City to Buffalo. On foot, on horseback, or in a coach, a traveler would be lucky to cover forty miles a day. The 440-mile distance between the two cities would require eleven grueling days of travel for those hardy enough to make the trip at all. After 1825 a trip on the Erie Canal was much less physically demanding but not much faster. A decade later, in contrast, a traveler could step onto a train in New York City and after a single day spent in the comfort of "the cars" could step off in Buffalo.

Steamship service began on Lake Erie in 1818, before the Erie Canal was even completed. From Buffalo, the lake opened a route to Michigan. Western New Yorkers like the Ranneys took advantage of the opportunity and went west to work or invest on the frontier. After moving to Phelps, George Ranney and some of his sons spent at least one winter logging in Michigan. In July 1833, the New York speculators Charles Butler and Arthur Bronson left Detroit to explore the new lands available in southwestern Michigan. After passing through the new townships of Coldwater and Sturgis, they stopped on the large prairie surrounding the village of White Pigeon. Butler wrote in his diary, "White Pigeon is a pleasant little village . . . situated in the center of an extensive and beautiful prairie 6 or 7000 acres. What is a prairie? It looks like the great ocean, for there is nothing to obstruct or intercept the view except here & there a house; a perfectly level plain without a tree or bush or stone; encircled in the background with the dense & noble forest which looks like the frame of the picture."[17]

Some of the first New Yorkers who visited land offices on the Michigan frontier were speculators, but their numbers were decreased by President Andrew Jackson's Specie Circular, the 1836 executive order that required land-office purchases to be made in hard currency rather than on credit or using banknotes of questionable value. During the winter of 1836–37, George Ranney worked in western Michigan with two of his sons and his son-in-law, cutting timber on the Grand River.[18] George had been the first member of the family to move to western New York, and within a few years of his arrival he had expanded his interest to the new territory, which became a state in January 1837. On April 15, 1837, as previously mentioned, Samuel Ranney and his son William bought two parcels at the Detroit Land Office. Two weeks later, on May 1, Leman and Hiram Hotchkiss of Phelps bought 1,327 acres of western Michigan land, and their uncle Calvin Hotchkiss bought 1,325 acres. A year and a half later, after Samuel Ranney's death, his son William returned to the frontier to visit the newly opened Bronson (Kalamazoo) Land Office and purchase another 560 acres in September 1838. Henry Ranney's brothers and cousins were on the move to Michigan.[19]

The Ranney family correspondence preserved in the file cabinets of the Ashfield Historical Society tells the story of a tightly knit extended family that worked very hard to maintain connections across time and distance. Henry Ranney saved the letters he received over six decades from relatives in Boston, New York, Michigan, Arkansas, the Indian Territory (Oklahoma), and California. Family members shared information and provided both emotional and financial support to each other throughout the nineteenth century. Ranneys who went west to New York, Michigan, or even the distant goldfields of Pikes Peak and California remained securely attached to their family. They visited each other regularly, over the years, and between visits they wrote.

In May 1839, Henry Ranney received the first letter in a correspondence that spanned six decades. George Lewis Ranney wrote from Phelps to his brother Henry in Ashfield. The twenty-four-year-old, who

went by his middle name, Lewis, opened his letter with the most important news: "Our folks are well as usual." Lewis continued with news of
his business ventures: "I am working at home this season. . . . We have
planted this season about 6 acres of mint, 9 acres of corn, 6 acres spring
wheat, potatoes and oats sufficient, &c. Our people are going into the
poultry line considerable this season, with near 50 chickens already."
Lewis then passed along news of their cousins, Samuel Ranney's sons.
"Dexter is yet in Michigan I suppose, William is a-building a new house
in the West Village, Frederick is about here as usual." Frederick, who had
been a minor when his father Samuel died in 1837, had just turned twenty. Lewis concluded, "Mother says she calculates to send to you three
pairs of socks. Father wishes you to send them $50 or $100 if you can,
as he has had none from Michigan. Money is very scarce here now,
probably will be until after harvest."[20]

Lewis's letter sets the template for the Ranney brothers' correspondence. News of the family came first, then business and occasionally
politics and neighborhood gossip. Although they would ultimately be
spread across the nation, the brothers not only kept in touch but also
regularly did business together. Henry Ranney and Jasper Bement's peddler operation in Ashfield was the market for Lewis's peppermint oil.
And the call of their father, George, for money from Ashfield, since he
could expect none from Dexter in Michigan (presumably the return of
a loan to his nephew), was not unusual. Information, money, and people all flowed freely between Massachusetts, New York, and Michigan.
Later, celebrating the close family connection enabled by improved
transportation, the brothers' aging mother, Achsah Sears Ranney, began
splitting her time between the three regions after the death of her
husband, George, in 1842.

The Ranneys and their close friends prospered in Phelps even as
they looked westward. Alonzo Franklin Ranney, Henry's oldest brother,
considered moving to Michigan several times but ultimately spent his
life in Phelps. Cousin William stayed in Phelps for a few years before
moving to Michigan. Relative-by-marriage Russell Bement lived on a
281-acre farm in Phelps and owned a brick store downtown. Russell's
son John moved to Philadelphia, where he worked for a glassmaker,
sold essence vials to Henry in Ashfield, and later represented Hiram

Hotchkiss's brand of peppermint oil.[21] As these relatives and former neighbors fanned out across the growing nation, they retained the bonds of familiarity and trust formed in Ashfield.

By 1837, Henry had completed his commercial apprenticeship with Jasper Bement and had opened his own store. In the spring of 1840, Henry's cousin Luther Ranney peddled essences, carrying sixty-three dozen vials in March and returning for another fifty-three dozen three weeks later. In July, Ashfielder Horatio Flower bought eighty-four dozen vials of essence for a peddling trip to the west that resulted in Flower's relocation to Phelps.[22] The R. G. Dun credit company's correspondent reported in 1842 that Ranney was a "clever young man." A few years later, Henry and his partner, Richard Cook, were "reputed safe and doing good business." On the tenth anniversary of their partnership, the R. G. Dun investigator described Cook and Ranney as "good character business men, credit and business fair. Worth 2 to 3,000. Considered good for [credit] engagements."[23] By this time Ashfield was no longer producing its own peppermint oil, and the change had been noticed by newspapers like the *Boston Daily Courier*, which ran a feature article entitled "How Ashfield has gone out of peppermint business."[24] But Henry Ranney remained the center of a wide web of peppermint oil distribution.

In April 1842, John Bement wrote from Philadelphia to Richard Cook's brother Moses in New York City, "I have shipped this week 200 gross of vials of 1 3/4 oz, the very kind that is used in Ashfield." In a postscript, Bement added: "I wish Ranney would come here and see me."[25] It's unclear whether Henry visited his friend in Philadelphia, but soon he would have an opportunity to see Michigan. In May 1842, twenty-three-year-old Lucius wrote to his older brother of his arrival in Allen, Michigan, after a ten-day journey from Phelps. To cover the 475 miles between Phelps and Allen in ten days, Lucius almost certainly took a steamer between Buffalo and Toledo, some three hundred miles away on the other edge of Lake Erie. "I have a warranty deed for 160 acres of as good land as there is in Michigan," Lucius wrote. "For said land I paid $148." The property is well situated, he continued, only "6 miles from Hillsdale Center which the railroad will be completed to from Adrian this season."[26] Lucius's prediction was accurate: a line of the Michigan Southern Railroad reached Hillsdale in September 1843.[27]

Lucius wrote his brother again from Allen in April 1843. "I traded one of my lots of land the other day for a lot with 35 acres improved, house and barn." Lucius said he would delay a planned visit to Phelps because he had gone into the potash business. "We have made three times and we find it profitable," he reported; "therefore we intend to follow the business." Potash, made from the ashes of trees burned to clear farm fields, was often the first product western settlers shipped east to raise cash. "This part of the country is settling fast," Lucius wrote. "Just where there was forest one year ago, the same surface is now waving with wheat. The cars will run to Hillsdale Center this summer, 6 miles east from where this child is, and then you can come out here in a hurry if you please." Regarding the extended family, Lucius wrote: "As for Lewis, I saw him a few weeks ago. He was well and is doing well I guess. He and his partner will have about 50 acres of mint to still this fall. You had better come out this fall and buy their oil. What is it worth now?"[28]

Lewis Ranney had migrated from Phelps to Michigan with peppermint roots in 1835. He was probably the first farmer in western Michigan to grow peppermint. He settled on the prairie near White Pigeon and got right to work growing and distilling peppermint for Henry's peddler business. But Lewis soon discovered that Ashfield was not the only market for his peppermint oil. He wrote to Henry from Phelps in November 1843: "I ought to have written a long time since but through the fall I occupy 20 hours in the 24 a-stilling therefore I wanted the rest for sleep." Peppermint oil was distilled from "hay" cut and dried on the fields in the fall. Lewis reported that he had left Florence, Michigan, with a load of newly processed oil in mid-October. "We brought down 594 pounds of oil we sold to Wells of Lyons at two dollars in advance and the rise [for] eight months. I have been here about three weeks. I shall tarry until good sleighing, and then go back." Phillip C. Wells was a peppermint oil broker working in western New York and, later, Michigan. Wells and Hiram Hotchkiss often worked together, and both offered terms that included an advance payment at the current market price and a guarantee to pay whatever the price might rise to in the months between contract and delivery. In this instance Lewis seems to have negotiated an even better deal, being guaranteed a share of the price rise for eight months after he delivered his oil to the broker, Wells.

"Smith and myself intend planting 30 acres in the spring of mint," Lewis concluded. "It is rather hard business, but I think it better than wheat."[29] Lewis's yield of a little over ten pounds of oil per acre was fair for a newly planted field. Growing peppermint involved planting root cuttings called stolons in plowed fields and cultivating them throughout the season to keep out weeds that could ruin the distilled oil's flavor. Peppermint was more labor intensive than wheat but also much more profitable. Lewis wrote again from Michigan in February 1844. He had waited for snow in Phelps, but when it did not come he set out in a wagon. "We found very good wheeling most of the way," he wrote. "We got two dollars per pound for our oil we sold to Wells of Lyons. He shipt it to New York, ours was to be sold with his. His agent sold sooner than Wells expected they were going to and when Wells was informed of the sale oil was worth $4.00 per lb in NY. Probably some Gum Game about it." Although Wells had promised Lewis a share of the price rise when he sold it on to a final customer, Wells had apparently been swindled. In spite of this disappointment, Lewis reiterated, "Smith and I intend putting in thirty acres this Spring to mint and that in addition to what we have already in I hope will give us some oil next fall for Pocket Change."[30]

Henry continued bottling peppermint essence for peddlers, and, like Jasper Bement, he expanded into other essences. In May 1844, his peddler Charles Sanderson wrote Henry from Leominster. He sent the letter with his brother, Henry's politically minded friend William, and asked: "If it is convenient you may pay him that last bill, one half in essence as follows, one half gross peppermint, one half gross wintergreen, one quarter each cinnamon, hemlock, lemon, aniseed and Sassafras, one quarter gross sassafras in large bottles if you have it. One half gross oil spruce, the balance proportioned as above."[31] A few months later, in August 1844, twenty-one-year-old Augustus Graves of Ashfield wrote to Henry from Franklin, Massachusetts, during a peddling trip. Instead of to Ashfield, however, Graves's envelope was addressed to 76 Union St., Boston. Henry had moved briefly to the city to begin a business partnership with George C. Goodwin, the brother of his new bride, Maria. The Goodwins were Ashfield natives whose father manufactured surgical splints. "I shall be in Boston in a week or 10 days at the most and I shall want an assortment of essences," Graves wrote. "I should like you to put up some essence of an <u>extra quality, twice as strong as any I have yet had of you</u>, without the alcohol being reduced. . . . I think I shall want about two gross of 4 ounce essence in peppermint, lemon, Wintergreen, hot drops etc. (and four or five gross 2 ounce ditto) I shall be in sometime next week and shall want considerable stuff if you have the right sort."[32] Although he became a Boston wholesaler, Henry Ranney continued supplying the peddler trade and soon returned to his home in western Massachusetts.

Although they were no longer technically partners, Jasper Bement and Henry Ranney remained close business associates and close friends. The two men also shared a political orientation favoring the abolition of slavery, as mentioned earlier. But their activism was much more substantial than simply preferring an end to slavery. Like William Sanderson, who had carried abolitionist tracts while peddling, Ranney and Bement continued in the Ashfield tradition of expressing their ideals on a national stage. In August 1844, Jasper Bement wrote to Henry Ranney from Syracuse, New York, where he had stopped on his way to Detroit. Bement touched briefly on business and then offered detailed descriptions of several conversations he had enjoyed with Liberty men and the reactions of strangers to whom he had offered abolitionist tracts at a political gathering. Bement gave Ranney some intelligence he had gathered on flour prices in Troy but then returned to politics and suggested a strategy for an upcoming Liberty Party convention. Bement confidentially advised Ranney against supporting Hooker Leavitt for the state Senate, because the voting public might become aware of his "disability" and reject him for public office. Leavitt was aiding runaway slaves on the Underground Railroad, which the men supported but were aware would disqualify him from election in 1844 in Massachusetts.[33]

A few days later Jasper Bement wrote to "Friend Ranney" from Buffalo, New York. Bement was unhappy his travels were taking so long and complained that the whole trip was likely to last six weeks. Although canal boats, railroads, and steamships on the Great Lakes had greatly reduced travel times between Massachusetts and Detroit, Bement was making several stops along the way to do business and talk politics. He mentioned he had lectured on abolition at a Liberty rally. Bement told Ranney he used Ranney's "notice," so apparently Henry had printed a handbill announcing talks about abolition. In addition to Liberty men, Bement found Whigs and Loco Focos (an equal rights faction of the Democratic Party) busily holding mass meetings. "Some of the Whigs," he said, "are most ready to vote for Liberty, but they think they must vote Clay in this time to keep Texas out." His prediction proved correct: the Whigs voted for Henry Clay in the next presidential election to prevent Democrat James K. Polk from being elected and annexing Texas. They failed to elect Clay, and Polk led the United States into the Mexican-American War.[34] Bement also described a visit to Niagara Falls, which he called a sublime spectacle. He mentioned seeing the monument at Queenston Heights, site of the first major battle of the War of 1812, and the battlefield of Lundy Lane. Bement closed by urging Ranney to write him care of Detroit. He addressed the letter to "Mr. Henry S. Ranney, Postmaster": the twenty-seven-year-old Ranney had returned from Boston and was becoming a substantial citizen of Ashfield.

When the R. G. Dun credit reporter visited Ashfield again in May 1847, he found Henry doing business on his own. The reporter wrote that Henry "manufacture[d] oil of peppermint at Ashfield" and had acceptable credit.[35] Augustus Graves wrote to Henry again from Middleborough, Massachusetts, on another peddling trip, to order twenty-nine dozen two-ounce essences, including six dozen peppermint; twelve dozen four-ounce essences, including six dozen peppermint; and six dozen half pints of peppermint in flat bottles, probably supplied by John Bement from Philadelphia. Graves also ordered cinnamon, wintergreen, hemlock, wormwood, spearmint, sassafras, anise, lemon, pennyroyal, goldenrod, Hot Drops, Balsam of Life, Balsam Honey, and Lee & B.'s Prestons Salts, "if you have them—no other."[36]

Henry Ranney positioned himself at the center of a commercial web that spread from the peppermint fields of western New York and Michigan to the wholesale market of Boston and the far-flung retail markets served by Ashfield's peddlers. Peppermint oil grown by his family and by trusted friends passed through his hands on its way to warehouses in the city or essence baskets carried by peddlers into the remotest corners of the nation. Throughout his career, Henry preferred to do business with people he knew and trusted. He continued this style of business well into the second half of the nineteenth century, in spite of the economic panics and credit crises many historians suggest began a shift toward a more impersonal style of commerce.[37]

In August 1847, as mentioned previously, Henry's cousin Frederick Ranney wrote from Centerville, Michigan, seeking payment for peppermint oil he had sent Henry the previous fall. In October Augustus Graves wrote again from Franklin, Massachusetts, to order fifty-four dozen two-ounce essences, including six dozen peppermint, as well as six dozen four-ounce peppermints and other patent medicines, including Carter's oil and opodeldoc.[38] The patent formula for the liniment Graves ordered was well known to suppliers like Ranney. Opodeldoc, attributed to the German alchemist Paracelsus, consisted of soap, alcohol, camphor, and wormwood.

In the spring of 1848, Jasper Bement wrote again to Henry. As he had done years earlier, Bement quickly left business behind and turned his attention to abolitionist politics. "So Cass is to be the slave holders tool," Bement wrote, "to do their infamous work and Northern Locos will fall down and worship. Already the Greenfield Democrat has him out with a long article and lauds him to the skies, puts on a thick coat of soft soap. Oh the full blaze of the 19th century!"[39] General Lewis Cass, who had been the territorial governor of Michigan, was running for president on a platform of popular sovereignty that advocated letting new territories decide whether to permit slavery. Cass's presidential campaign in 1848 drove many antislavery Northern Democrats into the arms of the Free-Soil Party. In addition to running a widespread peddler business with a far-reaching supply chain, Ranney and Bement continued to share a keen interest in national politics. And Henry's antislavery stance seems to have been shared by his brothers. In the spring of 1850 a younger brother, Lyman, wrote from Van Buren, Arkansas, where he was working as a store clerk. Lyman thanked Henry for sending him eastern newspapers but warned against forwarding any openly abolitionist Free-Soil papers. He reported, "Slavery exists here in almost all forms." Some slaves seemed to live under decent conditions, while others had it hard. The most alarming element of slavery, for the young man, seemed to be that "some slaves are black others are white. There is one boy around in town who is whiter than half the so called white children. He has very light colored hair, roman nose, and his features do not resemble a negro in the least. Yet this boy is a <u>slave</u>." Lyman said the boy was sold since his arrival for $150, less than half what he would have been worth if he had been visibly black. "If I had plenty of money," Lyman concluded, "when I go north I would purchase him and take with me and let them see what some of the subjects are that are held in bondage." Lyman did not purchase the boy, and he did not go back north. He took another job at a mercantile store in the "Indian Nation" at Tahlequah, where he died mysteriously in 1854.

In June 1850, George Goodwin wrote from Boston to "Brother Henry": "I received J. Bement's order and forwarded the goods in a day or two. Nothing particularly new. We would all be happy to see you Maria and children, can you come?"[40] In contrast with the findings of some historians of this period and region that kinship networks were losing their importance as the foundations of business relationships, we see that family bonds and close personal friendships were still central elements of widespread commercial networks such as those run by Ranney and his associates from Ashfield. Historian Paul E. Johnson, for example, seems to accept the idea popularized by Alexis de Tocqueville that very early in American history most kinship networks were disrupted, and "restraints of every kind were swept away by the market, by migration and personal ambition, and by the universal acceptance of democratic ideas." This does not seem to reflect the style of business Henry Ranney continued throughout his life.[41]

In addition to growing staples for the family and peppermint for the market, the Ranney brothers in Michigan were always on the lookout for business opportunities, and they and Henry continued to provide financial backing to each other across the miles. In February 1851, Lucius wrote to announce: "I and one of my neighbors bought a thrashing machine last fall. We paid $250 for it, we hired a man to work with us which we worked at thrashing about two months and thrashed about 10,000 bushels of wheat which come to $360." Lucius estimated that labor and wear and tear on the machinery would cost him only about $90 per season going forward, which would make the operation respectably profitable. "We can thrash and clean fit for marketing 80 bushels in 60 minutes," Lucius concluded, and "the town of Allen raised about 30,000 bushels of wheat this year."[42] Lucius also mentioned that he had been ill for a while, that he had rented out his farm for three years, and that he had had "a little daughter" in September—"healthy and of course a smart and good girl." Returning to business, Lucius wrote: "Lewis and [younger brother] Harrison intend to mint it some next season. They are doing tolerably well." Lucius concluded by requesting an extension on Henry's loan: "The money I am owing you if you wanted I will try and borrow it if I can. Sickness and building will bring me rather short until next fall. If you can wait until next fall it would favor me some. I rather think that Lewis cannot pay you until then." In addition to the business deals they were doing together, the brothers maintained a strong network of emotional and financial support across the miles.

In 1851, Henry Ranney bought an old (1792) tavern in Ashfield, which he remodeled as a home with several apartments, which he rented out.[43] Although he closed his general store, he remained active in the peppermint oil business. In October 1851, Lucius wrote again with news: "Lewis is very sick with a swollen leg, the doctors call it a species of irrasiplas." Erysipelas was a bacterial skin infection that was common and potentially deadly in an age before antibiotics. "Unless it is checked it will work up into his bowels and kill him," Lucius continued. Remembering his debt to Henry, he said: "The demands you have against me I am afraid that I shall not be able to send you this fall. But I think and hope that I shall be able to go down next fall myself and pay you. Times are uncommon hard in the state this fall. . . . As for oil peppermint, in consequence of Lewis's health they did not raise any."[44]

Lewis survived his infection, and he wrote to Henry in September 1853 to say, "My health in the main is quite good, able to do good fair days work. But not the nerve I carried in former years. I do not work very hard nor do not intend to." Lewis had reduced his farm to forty acres, which he thought he could work with the help of a local boy and his wife, who he reported "is quite a rugged woman and very ambitious and helps me a great deal from choice." Lewis informed Henry that their mother, Achsah, who had been staying in Allen with Lucius, planned to spend the winter in Phelps or Ashfield. The Ranney matriarch continued taking advantage of rail travel to move regularly between her sons' homes for the rest of her life. Lewis concluded by asking, "What is peppermint oil worth, I planted 5 acres last spring? It has been too dry for it.

Shall probably still about 30 or 35 pounds. I see it quoted at about 4.25 in New York papers."[45]

Lucius wrote a month later, saying: "The season has been so very dry that peppermint is very small indeed. There is some New York buyers about, they offer about $3.50 per pound. Lewis will have about 25 pounds. He has contracted a few pounds to the druggists in Hillsdale, Jonesville and Coldwater for five dollars per pound."[46] Although by this time New Yorkers like Wells and the Hotchkiss brothers were regularly visiting and sending agents to buy Michigan peppermint oil, family ties enabled Henry to maintain a foothold in an increasingly competitive market.

In June 1854, Lucius wrote to Henry and to their mother, Achsah, who was staying in Ashfield to nurse Henry's wife, Maria, in her final illness. Lewis had sold his farm and was looking for a small property near Lucius. Lucius added, "The Bements have sold to John Baggerly and he has moved out here so that we have got them for neighbors once more. Mr. Bement's folks have bought 3 miles South of Hillsdale. He sold for $2000 and bought for the same 80 acres."[47] Henry's wife, Maria Jane Goodwin, died in the spring of 1855, leaving behind a ten-year-old son, Ralph, and an eight-year-old daughter, Ella. Several of his brothers visited Henry that summer in Ashfield. In August 1855, Harrison Ranney wrote from South Allen, Michigan, to Anson Ranney, who had just arrived in Ashfield with their brother Lemuel. In addition to asking, "Why cannot Henry come out here this fall?" Harrison inquired about peppermint oil: "I wish you would ask Henry to find out if I could dispose of any Oil Peppermint, and how much and at what price, for if I could sell two three or four hundred pounds of Oil down there somewhere I would go down sometime this fall." Harrison said oil was worth three dollars per pound in Florence and wondered whether he could get four in Ashfield or Boston. "You be certain to find out about the Oil Peppermint," Harrison reminded Anson in closing. "I want to make one thousand dollars this fall. I may go to St. Louis with one lot of Oil. It is worth four dollars there."[48] Although the prices of commodities were beginning to become more uniform as information about distant markets was distributed over the new telegraph network, detailed knowledge of particular commodities and their markets continued to offer well-connected sellers like the Ranneys a competitive advantage.

When Lucius returned home to Michigan after his own visit to Ashfield, he wrote to Henry: "[Harrison] will start for Florence next Wednesday. He has not been out there yet but saw a young man from there a few days ago and he says they hold oil at four dollars a pound there. But Harrison thinks he can get it for $3.50 or $3 and rise, and will let you know the result as soon as he returns."[49] Henry brokered a deal for his brother, selling Harrison's peppermint oil to his late wife's brother George Goodwin in Boston. In November 1855, Harrison wrote to Henry: "I recd your letter containing the draft two or three days since and am glad Goodwin is satisfied with the oil, for I took some extra care to get that which was good and pure." Harrison reported that he and their brother Lemuel were visiting Lewis to help shuck his corn crop. Harrison concluded the letter with an apology: "Please excuse bad writing for I have been husking corn so long that my fingers are like sticks."[50]

Henry visited Phelps, New York, and Allen, Michigan, in 1856 with his children and his new wife, the Ashfield resident Julia A. Bassett. In July 1857, Lucius wrote to Henry: "There is not a day passes but what I think of you and also think of what a fine visit we had together last fall." As always, the letter begins with news of the family. "I suppose that you have heard that Harrison has a boy about three months old," Lucius wrote. "Anson's boy walks all over the house. . . . I moved the house from across the road over near where you and I staked out, and I find it much better or handier rather, it also looks better." Lucius continued, "Mother did not go out to Coldwater to see Mrs. Hathaway last fall, it did not seem to be convenient for her to go until she was afraid that Mrs. Hathaway was gone" Mrs. Hathaway was their cousin Lucretia, Samuel Ranney's daughter. Lucius added a postscript, to his twelve-year-old nephew and ten-year-old niece. "Ralph can't you take a basket of essences and take a trip out into Michigan and make a dime or two & see your kin, they would like to see you very much. Ella how can you manage to come out, try and study out some way can't you. If you cannot don't forget to write."[51] Although the Ranney letters were often filled with the details of the brothers' business dealings, they were always primarily concerned with maintaining the close bonds of the family across the distances that separated them.

Lucius made another trip to Ashfield in late 1857. Returning home to Allen, he wrote to Henry that he had stopped in Phelps on the way back. "I found Franklins folks well and Frank was making arrangements to move to Michigan in the spring."[52] With a national recession just beginning following the Panic of 1857, however, Franklin changed his mind and ultimately spent the rest of his days in Phelps. The next letter Henry received was from his brother Lemuel, who wrote at the request of their brother Lucius and his wife "to inform you of their affliction. They have lost their little girl. Little Cally is dead. We buried her last Wednesday. She had the scarlet fever in its most malignant form. . . . She suffered very much throughout her illness. It is a severe stroke on Lucius and Clarissa I assure you." In addition to the family tragedy, Lemuel filled his brother in on the local business climate. "The price of land has fallen 20 per cent since you were here last fall," he wrote. "How are the times down your way this winter? I hope not as tight as it is here."[53] The Panic of 1857 began a recession that lasted for two years and has been characterized as the first global recession. Many historians consider the widespread business failures in this period as the culmination of a trend that had begun two decades earlier, in the Panic of 1837. They describe a shift to a more impersonal style of business as "incremental movements in a long process of disentangling the claims of commerce from the claims of personal obligation."[54] As we see from the activities of the Ranneys here and from the business of the Hotchkiss brothers discussed below, however, the abandonment of a "moral economy" of kinship networks in favor of an impersonal "market ethic" was by no means immediate and universal.[55]

As his brothers in Michigan began to decrease their involvement with peppermint oil in the late 1850s, Henry cultivated other sources, again preferring to deal with relatives and close friends whenever possible. In October 1858, he received a letter from Harrison Hawley Lawrence responding to an inquiry about the peppermint oil market in Michigan. Lawrence was connected to the Ranneys through his wife, Mary, who was either a relative or a close friend of the family.[56] Lawrence wrote, "You say you would like to buy one or two hundred pounds of pure oil at a low figure. I have not got any oil on hand as I have just sold my crop of oil at two dollars per pound, but I know of good oil that can

Your notified

be had for 14/- per pound for the money. If you want old oil two years old I can get it for 13/- that I know is pure & free from weeds, for cash." Lawrence said most of the oil had already been sold but if Henry wished he would "get [him] a good article & fit it for transportation."[57]

The Ranney correspondence of the mid-nineteenth century and the Hotchkiss correspondence from the same period covered below frequently quote prices for peppermint oil in shillings rather than dollars and cents. Except during the inflationary Civil War years, the British pound sterling was worth between $4.80 and $4.90 throughout the nineteenth century. One British shilling (1/-) was one-twentieth of a pound, or, when exchanged for American currency, about twenty-four cents. This was not, however, the way the Ranneys and Hotchkisses understood shillings. When early American merchants who were not involved in foreign exchange used shillings, they were referring to a tradition in which a shilling was worth 12.5 cents, or one-eighth (one "bit") of a Spanish real. In this tradition, fourteen shillings equals $1.75. Oddly, in this alternate accounting, twenty shillings equals only $2.50, or about half the actual value of a British pound sterling.[58]

Henry relayed Lawrence's information to his brother-in-law and former Boston partner, George Goodwin, adding a markup to cover his services as broker. Goodwin replied, "I have bought a lower figure than you mention. I sell considerable quantities of oil of peppermint to retail apothecaries in the country, but as I said I have been supplied at a lesser price, genuine and pure, and can purchase now at the same price."[59] Lawrence wrote again, a few days later, and reiterated, "If you should want, or your brother-in-law, 200 pounds of oil you had better send soon as there is but little here. I know of 300 pounds of good new oil that can be had for 14/- [$1.75] per pound for the money."[60] On October 29, Henry wrote to Goodwin offering "100 lbs or more of pure, new, Oil Peppt, at $2.00 per pound." Henry offered his brother-in-law ninety-day credit terms to sweeten the deal and concluded, "I am not urgent about making any sales, for I have not ordered any oil yet."[61] George accepted the offer on those terms, and in late November Henry received another letter from Lawrence, stating: "I send by todays Express to G. C. Goodwin & Co. according to your order 100 lbs oil peppt of the first quality of new mint of this years raising. I have taken great pains in fitting it up for transportation." Lawrence passed along news of some other peppermint oil deals Henry had inquired about and concluded by mentioning, "I believe we intend paying your brothers in Hillsdale a visit in a short time."[62]

In the following weeks, Goodwin in Boston wrote "Brother Henry" to say, "The oil of peppermint has been received and I think it is a first-rate article."[63] And Harrison Ranney wrote to update his brother on the family. "Mother is making 7 lbs butter per week from her cow this winter," Harrison wrote. Achsah Sears Ranney had just turned seventy. And "Lem is not doing anything this winter but thinks or talks of going to Pikes Peak in the spring. There is quite an excitement here about the Gold in Kansas."[64] Until statehood in 1861, the Kansas Territory extended to the Rocky Mountains and included the Pikes Peak region that attracted more than a hundred thousand Fifty-Niner prospectors. In March 1859, Lemuel and Anson Ranney set off for the goldfields with three other local men. Anson rented out his farm and sent his wife and baby to stay with her parents.[65]

In the fall of 1859, Henry once again contacted H. H. Lawrence, to ask for four hundred pounds of peppermint delivered at $1.50 per pound. Lawrence responded: "Wells of Lyons is here at present. He is buying some and paying 12/- [$1.50]. So you can see I cannot make enough at the offer you make to pay me for buying and fitting it for transportation."[66] Lawrence asked for a handling charge of $2 per hundredweight, so he could make a small profit on the transaction. Henry agreed and sold two hundred pounds of Lawrence's peppermint oil to Goodwin for $1.75, making $46 profit on the deal, compared to $4 for Lawrence.[67] The Ashfielder was clearly in the driver's seat in these transactions, demonstrating the strength of the interstate network of friends and relations he controlled. But Henry's interest in the peppermint oil business was decreasing. Although the deals Henry occasionally brokered yielded him good profits for very little effort, Phillip Wells and his associates the Hotchkiss brothers (discussed below) were already buying most of the peppermint oil produced in Michigan. And unlike Wells and Hotchkiss, who were able to communicate between Michigan and New York by telegraph when necessary, Henry was limited to postal letters because the telegraph did not reach Ashfield until the 1890s.

In October 1860, Lawrence replied to Henry's annual query, explaining that "the crop was not large on account of the drought, it has been very dry the latter part of the summer here. I raised 140 pounds of oil, which I sold a short time since for two dollars per pound." Lawrence warned that "Messrs. Wells and Hotchkiss of Lyons New York has bought all the oil in the state. I do not know of a pound for sale. They paid two dollars per pound."[68] Henry used this information to close a transaction with his brother-in-law that had been left unresolved from the previous season. "A short time since I had advices from Michigan that Hotchkiss and Wells of Phelps and Lyons New York had purchased the whole of the oil of Michigan," Henry wrote to George Goodwin, "paying from $2-$2.50 for it, it is supposed, for the purpose of controlling the price. . . . In relation to the oil sold by you," Henry concluded, "I leave it for you to make the proper account of sales, or if not convenient to do it in detail, then the net result."[69] Goodwin replied apologetically, explaining that Henry's bill had been mislaid, and then sent Henry "our check for $172.51 in payment for 93 pounds of peppermint at $1.75 per pound and one years interest on the same at 6%. If this is entirely satisfactory to you we will call the account settled in full to date, if not we will try to make it so."[70] The close personal relationship maintained by Henry and Goodwin certainly facilitated the resolution of the outstanding issue. As we will soon see from the Hotchkiss brothers' story, business dealings between people lacking such trust—even when related—were often much less amicable.

Although Henry expended much less energy in his peppermint business than his rivals in western New York, his strong personal network allowed him to remain competitive. In 1861 he tried to get ahead of his competitors and contacted Lawrence a month early, in late August. Lawrence replied, "I have 10 acres of new mint that looks the best of any I have seen. I think there will not be half the oil this fall there was last fall. Mr. Wells and Hotchkiss of Lyons New York is coming out soon with the intention of buying the whole crop.[71] Lawrence included a wholesale price list clipped from the August 21, 1861, *Western Chronicle* in Three Rivers, Michigan, that quoted "Peppermint Oil, 2 25 a 2 50." A few weeks later, Lawrence wrote again, saying that he had distilled 218 pounds of peppermint oil from his ten acres of new plants, which he would let go for eighteen shillings [$2.25]. "It is rather early yet to sell oil," he wrote, "as most farmers are not stilling yet. But as you have dealt with me for some time past in the oil matter, I will offer as low as I dare."[72]

Henry relayed Lawrence's information to Goodwin, adding: "I think my information is reliable, and as I know Hotchkiss and something of his circumstances and management, I think it likely that he and his partner may buy up pretty near the whole crop."[73] Goodwin replied that he would buy one hundred pounds at $2.50 or the full 218 at $2.25. He mentioned the current price quoted in Boston was seventeen shillings [$2.125] per pound.[74] The day he received Goodwin's offer, Henry wrote to Lawrence with an offer. "My brother Frank at Phelps NY writes me that Hotchkiss is buying oil Pep there for $1.75 per lb and is to allow the advance or rise in price, if any, 'till the first of January." Henry told Lawrence that as they had been doing business with each other for several years, he preferred to continue dealing with friends and hoped they could settle a deal to their mutual advantage. Lawrence challenged Henry's information from Phelps. He wrote, "You stated that Hotchkiss was buying oil pepp at 14/- [$1.75] per lb. Oil cannot be had here for that price. Oil is held here at $2.00 per lb now."[75] But Lawrence accepted Henry's offer and shipped his peppermint oil for fifteen shillings [$1.875] per pound, after receiving a "package of money" totaling $410 in New England banknotes.[76]

While he was negotiating this transaction, Henry received a letter from his brother Lucius, who had been ill. "I was obliged to stop work entirely," Lucius wrote. "Of course I had to commence doctoring and the more I doctored the worse I grew, and I tried a second doctor and the third and so on until I got so debilitated from the top of my head to the soul of my feet that I could not eat sleep nor rest in no shape." In spite of his illness, Lucius reported that he had "just finished husking and digging potatoes. I had about 150 bushels of potatoes and about 1000 bushels ears corn. I had about 200 bushels wheat."[77] One of the most remarkable features of the Ranney brothers' letters is the apparent obligation the brothers felt to stay in touch, even decades after they had all gone their separate ways. In spite of his illness, Lucius began this letter to Henry with an apology for not writing sooner that was typical of the brothers' correspondence. "It is been so long since I have written to you that I am at a loss to know what to write first," Lucius wrote. "It is been some two years since I have written to you, and on the other hand you cannot boast much of writing to me that time and for my part I feel ashamed that such a state of things should have occurred, but so it is." There is no reason to believe the Ranneys were unique in this feeling; western archives are full of evidence of correspondence and visiting between extended families, friends, and even old neighbors from back east. Nineteenth-century Americans, at least in the Yankee West, were much more connected than history sometimes gives them credit for being. Perhaps we discount the connectedness of rural Americans in this period because, as historian Susan E. Gray has observed, the historiography of the Yankee migrations is complicated by the story Yankees created for themselves "coeval" with settlement, and by "an interpretation that reigned from the 1890s to about 1950, to which the works of Frederick Jackson Turner are central."[78]

The next peppermint harvest was affected by drought and also by the Civil War. Lawrence wrote to Henry in September 1862: "Of 14 acres I got but about 142 lbs oil and 4 acres of that was new mint. We are holding our oil at 22/- [$2.75] per lb." Three men from New York were in the fields, Lawrence wrote, and "they offer[ed] 20/- [$2.50] and the rise for oil," but the farmers were holding out for a better offer. "The war is causing some excitement here," Lawrence added. "Every young man has enlisted that is able to carry a musket. Drafting is soon expected here."[79] Henry offered Lawrence's oil to Goodwin at twenty-five shillings, or $3.125, a pound. "The practice of those Yorkers (Hotchkiss &c.)," he explained, "is usually to offer or make a stipulated price, and grant the seller the advantage of the rise for a few months. They make such offers this year."[80] Goodwin dragged his feet, possibly hoping for a lower price. By the time he gave Henry his order a month later, Lawrence had sold his peppermint oil and reported there was none left for sale in the region.[81]

Henry contacted Lawrence early in the 1863 season, and by the end of August Goodwin had agreed "to engage about 200 lbs oil peppt." This time, Goodwin wrote, "I am willing to pay the market price, but wish to secure it so that it should not this time slip through my fingers."[82] The following year, wartime inflation and drought combined to drive prices to levels that had not been seen since the early days of peppermint growing. "There is no established price," Lawrence wrote in September 1864. "Those having any amount are holding at from $8.00 to $10 per lb. The crop is not ¼ of a yield to what we have formerly raised. . . . I had but 120 lbs from 20 acres of land. . . . I say to you if you want what I have, 120 lbs at $6.00 per lb, you may have it."[83] Lawrence also wrote that he planned to hold his five-hundred-bushel wheat harvest "until next Spring. If gold should advance much more, wheat will, which the prospects looks favorable for gold to advance still more yet."[84] Peppermint farmers were well aware of the risks and opportunities presented by inflation in the Civil War's greenback economy, as we will soon see in greater detail.

After the wartime price spike, Henry's interest in the peppermint oil business waned. In 1867, Lawrence reported that oil was scarce because the crop had been winter-killed, and Henry bought just twenty pounds for Goodwin.[85] The following September, Henry bought two hundred pounds for three dollars a pound.[86] He also heard from his son Ralph, who had survived his Civil War service in the 34th Massachusetts Regiment and had taken up peddling.[87] Ralph wrote from Northfield, Vermont, while peddling in the Connecticut River Valley. "I can't think of anything that will impress one of the greatness of our country," Ralph said, "[more] than to travel mile after mile by rail in a state like this and then look at the United States map and compare distances."[88] A few weeks later, Ralph wrote again: "A man was run over by the cars near the Depot at the crossing last night and his leg and arm cut off and otherwise badly mangled. He is yet alive. He was intoxicated at the time. Is now sober!"[89]

Henry effectively retired from the peppermint oil business when he was elected for a second time in 1868 to represent Ashfield in the Boston legislature.[90] Goodwin approached Henry for more peppermint oil late in the 1868 season, and Lawrence responded to Henry's inquiry, "I am out of the business at present. . . . I find I can get you two cans of oil 40 lbs at $4.75."[91] Although also nearly out of the business, Henry brokered a final deal, selling Lawrence's oil to Goodwin for $5.50 per pound.[92]

In August 1869, Lemuel Ranney wrote to Henry: "We buried our mother a week ago today. She died on Saturday night August 7 at 11 o'clock, entirely conscious and able to talk up to the last moment. . . . I suppose you know mother's age. It was 80 years three months and

27 days."[93] Born in 1789, Achsah Sears Ranney saw remarkable changes in her lifetime. A pioneer settler of western New York, in later life she took advantage of the transportation revolution to travel regularly by rail between her children's homes in Massachusetts, New York, and Michigan. After her death, as the Ranney brothers aged, their letters became less frequent and more filled with news of the deaths of family and friends. In 1877, Alonzo Franklin Ranney wrote to Henry from Phelps: "I think sometimes of selling my farm in order to get rid of so many tears and hard work. But just now it would be hard disposing of it except at a sacrifice." Alonzo invited his brother to visit: "It will be 20 years this fall since you are out here."[94]

An element of the Ranney letters that should not escape notice is that throughout the decades of their correspondence the brothers never addressed religion or wrote to each other about faith. Even events like their mother's death and the jarring loss of Henry's wife and Lucius's young daughter never elicited an expression of religious sentiments. The Ranneys all seem to have shared their uncle Samuel's secularism; if not in the affirmative sense of Samuel's materialism, at least in their apparent lack of interest in religion. They lived in the "burned-over" district of western New York while the fires of the Second Great Awakening were raging but were apparently untouched by the flames. Perhaps historical accounts of the overwhelming influence of religion on rural American society are overstated.

Toward the end of the nineteenth century, the Ranney brothers began to die. In early 1881, Anson Ranney wrote to Henry, "I have sometimes thought that we would hardly know how many there were left of us, if we did not write each other and find out how many were living in how many dead." Anson related the details of the recent death of their brother Lewis. "Sarah [his widow] still lives on the place and Everett our boy is going to work it this summer."[95]

Anson closed his letter to Henry with an invitation to "[you] and your wife to come out here to Mich on a visit. I would so much like to have you come and make us all a long visit. We ought to write each other oftener than we do." Harrison Ranney wrote in 1885 from Clearwater, Minnesota, with news of cousins and old neighbors.[96] In early 1886, Lemuel Ranney wrote, "I come to you with sad news. Brother

Anson died last Wednesday after a short illness of one week. . . . He says I intended to write to Henry today but I don't feel able to and probably never shall again. I went up again on Tuesday morning and stayed with him until he died Wednesday about 11 o'clock." Lemuel also passed along information on the health of the surviving brothers and the death of Frederick, the son of their cousin Samuel Ranney. "I saw his son Frederick in Detroit about two months ago," Lemuel wrote. "I also saw Charlie Hathaway [Lucretia's husband] who is city inspector of buildings in Detroit."

In 1893, Henry wrote a long letter to the editor of the *Phelps Citizen*, in answer to an inquiry regarding the Massachusetts peppermint oil business. He narrated the introduction of peppermint to Ashfield by Samuel Ranney, its transportation to Phelps by Archibald Burnett, and the migrations of the Ranneys to Phelps. After more than a thousand words, Henry remarked: "I find I have written more than I intended, but have been led on by personal interest with regard to the mint business, for in my youthful days I assisted my father in its cultivation and distillation, and later, during the 25 years that I was in the mercantile business. I manufactured and sold thousands of gallons of essences—mostly at wholesale rates in supplying peddlers."[97]

Henry Ranney died on January 23, 1899, at eighty-one years of age. Although he had been a Free-Soil abolitionist and a key figure in the essence-peddling and peppermint oil businesses, the obituary in the local newspaper remembered him primarily for the unprecedented fifty years he had served as Ashfield's town clerk.[98] His two wives and five children all predeceased Henry, but four grandchildren and his brothers Alonzo Franklin in New York, Lemuel in Michigan, and Harrison in Minnesota survived him and carried the Ranney family legacy into the twentieth century.

The history of the Ranney family's involvement in the western expansion of the peppermint business illustrates the important role played by family networks in rural commerce. Although nineteenth-century economic changes tended to decrease the importance of personal loyalty and kinship networks, especially in cities, the close ties maintained by the rural Ranneys and their associates gave them a competitive advantage against rivals lacking these secure networks. Next, we turn our attention to the Hotchkiss brothers, Hiram and Leman, who were the first Americans to declare themselves peppermint kings. Although their activities overlapped with those of the Ranneys, the Hotchkisses struggled throughout their careers with the limits of trust, both with strangers and with close family members.

Prize Medal Oil of Peppermint

As discussed above, the early history of the peppermint oil industry featured serial migration and the development of a strong family business network that gave Ashfield native Henry Ranney a competitive advantage over his rivals. The second part of the story overlaps significantly with the first, taking place primarily in New York and Michigan during the middle years of the nineteenth century. It is mainly the story of Hiram and Leman Hotchkiss, brothers who dominated the local business, created a national brand, and declared themselves peppermint kings. Like Ashfield's family-dominated peppermint business, the Hotchkiss enterprise was operated by two brothers and their families. Unlike the Ranney operation, however, the Hotchkiss peppermint business involved a shift toward modern business practices that aligned with the Hotchkiss brothers' predilections for conflict and controversy. Although born and raised in rural western New York, the brothers operated an international business that included essential oil distilling, brokerage, branding, exporting, and banking—but also bickering, name-calling, and quite a bit of litigation. Their story illustrates the difficult economic transition of the nineteenth century and suggests Hiram and Leman Hotchkiss viewed themselves not as peripheral players in a changing world of trade and finance dominated by New York City but as formidable competitors at the center of their own commercial network.

Peppermint oil production in western New York began in the 1810s following the introduction of peppermint roots by the peddler Archibald Burnett. By the time the Ranneys had begun settling in Phelps, many of their former neighbors were already living in the area, raising peppermint, distilling it, and shipping the oil to Ashfield for the peddler trade, and to Boston and New York City for use in medicines, confections, and cordials. But this is not the history of peppermint remembered by contemporary western New Yorkers. The story of peppermint in Phelps and Lyons has been retold to put the western New York region and the Hotchkiss brothers at the center, often by writing out anything that happened before New York's peppermint kings ascended their thrones.

A 1903 newspaper article, for example, described Hiram Hotchkiss as merely a small-time storekeeper in 1841 to emphasize the way his fortunes grew when he "discovered" peppermint oil, and it included an account of Yankee peddler "Jim" Burnett dickering with Phelps farmers over small quantities of oil.[1] The 1903 account became a key source for a charming but inaccurate article published in *Yankee Magazine* in 1957, and it is still typical of the error-filled storytelling perpetuated in commemorative celebrations such as Lyons's annual "Peppermint Days" and interpretive materials at Lyons's H. G. Hotchkiss Museum and the Museum of Wayne County History. Local accounts not only give Hotchkiss undue credit for developing the New York peppermint oil business, they understate his prominence in regional business *before* his entry into the essential oil trade. Local histories of Phelps and Lyons, New York, uncritically build on these accounts, giving credit to the Hotchkiss brothers as the originators and first kings of the peppermint oil business. In fact, Hiram and Leman Hotchkiss originated little but rather were important innovators who created one of America's first globally recognized brands and changed the way essential oils were marketed.

The Hotchkiss brothers were sons of a western New York merchant named Leman Hotchkiss and his wife, Chloe Gilbert, who had arrived in Phelps in 1811, about the same time as peppermint. Like the Ranneys, the Hotchkiss family was a widely distributed clan, whose first home in America had been in southern Connecticut, near New Haven. Leman Hotchkiss had moved to Phelps from Oneida Castle, about eighty-five

miles to the east. Leman's brothers William and Calvin had also migrated to western New York about the same time, becoming a Niagara
County judge and a wealthy landowner, respectively, in Lewiston, near
Niagara Falls. Twenty-six-year-old Leman opened a gristmill on Flint
Creek, which he named the Eagle Mill after noticing a bald eagle perched
on its roof. The Eagle Mill prospered, and Leman opened a general store
that became the region's largest, reputedly doing more than a hundred
thousand dollars in annual business in the early 1810s.[2]

In 1816, Leman opened a second store, in Lyons, about ten miles
north of Phelps, and then opened a third store, in nearby Newark, in
1822, sending his twelve-year-old son, Hiram, to work there as clerk while
he trained his younger son, Leman Beecher, at the Phelps store. When
the elder Leman died unexpectedly in 1826, his two sons took over the
family businesses, while their mother, Chloe, and their uncle William
managed Leman's substantial estate. Chloe and William retained control
of the estate well into the 1830s, long after Hiram and Leman B. had
reached majority. The Hotchkiss brothers probably received their first
exposure to litigation and to trading in distressed assets while watching
the ongoing administration of their father's complicated estate.[3]

The brothers learned the milling and mercantile trades well. By
1829, eighteen-year-old Hiram, his sixteen-year-old brother Leman, and
their cousin William T. Hotchkiss were partners in a general store and
owned two mills in Phelps and a third mill in Seneca Falls. The combined capacity of the Hotchkiss mills was more than five hundred barrels of flour daily.[4] The opening of the Erie Canal, completed in 1825,
provided the Hotchkiss mills with a ready market for flour in New York
City. The Hotchkisses partnered with fellow western New Yorkers at the
prominent Manhattan brokerage firm of Dows and Cary.

Ira B. Cary's first business had been shaving shingles on the banks
of the Mohawk River during western New York's long winters and float-
ing them to market in the city each spring. When New York's governor,
DeWitt Clinton, began constructing the Erie Canal in 1817, Cary and his
partner, John Dows, immediately recognized the opportunity and became the first shippers to operate canal boats on the new waterway.[5]
Dows and Cary opened offices in Albany and New York, and they were
running fifteen boats on the canal by 1829.[6]

In the early 1830s, the Dows and Cary firm was one of the leading flour commission merchants in New York. The firm sold flour shipped to it by merchant millers like the Hotchkisses, taking a commission on each transaction as well as charging fees for shipping and storage. As their business expanded, Dows and Cary also advanced money on inventories, charging interest, and discounted notes for its upstate clients. Discounting was a method of converting debt obligations to cash by selling promissory notes to financial institutions at a discount from their face value that reflected the interest. Discounting involved risk because the discounting firm was liable if the maker of the note defaulted. David Dows, John's younger brother, joined Dows and Cary in 1833 at the age of nineteen and became increasingly involved in managing the firm in the early 1840s during his brother's illness prior to John's death in 1844. As a young businessman of similar background, raised in Saratoga, apprenticed in Utica, and roughly the same age as the Hotchkiss brothers, David Dows was the firm's main contact with Hiram and Leman.[7]

By the mid-1830s, travel and shipping time from Buffalo to New York City had been halved, from twenty days to ten. More important, freight costs fell by a factor of twenty, from one hundred dollars a ton to five dollars. More than 150,000 tons of freight was shipped through the canal to Albany annually, including nearly three-quarters of a million barrels of flour.[8] Although the Hotchkiss brothers' shipments were a small part of this total, they were not insignificant. In December 1842, for example, David Dows wrote Hiram to acknowledge "receipt of your flour, 8442 barrels 948 half-barrels ... amounting to $3915.76."[9] Dows also warned the brothers that the company had already advanced Hotchkiss more than ten thousand dollars on the season's flour shipments, adding: "It is quite certain we shall need some remittance and you may as well send at once say $2,000." A week later, Dows wrote again to say he had sold 1,388 barrels and one hundred half barrels of Hotchkiss flour for $6,174.18. The proceeds would be applied against Dows and Cary's advances, but Dows noted that he still had more than three thousand barrels on hand; "the demand is quite small generally."[10]

A year later, Dows wrote Hiram to warn him that his balance due had risen to $32,840.44, and that "against this we have in hand unaccounted for 4993 barrels and 445 half barrels."[11] Although at 1843 flour prices the inventory held by Dows and Cary would easily cover the debt, David Dows's concern that the flour was not accounted for shows the seeds of a disagreement. Dows expected to have his advances repaid when the notes associated with them came due, typically in sixty days. Hotchkiss, on the other hand, felt no urgency, believing that the value of the flour held in New York was adequate security to extend the debt. Hotchkiss expected to roll over his paper into new notes, adding interest and fees to the principal carried forward. After a few more months, Dows had sold off another 3,600 barrels worth nearly twenty thousand dollars, and the proceeds had paid down the outstanding balance.[12] Although Hiram's perspective differed from Dows's, it was defensible for a product that sold quickly and at fairly consistent prices. If Dows wanted his money faster, Hiram reasoned, all he had to do was sell the flour. As we will see, Hiram's assumptions regarding a ready market and stable prices were not so easily transferable to the peppermint oil business.

As merchants in Phelps in the 1820s, the Hotchkiss brothers were surely aware that families such as the Burnetts, the Vandermarks, and the Ranneys were all deeply involved in growing peppermint, distilling oil, and selling their output to merchants in Ashfield, Boston, and New York City. A publicity campaign begun by Hiram Hotchkiss and proudly carried on by his descendants after his death has, however, distorted the facts to the point where newspapers, regional historians, museums, and even a published history of the peppermint oil industry incorporate the misinformation Hotchkiss had originally promulgated to boost his essential oil sales.

According to the H. G. Hotchkiss Company's retelling of the peppermint story, sometime in the 1830s farmers began taking peppermint oil "with their wheat to the Hotchkiss store where Hiram accepted jugsfull in trade for goods. The supply grew until there were 1,200 pounds stashed in the store cellar." Hiram drove a wagonload of oil down to New York City, says the story, only to discover that American oil was considered unmarketable—especially when compared to the premium oil produced in Mitcham, England. Undeterred, Hotchkiss discovered that the arbiters of quality peppermint oil resided in Germany, "bottled some, shipped it to Hamburg and then waited." After a long wait, Hiram was informed that "his peppermint oil was declared by Hamburg authorities as the purest in the world." So, discovering "there were no large markets in America for the product," Hotchkiss decided to challenge the formidable international competition.[13]

While the Hotchkiss account exaggerated the details that favored Hiram, there are some important elements of truth. Hiram's first international sale consisted of an unsolicited bulk shipment of peppermint oil to Hamburg, Germany, around 1839. The tale of this first shipment is told in several local histories and repeated in James E. Landing's agricultural history *American Essence*, which to a great extent is an uncritical compilation of such stories. The Hamburg shipment is considered the beginning of the H. G. Hotchkiss Company, which dates its establishment from 1839—although, as we will see, the changing nature of the Hotchkiss brothers' business and the ongoing, semisecret partnership between Hiram and Leman makes setting precise dates problematic.[14] Hiram shipped his oil in metal containers marked "Peppermint Oil from Wayne County, U.S.A. Guaranteed Pure by H. G. Hotchkiss." After waiting several months for a decision on the quality of their oil, the brothers received an acknowledgment that their shipment had been judged suitable for Hamburg customers. The notice included an order for more oil than Hiram had originally shipped. The Hamburg endorsement of Hotchkiss's oil was considered a turning point for Hotchkiss's business, although Hiram had already begun moving his business from Phelps to Lyons in these years to take better advantage of the canal for shipping flour, and he began acquiring properties in foreclosure after the failure of the Bank of Lyons in 1842. And there was a final motivation for Hiram to move to Lyons. In 1833, he had married a Lyons resident, Mary Ashley, daughter of the town's physician, who had migrated from Deerfield, Massachusetts, around the turn of the century. Hiram and Mary settled on a large estate known as the Hecox mansion in the center of Lyons, where they had twelve children.

Hiram's brother, Leman, remained in Phelps, where he married Lucretia Oaks in 1844 and began raising three children with her before her death in 1855. After losing his wife, Leman tried unsuccessfully to scale back his activities as part of the partnership with Hiram and to focus more on his own business and less on supporting his brother's. Leman and Hiram officially ended their partnership in the essential oils business in 1855, but their business interactions only became more complicated. The convoluted family-business dynamics of the Hotchkisses are examined in detail in chapter 7.

There is also truth in the assertion that there was not much opportunity for domestic sales of essential oils for the Hotchkiss brothers until they found a market not dominated by their neighbors the Ranneys. Shipment of peppermint oil from Phelps to Massachusetts for the peddler trade was controlled by an earlier generation of men such as Roswell Ranney in Phelps, working in coordination with Henry Ranney in Ashfield. Although Henry later stated he knew Hiram and his business practices, there is no evidence the Hotchkisses ever made any significant inroads into this older peppermint business or supplied peppermint oil to Ashfield. Hiram and Leman did, however, take advantage of opportunities to buy oil from local farmers and ship it to New York City on the canal, along with their flour.

In an era before rolling mills and the grain elevators invented in 1842 in Buffalo by another Erie Canal shipper, Joseph Dart, flour from different sources was readily distinguishable on the basis of quality.[15] Historian William Cronon has described the standardization and commodification of flour in the later nineteenth century, and the corresponding decrease in the power of farmers relative to processors. But when the Hotchkiss brothers were merchant millers, a local miller with solid connections to urban brokers had considerable power in the local market. The standard for acceptable flour was relatively easy to achieve, and the processes employed were well-known. By all accounts, the Hotchkiss mills produced quality flours.

Unlike staples such as wheat and corn that required postharvest processing by millers who added value, peppermint was traditionally distilled on the farm. Buying already-distilled peppermint oil complicated the Hotchkiss brothers' ambition to differentiate the end product based on quality. The Hotchkisses branded their farina and other mill products. Similarly, they wanted to create a peppermint oil brand they could sell at premium prices. It took the brothers several years to determine how selling oil differed from selling flour.

Because they focused on selling oil in wholesale quantities to makers of medicines or confections, Hiram and Leman needed to convince their customers that not all peppermint oil was equal. Their innovation was to build a brand name associated with consistency and quality. Although both brothers accumulated several hundred acres of land over the years and grew some peppermint of their own, most of the essential oil sold under Hotchkiss labels was grown and distilled by independent farmers, first in western New York and later in Ohio, Indiana, and Michigan. The development of a Hotchkiss brand thus hinged on strict quality control and on effective marketing. The main focus of the Hotchkiss brothers' effort was a decades-long campaign to raise the prestige of their peppermint oil by comparing it with foreign oil rather than American competitors'.

Since peppermint's earliest days, the Hotchkiss brothers claimed, British peppermint oil had always been considered vastly superior. It was true that British peppermint oil produced in Mitcham, England, where the plant had first been commercially grown, sold at prices three or four times greater than those received for American oils.[16] British peppermint oil was considered the world's best, but its production was also limited by the availability of farmland in the area surrounding Mitcham. Demand was increasing both in Britain and on the Continent. The price difference between scarce British peppermint oil facing high demand and abundant American oil may have been due more to supply and demand than to quality. Hiram and Leman recognized that there might be a substantial foreign market for Hotchkiss peppermint oil that their American competitors had not yet tried to serve. The brothers realized that if they could convince foreign buyers that Hotchkiss peppermint oil was comparable to British oil, they could sell their product in foreign markets at much higher prices and use the prestige derived from that success to command premium prices in America. They also understood that if they convinced Americans that the premium paid for British oil was due to its higher quality, then any success they had selling their own peppermint oil overseas would set them apart from any other American brand.

Throughout his career, Hiram Hotchkiss had an unfailing confidence in his unique personal capability to distinguish the quality of peppermint oil. He considered himself an infallible judge, easily able to spot oils tainted with weeds during distilling or deliberately adulterated afterward. When he grew his own peppermint, he paid crowds of farm-workers to hoe his peppermint fields three or four times a season, to ensure that at harvest time there would be minimal contamination of the mint hay. The difficulty he often faced was convincing other people of his expertise, especially when this insistence frequently took the form of claiming that his own oil was obviously superior or that a rival was willing to sell oil for less because it was old, of poor quality, or had been cut with turpentine. Although apothecaries and medicine manufactur-ers remained an important market for Hotchkiss oil, a rapidly growing confectionary market offered the Hotchkisses their most significant opportunity. Mass-produced brand-name candies would not reach con-sumers for another half century, but by the middle of the nineteenth century Americans were developing a sweet tooth, and small candy-making concerns operated in every city. Although Hiram focused most of his energy on developing a distribution channel through commission agents and later exporters, confectioners were his target clientele. A twenty-one-ounce bottle of peppermint oil, he announced, would fla-vor a thousand pounds of candy.

Despite Hiram's claims, there really was no objective standard for peppermint oil quality. And sometimes his own product did not meet the standards Hiram claimed for it. In February 1843, for example, Da-vid Dows wrote to Hiram acknowledging receipt of nine crates contain-ing fifty-three cans of peppermint oil, valued at $1,916.63. Unfortunately, Dows reported, the oil had been contaminated with water, which had rusted the insides of the containers and then frozen during shipment, bursting some of the cans.[17] Luckily for Hotchkiss, occasional quality issues with the peppermint oil did not prevent Dows from doing busi-ness with the brothers, and in August 1843 the two companies entered a joint venture to operate a flour mill in Seneca Falls.[18] The soft demand for Hotchkiss's peppermint oil, however, did cause Dows and Cary to regard the product more skeptically than it did flour. In February 1844, David Dows wrote to Hiram: "We have had a number of applications for HG&LBH oil but as yet none take hold."[19] Hotchkiss believed Dows and Cary did not push his peppermint oil as aggressively as it ought. For its part, Dows and Cary was frustrated that the oil, which Hotchkiss ex-pected the company to advance money on as readily as flour, languished in its warehouses. Later in the year, when the peppermint oil had been sold and Hiram had shipped another batch, Dows reacted to the request from Hiram to begin advertising his oil before Dows and Cary had received it: "It will not answer for us to advertise the oil till it arrives. It would be unpleasant to advertise an article and have a purchaser call and have to say to him we have not got it but expect to have this."[20] Hiram responded, "When the 21 boxes oil peppermint arrive containing 1820 5/16 pounds please advertise . . . that you have just received 89 cans of pure oil of peppermint from Ontario and Wayne County containing 1820 pounds and that the same will be warranted by you to be pure and unadulterated and that same is believed to be equal to the best English oil." Hiram noted that he wanted Dows to try to sell the oil in a single lot because he suspected that people buying oil in small parcels would be more likely to adulterate the product to "stretch" it.[21]

Hiram's suspicions of adulteration were not limited to buyers of small batches, however. A few days later, Hiram wrote to Dows again: "We notice in the Journal of Commerce of the second instant and Express of the sixth instant the sale of 2500 pounds pure oil peppermint at $2.63 1/2 per pound. This is no doubt the Wells lot and it was probably sold to Miller who no doubt will soon adulterate it." Phillip Wells was a peppermint oil broker with whom Hiram later worked closely, but Hiram suspected anyone who beat him on any deal. Hiram told Dows, "We believe our lot nearly the only lot Pure in your city. We want you to keep our lot of oil advertised till sold."[22] Dows responded with a clipping of the advertisement he had placed, which unfortunately had failed to bring any buyers.[23] Three months later, Hiram wrote to Dows again: "Our oil of peppermint does not seem to work off satisfactorily but is worth all we ask for it and why it does not sell is a mystery."[24] Dows responded, "Miller says he sold his oil bought last fall without touching it. There appears to be no disposition on the part of any of the oilmen to buy . . . we do not believe a sale could be made here at over 16 shillings [$2.00]."[25]

Hiram's patience with Dows began to fray. The day after he wrote to Dows, Hiram wrote to an exporter named George Morewood proposing a consignment deal to ship peppermint oil directly to Liverpool. "We are extensive dealers in the article and our object in making shipments to

England would be to get the value (if possible) of a pure and unadulter-
ated article, and if we could do so our shipments to England would be
quite large, say about 5000 pounds annually." Hiram noted that a pound
of American peppermint oil usually sold in England for between eight
and twelve shillings ($1.00 to $1.50), while British oil commanded at least
thirty shillings ($3.75). "There can be no doubt in our minds," he con-
cluded, that a pure article of American oil is equal in value to the English.
We would like to have your opinion in regard to this matter and whether
your partners in England would be able to discriminate and get for a
pure article its real value?"[26] In May Morewood agreed to advance Hiram
$342 for 120 twenty-one-ounce bottles of peppermint oil, which would
be used as samples to attract customers in England.[27] Dows and Cary
continued to insist, "Nothing new in oil of peppermint, had no calls for
it."[28] Several weeks later, David Dows reiterated his position: "We have
had one applicant for oil since we wrote you, but he would not talk about
it at your price and such has been the case with all that have applied."[29]

The Hotchkiss brothers soon discovered they were no longer Dows
and Cary's only contacts in the peppermint oil business. Leman wrote to
Hiram in late summer 1845 that "Cary says he has just received a letter
from a Gent in Michigan (White Pigeon) which says he shall during
September have in about 6000 pounds oil of peppt & wants an advance
of 8/- per pound."[30] A few days later, Leman reported about "a sample of
oil belonging to Hale which old Ranney took to David Dows and requested him to ascertain the most he could get for it."[31] Alfred Hale was
a peppermint farmer in Alloway, a village along the road between Phelps
and Lyons. Although less famous than the Hotchkiss brothers, Hale and
his sometime partner, banker William Parshall (whose son DeWitt married one of Hiram's daughters), were also successful peppermint oil
merchants. The illustration of Hale's farm included in an 1877 *History of
Wayne County* contains an inset showing workers loading mint hay into
a still.[32] And according to Leman's information, Hale was cooperating
with "Old" Roswell Ranney, who also had a working relationship with
David Dows.

This was the last straw for Hiram Hotchkiss. Receiving a letter acknowledging the arrival of his samples in London, Hiram turned his attention to the problem of cracking the British market.[33] He immediately

wrote to Morewood to request "the best sample of English oil of peppermint they can procure in London. . . . We wish to compare it with
some we have on hand. We feel sanguine that we hold an article equal to
the best English." Hiram then added a postscript, soliciting his agents "to
inquire of your friends in London whether we could in their opinion
pack our oil menth pip in any more desirable size bottles or any better
quality of bottles in our recent shipment for their market?"[34] Morewood
responded, "A sample of the best peppermint oil grown here will be sent
to you. It comes from Mitcham. The superiority arises from the soil we
think. The cultivation has been attempted in other parts of England
without the same success which attends at Mitcham."[35]

Morewood also mentioned he did not think the bottles were an issue, but Hiram held on to the idea that distinctive packaging would help
him differentiate his oil. Although many histories of marketing focus on
the advertising of products to attract the attention of consumers, before
a brand could be advertised it had to be created. For example, when the
sons of beverage merchant John Cadbury turned their attention exclusively to selling packaged cocoa in the early 1860s, they began creating a
recognizable brand. According to historian of advertising Mark Tungate,
Cadbury "started packaging their products, not simply to protect them
and preserve their quality, but also to *establish* their quality by the use of
the company's own name. Instead of leaving it to the retailer to determine which company's products a customer would buy, they began to
build their own relationship with the customer."[36] Ultimately his focus on
packaging led to Hiram shipping his oil in twenty-one-ounce cobalt blue
bottles from the nearby Clyde Glass Works. The bottles, which each contained one pound five ounces of peppermint oil, had originally been designed to carry ink and had convenient fluted spouts. To guarantee his oil
against the adulteration he insisted was so rife among his competitors,
Hiram sealed his bottles with labels bearing his signature. In addition to
his peppermint oil, Hiram shipped five hundred barrels of flour to
Liverpool. The Irish famine was driving up the price of flour in England,
and Hiram got five dollars a barrel for his shipment.[37] In early winter, Leman wrote: "The Brittania [*sic*] arrived about 5 minutes before the cars
left . . . there is great excitement in England and Ireland about wheat and
flour and potatoes. . . . Starvation seems inevitable. All excitement in

England . . . therefore buy all the wheat you can. . . . We have about 450 bbls in Lockville—get it shipped."[38]

In addition to handling the brothers' flour exports, Morewood managed to sell the sample bottles of Hotchkiss peppermint oil for seventeen shillings [$2.125], which he informed Hiram was much better than the seven shillings [$.875] most other American peppermint oil received in London.[39] Hotchkiss continued negotiating with Morewood, pushing him to take shipments of a thousand pounds of oil packed in bottles and at the same time insisting on a price of at least sixteen shillings [$2.00].[40] Morewood countered that he could advance no more than $1.50 per pound, and then only on the condition that Hotchkiss ceased shipping any additional oil to other British brokers.[41] His dealers, Morewood said, had been embarrassed to discover they were not the only source of Hotchkiss peppermint oil in their market. A few months later, Hiram again asked Morewood to take a shipment of a thousand pounds of peppermint oil and also asked Morewood to ship him a supply of the best Mitcham peppermint roots.[42] Hotchkiss was planning on cornering the peppermint oil market and wanted to plant only the best peppermint while everyone else was plowing under his old mint.

Hotchkiss planted the Mitcham roots he received, but there was not a widespread transition from the older peppermint, which had also originated in Mitcham, to the new. This may have been due to the fact that Hiram immediately set about trying to reduce the overall planting of peppermint, and that he and Leman were both reducing their focus on peppermint culture in favor of aggregating and marketing oil produced by others. They both owned substantial acreages, and Hiram seems to have introduced the practice of flooding his peppermint fields in the winter to protect the roots from excessive cold.[43] But by the mid-1840s, the brothers were more interested in cornering the peppermint oil market than in improving peppermint cultivation.

In late 1845, Leman had written his brother from Phelps with alarming reports of his conversations with "Old Ranney" about Roswell Ranney's recent trips to Boston and New York City. Hiram suspected that Ranney had considered trying to corner the peppermint oil market, which led him to consider trying it himself. In 1846, peppermint farmers produced nearly forty thousand pounds of oil in western New York, ten thousand pounds in Michigan, three thousand pounds in northeastern Ohio, and nearly a thousand pounds in Indiana.[44] Working with information from his British contacts, Hiram estimated that the next year's demand in European markets would be about twelve thousand pounds. In order to reduce the oversupply of American peppermint oil to a level where the Hotchkiss brothers could meet European demand at a reasonable profit, Hiram partnered with a New York brokerage called E. C. Patterson and Company, to pay Ohio, Michigan, and New York peppermint growers to plow under their fields.[45] In one of the earliest recorded attempts at market cornering, Patterson and his men contracted with 128 of the 210 peppermint farmers in New York, paying $19,393.35 to take about a thousand acres out of production for two years, beginning in March 1847.[46] Growers were allowed to keep only as many "seed" roots as they would need to replant after the contract expired, and they agreed to sell all their remaining oil to the partnership for $2.50 per pound.[47] By June, Patterson reported that his agents had reduced New York and Michigan plantings substantially and added, "We have contracted for nearly the whole Ohio crop."[48] Many peppermint growers in Michigan ignored Patterson and his agents and continued supplying peppermint oil to meet Henry Ranney's needs in Ashfield. Hiram seems to have ignored the Ashfield-oriented peppermint oil market in his calculations, and the Ranney brothers never mention the Hotchkiss-Patterson plan in their correspondence, suggesting that the cornering attempt was more successful in New York and Ohio than in Michigan. Patterson may have exaggerated his agents' successes with western growers in his correspondence with Hiram; and even if his reports were accurate, Michigan production rebounded quickly when the contracts expired. But the cornering was a success in Ohio, where farmers never replanted. By 1850 Ohio had ceased being a significant producer of peppermint.

Rumors of Hotchkiss and Patterson's activities began to circulate in England, and in midsummer Leman wrote to his brother from New York City, where he had met with Morewood. Rather than selling peppermint oil at current prices, the brothers wanted to hold it until scarcity drove up its value. "The price must advance to $3 ½ to $4 I think—perhaps to $10," Leman wrote. The brothers decided to pay Morewood a fee of one hundred dollars to hold their oil in inventory for an additional four months and to release it only after the conclusion of the next harvest.[49] But their control over the market was not as absolute as the brothers imagined. Hiram approached Stevens Trott and Company in Boston with an unsolicited sample of peppermint oil, which he assured them "will compare in quality to any ever sent to Boston." Hiram had gone on to boast, in the draft of his letter, that "we understand the article is mainly monopolized for about two years to come by a New York house," but he scratched out this section. He concluded, "If you could sell this lot say about 200 pounds at $4 per pound . . . you may do so and we will forward the oil without delay . . . although we are inclined to think the article will go much higher before 1 January next."[50] Stevens Trott replied that it had received Hotchkiss's sample and would show it to its largest buyer but noted, "This article has receded in value as rapidly as it rose and would not bring above $2.50 today."[51] A couple of weeks later, Hiram received a telegram from Stevens Trott reporting that the buyer would take one hundred pounds of oil for twenty-eight shillings ($3.50). Hiram accepted the terms, remarking: "We are inclined to think oil will go to 40/- per pound before 1 January next but we want to realize on part of ours immediately and we may be mistaken about its advancing so much."[52]

E. C. Patterson continued to assure Hotchkiss that "the news from abroad are very favorable, considerable view having taken place in London, all is working right, it only requires time to carry the price very high, both there and here."[53] The Ranneys and their network were still very active at this time, however, both in New York and in Michigan. This was the summer Henry Ranney received the letter from his cousin Frederick mentioned previously, looking for payment on a recent shipment of oil.[54] And in the fall, Leman wrote to Hiram from Phelps that the Ranneys' longtime associate "Mr. Belden [Belding] returned from New York today. . . . I think he wants to buy some oil Peppt . . . he seems to think 3 ½ is all that it is worth and said he would like to buy a few hundred pounds. . . . I do not like the idea of selling to old Belden but still we must do so if we cannot get along for money we must have."[55] A few weeks later, Leman wrote from New York City, "I have been round to ascertain the present value pept oil and I can assure you that there is no price to this article." He said he did not believe oil could be sold at even three dollars, so "if you can sell our oil at 3 1/2 dont hesitate a moment." He said he had visited Morewood and authorized the broker to sell enough of the Hotchkiss brothers' oil to pay the advances coming due. Leman concluded his letter with the suggestion, "Suppose you go & see old Belden it seems to me he would like 3 or 400 pounds."[56] By the end of the year, he announced: "Pept oil is very dull, everybody appears to be afraid of it. I think I shall ship 800# in Morewood's hands and order it sold in London at once. My opinion is decidedly in favor of settling & not wait."[57]

    As more time passed, Hiram's British agents began to lose confidence in Hiram's ability to limit the supply of peppermint oil and drive up the price. Hiram suggested to E. C. Patterson that the partners should make an arrangement "with some new house in the city of New York not now at all interested in oil of peppermint . . . and that holders agree to deposit all their pure oil and let this house advance in money or their credits to the extent of 12/- per pound . . . then have all sales made at a certain and fixed price." Hiram concluded, "We have all had so much trouble that it seems like a pity if nothing favorable should grow out of it. A concert of action would give tone and character to the market that would in my opinion be beneficial to all parties."[58] He was playing for time: this was the substantially the same deal he had already made with Morewood, and the exporters were no longer receptive to his argument. "You cannot with any degree of fairness," Morewood wrote, "ask us to hold the mint any longer under cash advances. . . . When you consider the length of time we have been over advanced, the commission you are to pay is but little consideration. We therefore must settle a sufficient quantity to cover our advances and if it will not bring $3 we must sell it for less."[59] Hiram offered to repay $1,500 of the advances in exchange for the return of 750 pounds of oil in Morewood's warehouse, and Morewood responded that he would take the money but would return only six hundred pounds of oil.[60] Morewood's agent in London reported: "Of your oil peppermint we have yet been unable to make any sales. It was put up at public sale last week in order to bring it before the trade, but not a single offer was made for it." After the sale, an offer of twelve shillings sterling ($2.88) was made for the whole lot, but the agent had followed instructions and refused to sell below three dollars. The agent concluded, "Regarding the probable sales for any further quantity which your friends Messrs Hotchkiss may be inclined to send over, it is really almost impossible to offer any opinion."[61]

Hiram responded to Morewood, holding out for higher prices and arguing that the current low price of peppermint oil was actually deliberate. He and his partners, Hiram claimed, "intend to keep the oil market depressed till after setting time is over for the reason that should the market at this time be at a high figure if might induce the growers to break their contracts with peppermint company not to grow any this year."[62] Morewood was not taken in. "The price at which you are willing to sell ($3 per pound) cannot be realized," he wrote, and "pure oil is now offered at $2 cash." Morewood concluded, "We have in our opinion done all which can reasonably be expected from us by holding it for so long a time against cash advance, and had you followed our advice you would have sold it when we could have got $4 ½ for it."[63]

Hotchkiss's domestic sales were also suffering. John Bement, the Ashfield native who supplied Henry Ranney with essence vials for his peddlers, wrote from Philadelphia: "I find by making a little inquiry about oil that I cannot sell any at the price you ask." Bement reported that Mr. Miller, the dealer Hiram had accused of adulterating oil, "does not wish to do much in the article at present." Although, Bement wrote, "[I] called on two or three of my old drug friends, I thought it would rather injure the sale of what you have with Mr. Miller for me to be running about offering oil all over the city."[64] Hiram tried contacting other exporters but was informed they were aware he was already consigning peppermint oil to dealers in London. Miller wrote, "I do not think you will ever obtain two thirds the price for English oil for any to be made. You have the best name now and I have no doubt you will keep it, but although we think your oil to be very good, it does not appear that any great difference in price will be given and I much fear the only principle use for your finest oil would be to mix with our Mitcham."[65] Miller also sent a sample of Mitcham peppermint oil and asked Hiram to enter it into the American Congress exposition in 1850.[66] Although Hiram declined to enter the British peppermint oil in the exposition, he was inspired to send his own oil to the upcoming Great Exhibition at London's Crystal Palace. Hotchkiss's success at the first world's fair was a turning point for the brand and an opportunity for Hiram to focus more exclusively on his essential oil business.

London's Exhibition of the Works of Industry of All Nations ran from May through October 1851. The event was attended by six million visitors and more than fourteen thousand exhibitors from twenty-seven countries. Among the stars of the American delegation to the Crystal Palace were Borden's Meat Biscuit, Dick's Anti-Friction Press, Bond and Son's Astronomical Instruments, Goodyear's India Rubber, and McCormick's Reaper, which each won a prestigious Council Award. Hiram and Leman Hotchkiss's peppermint oil was among the 519 products entered from the United States and won one of the 102 prize medals awarded to Americans out of a total of 2,987 awarded.[67] A bronze medal with portraits of Queen Victoria and Prince Albert was accompanied by a certificate signed by the prince, which still hangs in the lobby of Hiram's former headquarters in Lyons, New York.

The Hotchkiss brothers entered their peppermint oil and also kiln-dried cornmeal from their Eagle Mill with the help of their friend Benjamin P. Johnson, the secretary of the New York State Agricultural Society, who had been appointed by the governor to attend the exhibition.[68] Johnson's influence on the judges helped secure a prize medal for the peppermint oil, the first of many. The Hotchkiss brothers capitalized on the publicity surrounding the award and began to call their product "International Prize Medal Oil of Peppermint." Sales increased, and the Hotchkisses took advantage of every opportunity to show their essential oils, receiving additional awards at shows in New York (1851), Paris (1855, 1873), London (1862), Hamburg (1863, 1868), Paris (1867), Vienna (1873), Philadelphia (1876), and Chicago's World Columbian Exposition (1893). In his 1862 *Report on International Exhibition of Industry and Art*, Commissioner Benjamin P. Johnson observed that following Hotchkiss's 1851 London award, "large sales of his oils are made in England and on the continent."[69]

The Hotchkiss brothers' campaign to brand their peppermint oil was one of the first such efforts in American history. Historians of branding draw a critical distinction between bazaar economies, where products are "unbranded and ungraded," and brand economies, where goods are "standardized, strictly graded, and directly substitutable for one another."[70] The market the Hotchkisses operated in was beginning a very slow transformation from the bazaar to the brand. The key issue for an early brander like Hiram was to raise the perception of his product *out of* the bazaar. He aspired to leave his generic American competitors behind and make his peppermint oil the sole substitute for what he claimed was the world's undisputed leader, English oil from Mitcham.

Although Hiram remained deeply concerned with defending his essential oils' content and reputation as the purest, highest-quality products available, after 1851 a greater part of his effort went toward branding and packaging. He wanted his peppermint oil to be immediately recognizable as superior to its generic competitors. He spent a great deal of time and money developing elaborately engraved labels for his bottles that reproduced the images of his prize medals. Innovative marketers like him were beginning to register a few specific names and labels with the Patent Office in the 1870s, years before U.S. trademark laws were passed in 1881 and the nation's first major brands such as Coca-Cola (1887) and Quaker (1895) began to appear. In an era before the widespread use of trademarked names and logos, Hotchkiss was a pioneer. Years later, another agricultural prize winner became a household name: the Washburn-Crosby Company in Minneapolis branded Gold Medal Flour after it won gold, silver, and bronze medals at the 1880 Miller's International Exposition in Cincinnati. When the company was merged into General Mills in 1928, the brand was retained and remains a staple on supermarket shelves. Although Hiram never managed to achieve price parity with English peppermint oil, his higher profile enabled him to increase the distance between his own prices and those of less well-known American oils. By the end of 1855, Hotchkiss peppermint oil was selling for twenty-four to twenty-six shillings sterling ($5.76 to $6.24), which although still less than the thirty-six to forty-five shillings ($8.64 to $10.80) received at the time for Mitcham oil, was a great improvement.[71]

Although professional advertising and especially the creation of registered brands and trade-marked slogans became more significant elements of national culture after the Civil War, American newspapers had been carrying advertisements, including the ads for peppermint oil mentioned earlier, since before the Revolution. Patent medicines were among the earliest products extensively advertised in print, and their outrageous claims alienated many consumers and damaged the credibility of advertisers in general.[72] Essences like those sold by Ranney's and

Bement's peddlers had not needed elaborate labels, since the peddler was always there in person to make the sales pitch. Hiram's challenge was to create the perception that Hotchkiss was a premium product without making ridiculous assertions customers would immediately reject.

Third-party endorsements offered an opportunity for advertisers to print positive statements about their products without losing credibility. Hiram was not selling his products directly to household consumers but rather through dealers to druggists and confectioners. So instead of running advertisements in newspapers, he printed pamphlets he could send to potential customers and use as packaging for his oils. Among the first was a pamphlet advertising "Hotchkiss' Prize Medal Oil of Peppermint, Spearmint, and Wintergreen." The pamphlet was dominated by an engraved image of the two faces of the medal awarded to the Hotchkisses for their peppermint oil in 1851, followed by an excerpt from a letter written to them by Benjamin P. Johnson, New York's commissioner for the exhibition. Johnson wrote that he had "called the attention of the Jury to your Oil of Peppermint" and assured his readers that "the attention which it has received from persons interested in the trade is evidence of its value, and I have no doubt you will find a ready market for it here."[73] The letter was reprinted in German, French, and Spanish. The reverse side of the pamphlet included letters from the U.S. commissioner to the exhibition and from President Millard Fillmore congratulating the Hotchkisses on their medal, along with a list of the names of the jurors. These letters were also printed in four languages. Hotchkiss mailed pamphlets to dealers and potential customers and used them as wrappers when packing his bottles into cases. The most important part of this promotional literature, however, was the Hotchkiss product label itself. Hiram had labels for his bottles engraved and printed by the American Bank Note Company. The labels included a main wrap-around label for the distinctive blue Hotchkiss bottle and a special sealing label that would be signed by Hiram and glued over the cork. Hiram redesigned these labels every time his oils won another award. Cultural historians have suggested that advertising and packaging create a link between distant, impersonal manufacturers and consumers. "Wrapping gifts, tying bows, and attaching greetings," historian

James Carrier has noted, "works to overcome a contradiction between the generic qualities of (modern) branded products and the social requirements of ceremonial exchange in contemporary American households."[74] While advertising is now understood by cultural critics, advertisers, and even to some degree the public itself as an attempt to imbue market exchange with personal significance and even identity formation, it is important to remember that when the Hotchkiss brothers created their first labels, they were pioneers in uncharted territory.[75] By creating a sealed product that the user would have to open, Hiram allowed his customers to participate in creating a heightened significance for his products.

By the 1870s, the main label for the twenty-one-ounce bottle included the images of twenty medals. Leman, after splitting his essential oil business from his brother's, continued using images of the awards "H. G. & L. B. Hotchkiss" had received together and added facsimiles of the additional awards he won on his own. Leman may have been involved in the original design of the distinctive Hotchkiss packaging, but he was not the only other essential oil producer to adopt these techniques. While the extreme attention Hiram gave to the details of his labels might have been expected to ensure that his packaging would be unique, the result was actually the opposite. Not only did Leman emulate the style of labeling and pamphlets used during the earlier partnership, but many Hotchkiss competitors such as Hale and Parshall locally and Albert M. Todd in Michigan began showing their products at expositions, winning prizes, and printing images of the awards on their labels. And at least once, counterfeiters apparently went to the trouble of reproducing Hiram's labels to sell peppermint oil disguised as a Hotchkiss product.

In July 1857, Hiram published a pamphlet entitled "CAUTION," reprinting a letter from a dealer in Belfast, Ireland, who wrote that after purchasing "in London some Cases of your Oil Mint, we were led by low quotations to change the place from which we got it, and have been supplied by an article that has been returned to us by our customers, as of inferior quality." The dealer included labels from the returned bottles in his letter, which Hiram sent to his engraver. "The Counterfeits are so closely imitated as to deceive any one," the engraver reported, "rendering careful comparison with the original necessary, and a practiced eye, to detect the difference." Among the subtle differences were the volume of the bottles, which were printed "21oz." on the forgery where the original had been left blank so the volume could be handwritten, and a lithographed signature where the original had been handwritten. Hiram followed these letters with a notice admonishing dealers and customers to pay close attention to the labels on bottles offered by dealers, suggesting that when in doubt they were welcome to contact him and buy directly from his "Peppermint Oil Depot" in Lyons, New York.[76]

In spite of Hiram's clarification, confusion lingered in the minds of Hotchkiss oil customers. The issue, however, was less counterfeiting and more the ongoing presence of two Hotchkiss essential oil companies competing for the same dealers and customers. As Leman explained in a warning pamphlet he printed in 1876, "The co-partnership formerly existing between H. G. & L. B. Hotchkiss was dissolved in the year 1855. Please be particular and observe that each case is *wire corded*, and sealed with *red sealing wax*, and my seal affixed thereto." Leman went on to state that since the separation, L. B. Hotchkiss "has always been awarded the prize medal whenever his brands of Oils came in competition with any other brands, either in Europe or America." Leman urged "dealers and consumers to pay special attention to the 'signed' and other labels and wrappers appended to each bottle . . . and to intrust the execution of orders only to honest men, or address them directly to me at the European and American Prize Medal Oil Depot, located at Phelps, Ontario County, New York, U.S. America."[77] Leman repeated his warning in German, French, and Spanish for international customers. Although, as Hiram had done years earlier, he claimed to have discovered "bottles with spurious labels counterfeiting his own, and filled with inferior oil," Leman did not give a detailed explanation. It is unclear whether his warning was really about counterfeiting or rather about the increasingly acrimonious competition he was carrying on with his brother, Hiram, to which we return in chapter 7.

Peppermint Bank

The history of banking and business finance is a very specialized discipline, and the histories produced about them are often heavily freighted with equations and economic analysis. Insights shared in the discipline rarely find their way into mainstream histories and are understood only with difficulty by a public accustomed to living in an era of a single, national currency and federally insured banking. To make matters worse, the discipline has often been saddled with one-sided historical arguments, frequently designed for use in justifying new financial innovations. The histories of Civil War greenbacks, the demonetization of silver in 1873, and the resumption of specie payments in 1879, for example, were hotly contested by historians during the financial panic of 1907 and the debate over establishing the Federal Reserve.[1] In particular, the reactions of rural people to the elimination of state banking during the Civil War have most frequently been recounted from an urban perspective, using urban sources such as national newspapers, legislative debates, and the literature of trade lobbyists.[2] By contrast, the experiences of Hotchkiss family members in nineteenth-century upstate New York illuminate some of the attitudes of rural people toward money, credit, and banking.

The Hotchkiss brothers, Hiram and Leman, began their lives as the apprentices and heirs to a wealthy upstate New York merchant. Early in

their careers, they became successful merchants and millers in their own
rights. By the early 1840s, they operated several stores and mills and had
developed a business shipping flour to New York City for urban consumption and export. The addition of peppermint oil to the brothers'
businesses, and International Prize Medal Oil of Peppermint's success in
foreign markets, gave Hiram and Leman an opportunity to dominate a
specialty market that was small relative to the flour market but potentially highly profitable. As mentioned previously, however, the vagaries
of supply and demand for peppermint oil made it less attractive for traditional commission brokers such as the early Hotchkiss partner Dows
and Cary. In order to succeed as essential oil producers, the Hotchkiss
brothers needed to secure financing flexible enough to accommodate
the new business they were creating. When city commodities brokers
and local bankers proved less amenable to their demands than they
hoped, the brothers stepped into the financial markets themselves and
explored new ways to finance their operations.

As prominent businessmen in Phelps and Lyons, Hiram and Leman were members of a regional elite. Hiram married Mary Ashley, a
physician's daughter, and Leman married Lucretia Oaks, the daughter of
wealthy landowner Jonathan Oaks. As mentioned earlier, Hiram, Leman, and their uncle William Hotchkiss had all traveled to Michigan to
purchase land in the spring of 1837, within weeks of Samuel Ranney's
visit to the land office. The Hotchkisses had no intention of moving to
the frontier, however. Their investments were purely speculative, as were
many of their land purchases in western New York. The brothers had
watched their mother and uncle manage their father's estate in the 1820s
and 1830s and had become familiar with the practice of buying foreclo-
sures and distressed assets when opportunities arose.

The brothers received valuable experience in the evolving financial
sector when the Bank of Lyons failed on September 13, 1842. The bank
had a paid-in capital of two hundred thousand dollars and a circulating
currency of a hundred thousand, according to newspaper reports.[3] It
was one of ten New York banks established under the 1829 Safety Fund
Act to fail in the years following the Panic of 1837. The bank had been
incorporated by an act of the legislature in February 1832 and was profitable for several years, paying an 8 percent dividend to its shareholders in

May 1838 in spite of a deepening recession.[4] Early in 1842, the bank vigorously denied reports of its difficulties, but by the year's end a state-appointed receiver was auctioning bank property.[5] Using the close connections they had as major stockholders with the bank's directors, the Hotchkiss brothers determined that the bank's actual assets were $307,323.40 and its liabilities $692,173.75.[6] The bank owned $83,999.94 in real estate and had issued $389,204 in circulating banknotes. The Hotch-kisses were able to make a four-page list of the debts on the bank's books, which totaled $222,737.25. Hiram wrote to the state-appointed receiver, offering five hundred dollars for real estate valued at roughly eighty thousand dollars on the bank's books, slated to be sold the following month at auction.[7] One of the properties he acquired was the Hecox mansion and farm, which became the Hotchkiss family estate in Lyons. Hiram also bought a portfolio of debts and judgments, which he tried to collect. He paid $560.56 for a debt portfolio worth $173,216.57, or about a third of a penny on the dollar.[8] Over the next several years, Hiram wrote collection letters to individuals and businesses that had owed the bank money.

In one letter, Hiram informed a debtor's attorney, "I purchased at the receivers sale a judgment . . . docketed May 4th 1840 for $712.34." Hiram explained, "I was a large Stock Holder in said bank at the time of its failure, & am in hopes to get a part pay on my stock by purchasing some of the assets of the bank, that is the reason of my purchasing said judgment." He said he understood from the documents he had received from the bank that the "gentlemen" the attorney represented "have all taken the Bankrupt Law. I supposed they had when I made the purchase, but I am one of those who believe the Bankrupt Law will be declared unconstitutional." Hiram concluded that he would be willing to take two shillings on the dollar to retire the debt. With interest to the current date, the total came to "882.70. Say pay ¼ for it——$220.67. Yours very Respy. H. G. Hotchkiss."[9] There are several blank "waste books" in the Hotchkiss archives, filled with Hiram's handwritten notes describing conversations with and letters to debtors over the years. Collecting on debts and judgments, for Hiram, became a process of negotiation in which he usually offered to take a fraction of the original debt as settlement, in return for ceasing to dun the debtor or his representatives. In several cases, Hiram pursued the heirs of the original debtors and attempted to convince them to pay their fathers' obligations.[10] The experience seems to have taught him that, in contrast to the moralistic approach to credit taken by contemporaries such as Lewis Tappan, financial obligations were negotiable.[11] Hiram mentioned in his letter to the attorney that he expected the 1841 bankruptcy law to be overturned. It was at the end of 1843, and while as a lifelong Democrat he had probably opposed the Whig-sponsored act, his behavior also suggests that Hiram had little respect for the "application of moral principles to business" that led to the establishment of the Tappan—later called R. G. Dun—agency that would impugn his character throughout his later decades.

Early in their efforts to raise operating capital, the Hotchkiss brothers enlisted the help of their wealthy uncle Calvin Hotchkiss. A brother of their father, Leman, Calvin owned a large farm and invested in real estate around Lewiston, near Niagara Falls. In spring 1845, Leman wrote to his brother regarding notes Hiram was trying to get discounted with the help of Calvin's endorsement. "I shall be very surprised if you fail to raise the money with such an endorser as Calvin Hotchkiss," Leman averred. "Certainly no man would refuse to discount such paper if he knew the man."[12]

It is important to note that even in the early nineteenth century most commerce was conducted using credit. Early historian of American banking James S. Gibbons (1810–1892) explained in 1858 that "commerce, in its broadest sense, is carried on by promissory notes." According to Gibbons, the use of promissory notes at every step in the cycle of the production, distribution, and consumption was orders of magnitude greater than the volume suggested by the discounting of commercial paper by banks. He explained that most estimates of economic activity were incomplete because "New York City banks did not discount paper until it was within two or three months of maturity." But most merchandise, whether agricultural or manufactured, "is sold from first hands to the jobber on a credit of eight months, more or less, for which the latter gives his promissory notes. The jobber sells in smaller quantities (by the piece or single package) to the retailer, on a credit of six months."[13] Historian Bray Hammond (1886–1968) explained that "most traders of all classes were heavy borrowers, few having capital enough to pay till paid; and this condition supplied the banks with promissory notes." These promissory notes were the most common form of commercial currency "and had commonly been transferred already by endorsement from one merchant to another in settlement of debts by the time they came into the bank's possession."[14]

"The market," Gibbons had concluded, "carries millions of notes for what is already consumed and millions more for what is not yet sprouted in the furrow." Although Hammond qualified Gibbons's description, noting that in smaller markets such as Philadelphia it had been customary since the 1830s to discount paper at four to six months, most commercial activities were transacted without the aid of banks until the final stage, when debts that had been carried the better part of the year using commercial paper were finally converted to cash. This final conversion to cash was necessary because the products that had been grown or manufactured and had entered the distribution channel were finally reaching their ultimate retail destinations, where they would be sold to consumers for small-denomination banknotes or specie coins.

Leman and Hiram Hotchkiss spent a great deal of their time traveling from bank to bank in western New York trying to raise money for their business. They had accounts at more than a dozen banks, ranging from local operations in Phelps, Lyons, Geneva, Newark, and Lewiston to large institutions in Buffalo, Albany, and New York City. As the years passed, much of the responsibility for raising money fell to Leman. In the summer of 1845, he sent Hiram a packet containing $1,660.31 in cash, which he said were the proceeds of a draft drawn on the "Seneca County Bank at 4 months predicated upon our recpt for 2200 bushels wheat at Newark."[15] Leman warned Hiram to try to keep the cash from reaching the Bank of Geneva, "because Cook may think we are skimming." The brothers were operating on a larger scale than some local bankers found comfortable, but there was also already a degree of distrust between some of the more conservative bankers and the Hotchkisses. Leman concluded his note by saying he had tried to get yet another banker, Mr. Mercer, to discount three thousand dollars at ten days or at six months but had been refused the longer duration note. In the late fall,

Leman sent Hiram five hundred dollars, which, he wrote "[is] all I can possibly spare today. You must be aware that we are about out of funds. I drew our draft yesterday at 10 days through the Seneca Co. Bank to pay our note. . . . I also drew our draft yesterday through Bank of Geneva for $2250 at 4 months on our recpt of 1831# Peppt Oil which is all we have except the old oil. It is impossible to get our note discounted at this time. You must hold onto all the money you can."[16] A week later, Leman wrote again to warn Hiram: "I went to Bank of Geneva yesterday and made out to get our draft discounted for $3300 at 6 months, Mr. Cook hesitated some and said this would carry us through. . . . Cook evidently does not want us to have any more—even on shorter paper I think."[17]

As time passed, the brothers developed a division of labor in their partnership, in which Hiram negotiated with farmers and New York merchants while Leman handled the bankers. The archive is filled with hundreds of letters between the brothers regarding Leman's efforts to raise funds to support Hiram's deals. When they tried to end their partnership and separate their businesses in 1855 (unsuccessfully, as we will see in the next chapter), Hiram was forced to seek other financial partners. His first choice was his uncle Calvin Hotchkiss. In late 1855, Hiram wrote to Calvin, promising to be "as moderate as I can in respect to money calls as requested." Hiram assured him, "When once you get acquainted with the Superior Mercantile & Banking houses with whom my drafts (predicated on actual shipments of property) are drawn on, I think you will be pleased with doing my Banking business & I am now (at the prospect of you doing it) as happy as a Lark."[18]

Although by 1855 Hiram was doing a substantial business in peppermint oil, he described his operation to his uncle in the more familiar and comfortable terms of mercantile banking. Historian Horace White, in an essay describing George Smith, a Chicago-based contemporary of the Hotchkisses, illustrated the typical situation of a buyer of agricultural products raising operating funds. The buyer "makes his note at the bank and offers for discount a draft . . . secured by a bill of lading. The bank discounts his paper and the amount is immediately credited to him as a deposit, and will be drawn mostly in the form of bank notes to be disbursed among the farmers."[19] In his illustration, "each deposit is a discount," and White notes that it is an efficient way to expand the money supply as needed because "as this is what the bank exists for and derives its income from, it will, in ordinary times, discount all of such paper that is offered to it by its regular customers." This arrangement worked fairly well in the early stages of Hotchkiss's career. The merchant (Hotchkiss) in White's example would receive credit from his "correspondent" (Dows and Cary) when customers bought his flour. Customers' cash payments in New York City would be used to offset the drafts Hotchkiss had written to draw on Dows and Cary at western New York banks. As mentioned earlier, David Dows and Hiram Hotchkiss differed on how long Dows was willing to wait for his ultimate reimbursement. Dows preferred to have Hiram pay his notes when they matured, usually in sixty days. Hiram believed that the flour in Dows and Cary's warehouse was Dows's responsibility. It was up to Dows to turn that flour into cash to repay the note Hiram had written. There was a certain logic to the argument, from Hiram's perspective. In any case, Hiram would have long since spent the money he had drawn at the Lyons banks, paying local farmers for the wheat he had ground into flour and shipped to New York in the first place.

From his own perspective, Hiram had monetized the flour. Once his barrels were on flatboats bound for the city, fully insured against accidents along the way, the transaction was complete in his mind. Hiram could turn his attention to the next wagonload of wheat arriving at his mills. He considered himself a sort of Rumpelstiltskin in this story, spinning western New York's harvests into gold. This is also an accurate depiction of how Calvin and Leman operated on behalf of Hiram. The difficulty arose for them, and for Hiram, when he became a banker himself, when the chain of payments broke because the product he was monetizing failed to become cash as automatically as flour.

Calvin was less than impressed with Hiram's claims, and he responded a couple of days after receiving his nephew's effusive letter: "You appear to rush ahead as if my funds was inexhaustible. I would simply inquire the necessity of crowding every thing to such a pitch as formerly, in the flour business." Although Hiram had presented the opportunity presented by peppermint oil to his uncle as if it would follow the same logic as the flour business, Calvin apparently saw through Hiram's bravado. "You say you have this oil business under your control," he commented; "if so, why the necessity of pressing it to the greatest extent. It only goes to show you want to get rich at once." Calvin warned, "It is an old proverb, light comes, light goes ... your over anxiety has tendency to keep up the price at home & lessen it abroad."[20] Calvin concluded by calling Hiram's attention back to the present: a protested note enclosed with the letter. "Two or three protests of the same kind," he wrote, "& how would your drafts stand in Buffalo, about (X No. 24) instead of (A No. 1)."

A few weeks later, another of Hiram's forty-five-day drafts for two thousand dollars was returned for nonpayment, and the protest was sent to Calvin, who had endorsed the paper.[21] Hiram turned once again to his brother for help, but Leman responded: "I cannot get the note discounted to pay your note." Leman had more traditional ideas about credit than his brother, believing "it is no use to attempt continually of renewing paper—the only way is to pay up and then get fresh discounts. Now send the note to Buffalo & get discounted and pay your note and do not rely on me to meet your paper for I cannot do it."[22] Calvin wrote to Leman about the issue, reminding his nephew, "Above all other things, endorsed paper ought to be attended to in time, not to be neglected a day. It operates against my feelings to be subjected to this annoyance for bestowing favors, but it appears Hiram feels rather indifferent to such matters of late."[23] Although Hiram had learned from his experience of collecting defaulted loans and foreclosed properties that debts were fluid and negotiable, his opinion was not shared by his uncle, his brother, or most of the local bankers he looked to for credit.

When money failed to flow as wide and fast as he desired from local banks, Hiram decided he would be better off doing their business himself. He would open a bank of his own. Deliberately ignoring Calvin's expressions of frustration at Hiram's lack of attention to the details of his business, Hiram asked his uncle to be a principal in his new bank. Hiram believed he could avoid the difficulties he continually had with local bankers by opening his own Peppermint Bank. He asked Calvin to lend his name and reputation to the new venture—and also to lend him fifty thousand dollars in government bonds, which Hiram would need to deposit with the state regulator. Calvin responded, "I have only to say that I have so many objections to make on this subject that I have not time to enumerate them all at this time." Calvin's main objection was that he wanted nothing to do with Hiram's bank. "Did you think it would please me to be named <u>President</u>," Calvin asked. "If you did you are greatly mistaken. Such type of <u>Butterflys</u> does not take a deep root in my mind."[24]

Free banking, the dominant regulatory system for antebellum banks, has taken too much of the blame for economic instability before the Civil War.[25] Free banking refers to the ability of banks to be established without legislative charters, but the lack of state charters does not imply that the banks were allowed to print money indiscriminately. In states like New York with strict regulations, bankers were required to deposit government bonds with the state banking authority to back all the banknotes they issued. This allowed the banks to hold fractional reserves, issuing notes in greater quantities than their reserves of specie, but still maintain a level of security if "runs" or mass redemptions of notes for specie raised the danger of default. Banking historian Fritz Redlich highlighted the identity of currency, deposits, and credit when he explained that through issuing banknotes and taking deposits, "American banks relied for their profit on the creation of purchasing power (the creation of credit)."[26] But, of course, the state banks did not create purchasing power and credit from nothing. The notes they issued were, as mentioned earlier, tied intimately to a chain of agricultural and other production that was actually creating value. The firm foundation of most state bank currency on the economic activity of the regions the bank served was generally ignored by nineteenth-century critics of state banking and has been mostly forgotten by history.

New York's 1838 Free Banking Act imposed a minimum capital requirement of a hundred thousand dollars, later reduced to fifty thousand. New York banks secured their circulating notes with government bonds, which added a degree of safety but did not guarantee liquidity. The failure of the Bank of Lyons in 1842, which had an authorized circulating currency of a hundred thousand dollars but had issued $389,204 in circulating banknotes, illustrates the potential for trouble in a mismanaged bank. To combat abuse, New York law later required banknotes to be printed by the state comptroller's office, which retained possession of the printing plates. Later, however, banks were also allowed to secure half their note issues with real estate mortgages rather than government bonds, which gave them more flexibility but also made them more susceptible to market conditions. By the end of 1859, New York had "274 free banks with an aggregate paid-in capital of $100.6 million [that] secured their note issues with $26.5 million in bonds and $7.6 million in mortgages," according to Howard Bodenhorn, the one historian who has recently focused on state banks.[27]

Free Banks were highly leveraged, and it should have been easy for the H. G. Hotchkiss and Co. Bank to make money. Hiram deposited fifty thousand dollars in bonds (borrowed from his uncle Calvin) and received forty thousand dollars in circulating banknotes, which differed from promissory notes in that they were of small denominations (one dollar, three dollars, five dollars, and so on) and typically carried no interest. Hiram used ten thousand dollars of his initial borrowed stake to buy specie to cover note redemptions, leaving forty thousand dollars to lend. If Hotchkiss had made loans in the local market, the proceeds of these loans would have been used to pay for purchases and labor, ultimately finding their way back into the bank in the form of deposits. The banknotes would then have reentered the market in the form of new loans, and the bank's assets would have grown, since on bank balance sheets loans were counted as assets, banknotes and equity as liabilities. This was the type of banking Leman and his son Thaddeus did very successfully, several years later, in Phelps. Hiram, however, used his Peppermint Bank primarily as a payment mechanism for his essential oil business. Rather than loaning his notes into the local market, he spent them in western New York and in Michigan to pay for oil. In effect, he loaned all his funds to himself.

Recently, monetary historians Charles M. Kahn and William Roberds have observed that in today's economy "by value, most marketplace transactions in the United States are not paid for with government-issued currency or coin, but with privately-issued payments media," such as "checks drawn on bank deposits ... credit and debit cards."[28] They suggest that transacting business without cash was equally common in the past, and that historically the easy transferability of payments made in the form of drafts or promissory notes reduced "the incentive for monitoring by the original debtholders." In addition to state-printed currency, Hiram used engraved promissory notes to pay for his oil purchases. They looked like Hotchkiss's banknotes but provided spaces into which Hiram could enter amounts, like checks. He

often sent packets of these notes, written in twenty-five-dollar denominations, to his agents in Michigan to be used for paying peppermint
farmers for oil. He intended that both the denominated banknotes and
the engraved promissory "checks" would be considered as cash and used
by farmers to transact their business, rather than being returned immediately to Lyons for payment in the bank's limited specie. Hiram regularly urged his agents to get the notes "a good circulation," hoping that
they would be used as money in Michigan for a long while rather than
being immediately returned to the Hotchkiss Bank in New York State
for redemption.[29] The circulation of currency did not end in local markets when banknotes were returned to the issuing bank for redemption
into coin, since specie would typically be used to buy goods in the local
market and then deposited by merchants and immediately returned to
circulation in the form of new loans. If, however, specie was removed
from the bank and sent to Michigan, the cycle would be broken.

Silver and gold coins were not the most convenient form of money
for trading at a distance, however, since they were heavy and bulky and
would need to be carried home to Michigan and often might subse-
quently be sent to distant cities for purchasing items that couldn't be
obtained in the local market. When Michigan farmers sent Hotchkiss's
notes back to New York for redemption, the notes were often converted
into drafts that could be presented to other bankers or to merchants in
places such as New York City where the farmers might want to spend
their money. When Michigan residents or western New Yorkers wanted
to buy products in New York City, credit or banknotes could be redeemed in their local banks for drafts on city merchants or banks that
could be used to purchase goods or exchanged for cash in the city. The
local banker often collected a fee for facilitating this exchange and was
then able to put the banknotes back into circulation immediately in the
local market—or, in Hotchkiss's case, send the notes to Michigan again.
Clearing these credits and debits between banks, of course, required
trust and a stable relationship between the banks involved.

Bank money (defined as circulation plus deposits minus the
notes of other banks) in New York grew from $4.62 per capita in 1830 to
$9.35 in 1840, $20.73 in 1850, and $33.95 in 1860.[30] The money held by
Michigan banks, however, peaked in 1840 at $2.36 per capita and then

declined. Michigan residents may have been less economically active than New Yorkers, but they were also using money from eastern banks instead of their own. Similarly, while bank credit (defined as loans and discounts plus bills of exchange) in New York increased from $6.61 per capita in 1830 to $21.73 in 1840, $30.88 in 1850, and $51.63 in 1860, like bank money credit peaked in Michigan in 1840 at $10.14 per capita before falling precipitously. Although Michigan, like New York, had instituted free banking in the 1830s, by the 1850s and 1860s the state's banks were becoming less relevant as more Michigan residents became dependent not only on currency but also on credit and exchange services of eastern banks. In addition, a great deal of western money found its way into the vaults of New York City banks, where it was held as interest-earning bankers' balances to facilitate the settlement of commercial transactions in the city. These balances were the source of highly profitable "call loans" that New York banks made to brokers on the stock market, making "the deposits of rural organizations in New York City banks . . . the major source of profits for New York bankers."[31]

Western New York banks were probably only a small factor in the growth of New York bank money and credit, and western New Yorkers may have experienced changes similar to those seen in Michigan. Hiram Hotchkiss, however, seems to have fought this trend. He wanted his own bank and its notes to be a circulating currency in Michigan's peppermint-growing region. In a sense, Hiram seems to have recognized the growing center-periphery dualism of banking, and he wanted a piece of that action. This is not unlike the way Hiram touted the superiority of British Mitcham peppermint oil and then claimed that his own Prize Medal Oil of Peppermint was the next best thing. A rural entrepreneur, aware of a changing economy that would tend to reduce his agency, rejected that outcome and was determined to use the changes to his advantage by any means necessary. These means would not be comfortable for his allies and creditors.

A few months after declining to join Hiram's new banking venture, Calvin wrote his nephew again to complain at being asked by the sheriff to pay for a judgment against the brothers on an unpaid note. "So you see what I have been subjected to in consequence of your inattention to this business," Calvin wrote, noting that the charges and interest that had accumulated on the note since its due date probably amounted to more than a hundred dollars. "A man who suffers his endorsers to be sued & executions issued," Calvin concluded, "is something I did not calculate on when I endorsed your note. Such a man as will do this is deserving of no credit."[32] Soon after, Leman wrote to Hiram: "[I] recd the $1300 note this morning and I observe a protest attached to it. This is mortifying to me and causes me a good deal of trouble and I have got to spend my time now in writing an explanation to Uncle Calvin. It is just as easy to be a little ahead as a little behind if you will get accustomed to it. I fear you will never be a good Peppt Banker."[33]

In mid-1856, Hiram wrote to Abraham Bell and Sons, New York City merchants to whom he had been consigning flour and peppermint oil, and whom he had hoped to use as his "banker" in the city. Hiram complained, "It appears I have entirely misunderstood my arrangement with you. I supposed I was at liberty to draw any amount under $2000 if my business required . . . by leaving with you as collateral security my brothers paper endorsed by Calvin Hotchkiss, but it appears otherwise."[34] The Quaker merchant politely explained to Hiram, "The arrangement for keeping of thy account was based on accepting thy drafts (expected to remain out two or three months) drawn against cash or business paper (of which we now hold none) in our hands." Because the duration of these drafts was expected to be short, merely to facilitate transactions, Bell wrote, "such drafts to thee [are] considered cash when accepted and the interest not to be charged till drafts were paid." Hiram had not honored the standard operating procedure, however; he had "changed the mode of drawing," Bell continued, "and . . . we have since kept thy account to the usual way debiting and crediting all money received and paid for thy account and charging thee 1% on all time collections advising thee when overdrawn."[35] To Hiram's disappointment, Bell and Sons wanted to remain merchants and avoid being drawn into loaning Hiram money to operate his business.

Hiram turned once again to his brother for support, and despite commenting "I think you will make a hell of a banker if _you_ don't know when your notes fall due," Leman sent him a two-thousand-dollar note to forward to Bell. Hiram wrote to Bell, "I herewith hand you LB Hotchkiss note at four months for $2000, endorsed by myself and Calvin

Hotchkiss Esquire of Lewiston." Hiram invited Bell to verify Calvin's credit with officials of the Marine Bank and the Hollister Bank in Buffalo, assuring Bell, "You will find Mr. Calvin Hotchkiss is worth several hundred thousand dollars and entirely free from debt. The note you can rely upon it will be promptly met at maturity." Hiram assured Bell that Leman would pay the note when it matured and that Calvin's assets backed Leman's promise. He asked Bell to send him "$1500 in country currency per express, and balance please place to my credit."[36] Hiram was sending Bell a promissory note that would not be payable until after the end of the peppermint harvest season, and requesting cash to use with New York and Michigan farmers, offering a token payment to his account balance as a reward. Bell returned the note to Hiram, noting, "We are not at present discounting and therefore return Leman B Hotchkiss note $2000 which we have no doubt is very good."[37] Bell and Sons was willing to extend credit to facilitate deals in New York City, but it did not wish to be Hotchkiss's bankers.

As antebellum banking expert James S. Gibbons had explained in 1858, "The second common function of banks about 1857—the purchase and sale of exchange in the form of bills drawn for the sale of goods—combined the transfer of funds with lending." Gibbons elaborated: "Dealing in exchange fetched the banks a fee or discount for the service as well as interest on the credit advanced."[38] Interregional exchange, which had begun in international trade and had spread in the domestic market as westward conquest of native peoples increased the distances involved in commerce, entailed not only the lending of money but also its transportation from one city to another. Before the era of telegraphs and trains, the expenses and risks involved in moving money between distant cities had been substantial; even as technology made these transfers easier, the associated fees decreased only slowly. Hiram could have sought the services he expected of Bell at any New York bank, but his credit relationships in the city were already beginning to sour.

The final major function of banks before the Civil War was "the purchase and sale of domestic exchange in the form of bank notes, checks, or drafts." Dealing in local exchange "involved an enormous and continuous volume of small domestic transactions," Gibbons concluded, and "the bulk of these dealings were in bank notes, which were

bought, sold, or sent back to the issuing banks to be redeemed."[39] Thus
the four main functions of antebellum banks, in order of importance
and profitability, were discounting promissory notes, interregional exchange, local exchange, and lending money in the form of deposit credit. Technological change and legislation during the Civil War eliminated
the first three of these functions, leaving the fourth as the remaining "essential function of banks." To clarify this final function, bank historian
Bray Hammond noted: "It is perhaps advisable to repeat that though
bank deposits originate mostly in lending, most depositors are not borrowers but receive the money they deposit from others who are; they
receive it in payment of wages, salaries, and purchases."[40] While Hammond's description of deposits as credit may seem counterintuitive to
those of us among the traditional class of bank depositors, it represents
an important insight, which Hotchkiss understood: ultimately, all money is debt. Another way of understanding this is through the relationship between bank deposits, circulation, and the specie that backed
them. In 1859, for example, Michigan bank deposits and circulating
banknotes totaled $887,671, with the support of only $42,018 in specie
(4.73%). Michigan banking was based on the economic activity of the
state's residents rather than on vaults filled with silver and gold coin.
Even in New York State, with its financial center in the city and its conservative regulations requiring government bond deposits for note issue, $138,973,788 in deposits and currency were backed by only
$28,335,984 in specie (20.39%).[41] The relationship of bank assets to mon-
ey in circulation is very complicated, and confusion surrounding its history is exacerbated by the changing public understanding of money
resulting from the U.S. government's creation of greenbacks during the
Civil War and by political battles that raged throughout the balance of
the nineteenth century over a national currency based on a specie
standard. It is important, as we review national changes such as Civil
War monetary policy and the return to a gold standard in 1879, to consider the effects of systemic changes on the attitudes and actions of self-
interested rural businessmen such as Hiram Hotchkiss.

As noted earlier, for a number of reasons the price of peppermint oil
varied much more than the price of flour. Supply factors such as the

amount of peppermint harvested and the oil distilled each season were difficult to control, although the Hotchkiss brothers and E. C. Patterson had a significant negative influence when they set their minds to cornering the market. Demand factors, like the premium a customer might pay for a prize medal peppermint oil rather than the product offered by Hotchkiss competitors, were potentially more susceptible to pressure. In his mind, Hiram regarded all the factors as amenable to his influence—especially because, unlike perishable wheat flour, peppermint oil was a storable asset. His ability to bottle his peppermint oil and warehouse it for many years while he waited for the best price broke the simple equivalence of goods to cash described in Horace White's illustration of how commodity financing could create a stable money supply. Instead of a constant flow of commodities in one direction and money in the other, Hiram felt that peppermint oil might be able to function like the gold and silver specie that supported a bank's circulating currency, and he may have imagined himself at the center of a fractional reserve system where much more money circulated than the actual value of the commodity that might be called on to redeem it. This point of view caused problems when Hiram negotiated with other brokers and bankers. It became a disaster when he tried to become a banker himself.

Hiram always believed his oil should command a higher price than the market offered at any given time. He had several reasons for this belief, each of which may have been justifiable at different times. He believed that his peppermint oil was purer than the oil offered by his competitors. He regularly accused his enemies (and sometimes even his friends) of adulterating their oil, of buying tainted oils, of mixing good oil with bad, and of putting their labels on inferior products. Like the character in Herman Melville's novel *The Confidence-Man: His Masquerade*, Hiram had a complicated relationship with confidence (mostly in himself) and suspicion (of anyone who failed to act in accordance with his wishes).[42] He also believed that he could use his skills as a marketer to raise the perceived value of his oils, constantly pushing his prices toward the value of the English Mitcham oil he aspired to match. And finally, he believed he could control, or at least anticipate, changes in supply that would allow him to hold oil during periods of surplus and sell it only when scarcity had driven up the price. All these beliefs caused

Hiram to regularly break the straightforward flow of goods and cash that typified White's commodity model.

The difficulties began early in his career, when his peppermint oil didn't leave Dows and Cary's warehouses as smoothly as his flour had, causing conflicts over the drafts and notes Hiram had written to draw funds against his shipments. If the essential oil market softened and Hiram's oil languished in Dows and Cary's New York warehouse, the commission agent could be forced to carry both the advanced principal and a growing unpaid interest balance for months. Hiram regularly spent beyond his current means, using advances of the proceeds he anticipated receiving from the sale of each batch of peppermint oil to buy the next batch of oil or support his family, saving little or nothing as a reserve. This mode of operating was merely frustrating when Hiram and the agent disagreed on how low a price Dows and Cary should accept to clear its inventory. It became exponentially worse when Hiram entered the international market.

Hiram needed what came to be known at the end of the nineteenth century as an "elastic currency." An elastic currency is defined as a money supply that "will expand when there is an active demand for it and contract when the demand subsides," and has been something economists, bankers, and their historians have debated since the nineteenth century. In 1893, for example, when bankers argued over the merits and problems of the national banking system developed since the Civil War, Horace White delivered a lecture to the American Bankers' Association entitled ' "George Smith's Money' in the Early Northwest."[43] George Smith had run an insurance company and an unchartered bank in Illinois. After the Panic of 1837, Smith issued notes redeemable in gold and silver and backed by the solvency of his businesses. By 1854, Smith's was the only bank in Illinois, and "George Smith's money" accounted for 75 percent of the currency used in Chicago. White's lecture on Smith focused on the relationship between trade and currency. An elastic currency was needed, White argued, but: "How can we get this kind of currency? We cannot get it from the Government, because the Government cannot know when the demand for money is increasing and when it is diminishing."[44] White noted that both checks and notes were "pieces of paper promising to pay gold [that] came into use in the first place as

labor saving machines merely to avoid the trouble of carrying gold."
Smith's key innovation, White argued, was that his Wisconsin Marine
and Fire Insurance Company issued its "certificates of deposit . . . in denominations of $1, $3, $5, and $10." Occasional "runs on his institution
for specie . . . were always met with abundant bags of coin," and Smith's
money became a trusted currency, eventually reaching a circulation of
$1,470,235.[45] Smith operated a fractional reserve bank without govern-
ment supervision; the moral of White's story was that prudent business
practices could be relied upon to make such a system more responsive
to economic cycles than inefficient government intrusion.

Hiram Hotchkiss's story offers an important counterexample.
Chicagoan George Smith was technically a wildcatter issuing unsanc-
tioned currency, but his money was sound. Hiram, issuing legal
banknotes printed by the state comptroller, used them in a way that
damaged his own finances and the local economy. Like Smith, Hiram
understood that small-denomination banknotes made better circulating currency than randomly denominated promissory notes carrying a
string of endorsements on their backs. The main use Hiram had for his
currency, however, was as a means to pay his own debts, especially to the
large number of farmers who supplied him with peppermint oil. He
preferred sending engraved promissory notes, disguised to look like
currency, to Michigan, where they would get a "good circulation." He
intended his paper to be used in place of cash for long periods before
being returned to the Peppermint Bank for redemption—or ideally, to
stay in Michigan forever. And unlike Smith's, Hotchkiss's "money" actually depended less on local economic activity and bags of coins kept on
hand to redeem banknotes than on the elaborate web of credits and
debits in distant towns and cities surrounding his essential oil business.
Ultimately, the Hotchkiss bank was based not on gold or even on peppermint oil but on a shell game of credit transactions and relationships
Hiram continually abused.

It may seem strange that Hiram managed to convince Michigan
farmers to take his notes, New York bankers to take his paper, and his
relatives to support his banking venture. He was a leading peppermint
oil merchant, so he had leverage when dealing with farmers. And he was
not just a miller or a peppermint oil merchant. He was a charismatic

regional businessman from a prominent and well-respected family, interested in many of the economic-development schemes pursued by western New Yorkers. For many years, Hiram and Leman had been at the center of a series of legal and lobbying actions aimed at getting a line of the Auburn and Rochester Railroad built through their property in Phelps.[46] In the fall of 1856, Hiram engineered an opportunity for himself to ride with former governor William H. Seward, from Lyons to Geneva. He used the hours they spent together in a slow-moving coach to lobby for another of the Hotchkiss family's pet projects of internal improvement: a ship canal they wanted built around Niagara Falls through their uncle William Hotchkiss's property. Hiram reported his conversation to his uncle Calvin, who responded he believed that Seward "was very much in favor of the construction of the Niagara Ship Canal, but expressed a belief it would not be accomplished until a change in the administration (as much as to say when he became President)."[47] The Hotchkisses were rural businessmen who considered themselves the peers of the urban magnates and politicians who are the focus of so much history and biography.

The end of 1856 saw credit tighten, and cash became very scarce in western New York. It was bad timing for a canal but good for Hotchkiss banking aspirations. In spite of their disagreements, Calvin gave in to Hiram's entreaties and endorsed his project. By the end of the year, the Hotchkiss Peppermint Bank was operating, and Calvin wrote Hiram, "If the Peppermint Bank is discounting freely, to send me a good amount, and I will soon put the money in circulation."[48] In early 1857, Leman endorsed another two-thousand-dollar note for Hiram, although he again vented his frustration: "I think your way of continually asking for renewals of your paper has a very bad effect on your credit & prevents you getting accommodations when you might other wise get them." Leman reminded his brother that he had been working hard to repair Hiram's credit standing and had avoided protests or even renewals on his paper for more than a year. "It is disreputable," Leman concluded, "for any decent man not to perform his engagements."[49] Although Calvin welcomed a new source to inject some cash into the distressed local economy, he remained uncomfortable with the lax way his nephew attended to business. Several weeks later, Calvin wrote to Hiram regarding, he said, "your draft on Abraham Bell & Son for $2000 at four months, which I here return as I am <u>entirely</u> out of all kinds of Banking business or discounting or endorsing." Failing to convince Bell and Sons to take Leman's note guaranteed by Calvin, Hiram turned the tables and asked Calvin to advance funds on inventory in the broker's warehouse. Calvin said he planned to devote himself solely to his own business and chided Hiram sarcastically, "I do consider it is generally bad policy for (<u>a young man like me</u>) to branch out into many kinds of business, it is better for a man to attend to one branch of business well than 1/2 doz. neglected."[50]

But as Hiram soon discovered, his uncle Calvin had not really gone out of the banking business—he had just switched partners. Leman returned from a trip to Lewiston a few weeks later and informed his brother in a note, "I can make arrangements with Uncle Calvin to enter into the Banking and Brokers business, but it will be under stringent circumstances."[51] Leman would take over the role Calvin had played financing Hiram's businesses, but he warned Hiram, "You can readily see it will not answer for me to be associated with any man unless he meets his engagements—neither will I be. I speak plain for I know there is but one way for me to sustain a character." The next letter Hiram received from his brother was on letterhead announcing, "C & LB Hotchkiss, Bankers & Exchange Brokers," and signed as "LB Hotchkiss, Cashier."[52]

Later that summer, Calvin wrote to Hiram regarding a letter Hiram had received from William Seward, explaining why a Niagara River survey the Hotchkisses had requested had been delayed.[53] In early 1858, Calvin wrote again: "If Seward & Douglass would take up this subject my impression is something might be accomplished."[54] Like Henry Ranney and Jasper Bement, the Hotchkisses interacted with political figures who would shortly become nationally prominent in the newly formed Republican Party. Unlike the Ashfielders, the Hotchkisses pursued these political connections entirely for personal gain. And despite the Panic of 1857 and the recession that ensued, they were doing quite well. In the spring of 1858, a credit investigator for R. G. Dun reported on Calvin and Leman Hotchkiss's business, noting that "Calvin H is a bachelor and lives at Lewiston. LB is sole executor of his wife's estate, which is worth $60 to $70,000. And he is possessed of RE in the amt of nearly $80,000 and would certainly be worth $60,000 clear." Leman's wife, Lucretia, had died in the summer of 1855, leaving him with five children to care for, but with a substantial estate he held in trust for them. The credit reporter noted "Calvin H we are advised is worth $300 to $400,000. And LB is a widower and lives at Phelps. They do a lucrative Banking business, but confined to selling Exchange, buying notes, bonds, mtgs, etc."[55]

In May 1858, the Eagle Mill that the Hotchkiss brothers' father had built burned to the ground.[56] Hiram considered rebuilding but was unable to find an adequate source of capital for the project. This was the beginning of the end of Hiram's interest in the flour-milling business, though not of his dependence on family members for financing. In late 1859, Hiram again approached his uncle several times seeking financial support. Calvin responded, "I have rec'd your three letters, but did not think proper to answer them; for the reason that you did not mention a syllable in regard to the payments you were to have made me long ago." Calvin chided his nephew, "I think you have treated me in a most shameful manner, and I am determined not to put up with such treatment any longer. You & Leman have speculated on my capital about long enough."[57] When Hiram continued to pursue him, Calvin wrote: "I threw [your letter] down in disgust. The idea of heaping injury upon injury & insult upon insult was more than I could stand. . . . You and Leman ought to be ashamed to treat me in this way, after befriending you in advancing a large amount some 14 years since."[58] Several more months passed, and Calvin wrote to remind Hiram, "I do not wish, nor will I consent to have my name engraved as Banker, when in fact I have no immediate interest or supervision in the matter."[59] When Hiram went ahead without his uncle's approval, Calvin protested: "I was surprised & vexed to think you should go on in direct violation of my wishes & instructions." Calvin said he had expressly forbidden Hiram to engrave his image on banknotes with the title "Banker" and explained "my name should be used only as President and that was merely to give circulation to the notes, where I was known, and it was for your benefit that I consented to that." If he had been fraudulently described as banker, Calvin warned, "I will not advance one dollar toward forwarding the institution."[60]

On the first of September 1860, the New York Bank Department acknowledged receipt of fifty thousand dollars in bonds deposited for "H. G. Hotchkiss & Co. Bank" and the printing of forty thousand dollars in circulating notes.[61] The banknotes and the preprinted promissory notes Hotchkiss would send to Michigan for circulation were all engraved with Calvin's likeness on them, rather than Hiram's, to improve their prestige. Although some historians have argued that the first half of the nineteenth century was a period of "monetary chaos" during which wildcatters and counterfeiters prevented Americans from feeling safe about the nation's currency and economic prospects, this claim is based on a misunderstanding. Historian Stephen Mihm has suggested that antebellum schoolchildren were taught to discount because so many suspect notes were only accepted at a discount from par value. In fact, the reason children learned to discount in their heads was not because people feared banknotes were counterfeit but because so many promissory notes carried interest or passed from hand to hand at discounts from their face values. Finally, the primary evidence does not support the claim that currency was as widely discounted as Mihm's sources claimed. Even Hotchkiss banknotes were either accepted at par or rejected altogether until the federal tax imposed in 1866 created a de facto 10 percent discount that ended their circulation. And an 1857 newspaper reported, "It is a favorite maxim with some to to 'keep bad money in circulation' for they say it makes no difference whether a bill is counterfeit or not, as long as it will pass around freely."[62] A Michigan historian wrote in 1911 that "counterfeiting and issuing worthless 'bank notes' . . . was not looked upon as a felony as it would be today. Of course it was taken for granted that it was a 'little crooked,' but the scarcity of real money, together with the necessity for a medium of exchange, made almost anything that looked like money answer the purpose."[63] The relative lack of alternatives was one of the reasons Hotchkiss engraved promissory notes and banknotes could be used in place of cash in Michigan, although detective Allan Pinkerton remarked in his memoir that "they preferred a good counterfeit on a solid bank to any genuine bill upon a shyster institution."[64] It took Michigan farmers some time to discover that the attractively engraved currency Hiram sent his agents to pay for peppermint oil came from a shyster institution.

Calvin Hotchkiss may have allowed himself to be convinced to continue supporting Hiram's Peppermint Bank because the family was still deeply involved in lobbying for the Niagara Canal project. As the one family member with a personal relationship with Abraham Lincoln's new secretary of state, Hiram was crucial to this plan. In early 1862 he received a letter from his other uncle, William Hotchkiss, who wrote: "Our Niagara Ship Canal must be built. I hope you have had the desired interview with Seward, altho' his mind must be taxed heavily by the complication of our national affairs."[65] Even though the Democratic-leaning Hotchkiss family presumed their project would be among the most important issues facing the Lincoln administration, William Seward and the Republican government had problems more pressing than building a canal around Niagara Falls to compete with Canada's Welland Canal. The Civil War, which Republicans had expected to win quickly, dragged on at incredible expense. Foremost among the major projects the Lincoln administration needed to address was an overhaul of the national banking system.

Unable to raise funds in New York's money market, Republicans claimed they were driven to "emergency legislation when the banks suspended specie payments and destroyed the nation's money."[66] Before the formation of the Republican Party, "some Western Whigs, notably Abraham Lincoln, had called for a new national bank to provide a secure currency."[67] Like Lincoln's interest in railroads, developed while helping the Illinois Central receive the first major grants of public lands to a corporation in 1851, a strong central bank was a priority for the Whig Party, which had merged with abolitionist Free-Soilers to create the Republican Party that had nominated Lincoln in Chicago in 1860. Like the Pacific Railroad Act Lincoln quickly pushed through Congress, the Legal Tender Act of 1862 and the National Banking Act of 1864 achieved this Whig goal by creating a single national currency and a network of nationally chartered banks dominated by a handful of commercial banks in New York City.

The ability of state-chartered banks to issue their own banknotes was effectively eliminated in 1865 by a prohibitive 10 percent tax on state banknote circulation beginning in 1866, forcing a rapid increase in the number of state banks joining the national system. The original National Banking Act had included a section allowing state banks to issue national banknotes; the provision was eliminated only after the legislation had passed on the basis of this promised compromise. In the six months after the tax on state banknotes passed, the number of national banks doubled as many state banks "quickly realized that their future survival depended on allegiance to the national system."[68] Bank legislation had not been an apparent priority in the platform of the new Republican Party when it came to power in 1860, leading historians to disagree over the extent to which the government had intended the new laws as gifts to New York City bankers. Some argued the radical reforms had been "designed to accommodate the economic interests of Northeastern businessmen and capitalists, to the detriment of Western and Southern agrarians." Others countered that, in spite of including a large contingent of Northeastern Whigs, the Republican coalition was really based on a fundamental faith in the "political and social virtues of 'free labor' [and that] almost all of the early Republican leaders subordinated differences in economic philosophy to the basically moral question of slavery."[69]

What is clear is that as time passed, the new federal laws increasingly favored urban financial interests. For example, the first version of the National Banking Act in 1863 had included apportionment limits that required the three hundred million dollars of new national currency issued under the act to be distributed evenly among the regions of the nation. Since "country banks were the largest issuers of state notes, and conversion to the national system meant the loss of [that] privilege," there was legitimate worry that without provisions to ensure adequate currency outside the major financial centers like New York City, the economic activity that had been powered by free banking in states like New York and Michigan would be severely curtailed.[70] This concern was not addressed by the new Banking Act passed in 1864.

The U.S. Treasury suspended specie payments at the end of 1861, and two weeks later gold began to trade on New York commodity markets. Daily quotations were distributed by new telegraphic wire services and printed in newspapers nationwide, giving the value of one hundred gold dollars in United States notes. A quotation of two hundred, for example, meant that it took two hundred dollars in greenbacks to buy one hundred dollars in gold coins or that one dollar in the new, inflationary currency was worth only fifty cents in the old. At its worst, the value of the new greenbacks fell to 35.09 cents relative to the gold-based dollar, on July 11, 1864.[71] Government officials such as Treasury Secretary Salmon Chase attributed the devaluation of greenbacks not to inflation, however, but rather to "the rise in the value of gold caused by nefarious speculation."[72] Shipments of new American gold from California remained relatively stable, even as the destination changed. Gold shipped from California to New York City decreased from $32.6 million in 1861 to $10.3 million in 1863; but at the same time, shipments to England, which remained on a gold standard, increased by $24.4 million.[73]

Hiram Hotchkiss continued operating his Peppermint Bank in spite of the tax on his state-issued currency and the establishment of competing national banks. As a Democrat, he may have hoped the 1864 presidential election would put an end to his disagreement with federal banking policy. Hiram had benefited from being a New York banker. In the antebellum currency market, banknotes issued in eastern states "tended to have either the same contemporaneous discount rate, or discount rates that varied within a small band." During times of financial stress, banks, banknote brokers, and the reporting agencies that published discount-rate data "would advise their customers not to accept western banknotes, or to be wary of them."[74] Western banks were considered riskier, because information reaching eastern authorities was often incomplete, inaccurate, and untimely. Although the fear of counterfeiting was almost certainly lower than has recently been portrayed by historians, during periods of economic uncertainty it was safer for western farmers to use eastern banknotes even if they came from a less-than-ideal source like Hotchkiss.

Treasury Secretary Salmon Chase has been described by his contemporaries and by historians as a financial neophyte. Some have suggested that as a former Democrat, he came from a Jacksonian tradition of distrust of central banking. Others such as bank historian Bray Hammond have observed that whatever his initial inclinations, Chase became a principal actor in a "bloody combat" between federal and state authority. Hammond also noted that Chase, who would later take Roger B. Taney's seat as chief justice of the Supreme Court, disagreed with that court's decision in the Briscoe case regarding the legality of state banknotes. Chase argued that state banknotes "certainly fall within the spirit if not the letter of the constitutional prohibition of the emission of 'bills of credit' by the states and of making by them of anything except gold and silver coin a legal tender in payment of debts."[75] Economic historian Gary Gorton has observed that during the antebellum free-banking era "large numbers of firms entered banking and issued debt in the form of perpetual, non-interest-bearing, risky debt claims, offering the right of redemption on demand at par in specie."[76] Gorton claims that before the Civil War "there was no domestic coin between the 50-cent piece and the $2.50 gold dollar." This is not entirely true: the United States minted a wide variety of coins of lesser denominations, including half-cent pieces, several different sizes of pennies, two-cent and three-cent pieces, nickels, half-dimes, dimes, twenty-cent pieces, quarters, half-dollars, and (except for a period from 1804 to 1836) dollars. Gorton has sought to explain why "wildcat banking was not a pervasive problem during this period." Wildcat banking refers to the practice of issuing more currency than could possibly be redeemed with the securities controlled by the bank. Unfortunately, Gorton has not been able to quantify the significance of note issue in the commerce of the period. "It is not clear," he has admitted, "whether bank notes circulated across different states and regions in significant amounts."[77] In fact, despite the subsequent focus of historians on banknotes, they were far from the center of antebellum business finance.

The activities of the Hotchkisses in their flour and essential oil businesses during this period suggest that interest-bearing promissory notes and drafts written against inventories in transit or warehouses were much more common tools of trade than small-denomination banknotes. Another reason the practice of overprinting currency may have been less prevalent is that, unlike wildcatters such as Chicago's George Smith, many free bankers in western New York and the Yankee West considered themselves more as facilitators of business than as printers of money. Calvin and Leman Hotchkiss, for example, focused on exchange. Even Hiram, who was motivated by a desire to see his notes get a good circulation in Michigan, focused more on business credit for his own operation than he did on issuing notes. As economic historian Willford King remarked in 1920, "To the average citizen bank deposits seem entirely different from bank notes, but in fact they are very similar. Both are promises to pay on demand. . . . As a matter of fact, bank deposits are the principal circulating medium of the United States, nearly all important purchases being made through their use." This is the point missed by Gorton and many later historians. Even for bankers such as the Hotchkisses, the compounding of credit operations was more significant than the issuing of new notes. "The right," King argued, "to loan and reloan a million dollars for an endless period is practically equivalent to the ownership of a million dollars."[78]

Introducing the National Banking Act in January 1863, Senate Finance Committee Chairman John Sherman said: "All private interests, all local interests, all banking interests, the interests of individuals, everything, should be subordinate now to the interest of the government."[79] The federal government's consolidation of power using national banking and the destruction of state banks became a regional issue. In committee, "John Henderson of Missouri tried to set the minimum capital stock of a national bank at $300,000 in order to prevent the establishment of national institutions in rural areas at all" and to preserve some role for regional banking that reflected and facilitated rural economic activity. When the bill came to a vote, twenty-three Republicans from New England, New York, and New Jersey joined the Democrats to oppose national banking.[80] *Harper's Weekly* celebrated the law's passage, announcing that national banking would "institute such a connection between the public credit and the banking interest as shall, on the one hand, give the President virtual control over all the banks in the country, and, on the other, make every stockholder and banknote holder in the land an underwriter, so to speak, of the Government bonds."[81] A shift to centralized national banking did help the Union win the Civil War, but it did so by denying rural people a significant role in the national economy.

Arguing for the prohibitive 10 percent federal tax on state bank circulation the following year, John Sherman declared: "The power of taxation cannot be more wisely exercised than in harmonizing and nationalizing and placing on the secure basis of national credit all the money of the country."[82] Sherman did not explain why the national credit would be a more secure basis for currency than the regional economic activity that up until that time had been its basis throughout the United States. But it was clear to many observers that the banking legislation's goal was not to secure America's currency, which had been sufficient to the needs of commerce without government intervention, but to put the nation's financial system to work funding the war effort. Although all Democrats and even some Republicans worried about the "centralization of power and force here in the Federal Government . . . to destroy all the rights of the States . . . [and] to wield this as an empire," it became an accepted political truth that "Congress must either repeal the banking law or contract the circulation of state banks" to pay for the war.[83]

The federal government established national banks, suspended specie payments, and made greenbacks legal tender; but it did not immediately succeed in eliminating state banking. Government spokesmen mounted a media campaign to discredit the previous system, and "by April 1864 state banking had become identified with disloyalty . . . and gold speculation had become the Treasury's most pressing problem."[84] On April 15, Sherman introduced a bill to outlaw trading in gold "under penalty of a fine or a prison term or both." To support the federal government's control over the currency and the banking system, "the bill stipulated that only greenbacks or national currency, not state bank notes, could be exchanged for gold."[85] The government hoped that by outlawing the exchangeability of anything but the inflationary greenbacks with gold, they might halt inflation. Lincoln signed the bill into law in June 1864, but trading in gold continued, and the value of greenbacks relative to gold continued to drop. Embarrassed by the market's flagrant disregard of its authority, the government repealed the law two weeks later. Angry newspaper articles and congressional speeches identified defenders of state banking with the hated gold speculators. Lincoln replaced Treasury Secretary Chase with William Pitt Fessenden. Although Fessenden had at first opposed the Legal Tender Act, he now argued for "discriminating legislation" to shore up the national currency by forcibly eliminating state banknotes. In January 1865, he endorsed a currency bill that would make it illegal for national banks to circulate state bank notes. New York's Democratic senator Francis Kernan objected: "If the national banks, with the great advantages they enjoy, cannot compete successfully with the State banks, it simply shows that the latter serve the interests of the business community, and should not be destroyed."[86]

The senator did not bother stating the obvious: that state banks served the interests of the business community, especially the portion of it that operated outside the banking center of New York City. Kernan's fellow New York Democrat Hiram Hotchkiss not only continued operating his Peppermint Bank in defiance of the new federal banking policies, he took advantage of every opportunity to profit from the inflation caused by the Legal Tender Act. When New York banks and the federal government suspended specie payments, Hiram began redeeming his notes in greenbacks. As inflation drove the value of the federal notes down to thirty-five cents on the gold dollar, he profited from paying out greenbacks worth only thirty-five cents on each dollar he owed. Although peppermint farmers were also aware that the changing value of money required them to ask more for their oil, he managed to stay a step ahead. In early November 1864, he received a letter from his sons, in which they suggested: "The way gold is this morning we had better buy all the oil we can at $4.50 and $4.75."[87] The day after the 1864 presidential election, he telegrammed his sons: "Uncle Abe is elected & Gold is up to 258 at 1 o'clock PM. . . . I greatly <u>fear</u> that you are both <u>asleep</u> & do not try to secure the oil."[88] The sons responded that they would be happy to buy all the oil in Wayne County, if he would only send funds.[89] A week later, he wrote his sons again: "As gold is falling 235 today at 1 o'clock I should think farmers would sell a little . . . now at a fair price."[90] The next day, he observed: "Gold has declined as low as 218 today & Peppt Oil buyers are holding off. I guess I done well to sell ahead. So hurry up the packing as fast as possible."[91]

Although Hiram used his understanding of currency fluctuations to profit on inflation in the oil market, his attention to the details of his banking operation had not improved. Calvin wrote an angry letter to his nephew at 2:30 A.M. on the morning of March 9, 1864, complaining of five protested notes and one returned certificate of deposit, "which met me like the shock of an <u>Earthquake</u> and you may well Judge why I write you at this <u>unseasonable Hour</u>. The reason is that I <u>could not sleep</u> . . . this is something I never drempt of, when I went into this Banking business merely for your benefit." Calvin lamented, "As to giving you any advice, it would be like a feather in the wind, and you would perhaps consider it an insult."[92] The banking relationship was further damaged when Calvin sent Hiram notice of a "Sheriff Sale at which the county sheriff announced, By virtue of two Executions issued out of the Supreme Court ... I have seized & Taken ... about 60 acres of wheat on the ground, Five Horses, seven Oxen, four cows and fifty tons hay, the Property of Calvin Hotchkiss, which I shall expose for sale."[93] Calvin wrote that the sale of his property was "a transaction which never happened to me before," and warned Hiram: "If you do nothing to stop this sale, then my property must go for what it will bring. My health is quite poor, so that I am not able to travel, otherwise, I should be out to see you." A few months later, Calvin wrote again to "H. G. Hotchkiss Esqr., Banker &c.": "In six days my farm will be sold by the Sherriff of this County, to Pay Your debt you owe to DeWitt Parshall." Parshall was an attorney and rival banker who had converted the Lyons Bank he had established in 1857 into a national bank in 1864. Parshall's son William Henry had married Hiram's daughter Lissette in 1860, but the union of their families apparently did not reduce their animosity or increase the willingness of Hiram to pay his debt. Calvin urged his nephew, "Write me on the receipt of this whether You are ready to pay the debt to the Sherriff, or whether you intend to let him sell my farm. I want an immediate answer."[94]

At the end of 1865, Hiram received a final letter from Calvin, who told his nephew: "I will never write to Strong & Mumford to delay proceeding agt H. G. Hotchkiss & Co.s Bank another day. I have been humbugged about your damd Bank ... I do not want to hear any thing more about that cursed Bank which has given me so much trouble." Calvin complained of the destruction of his own reputation through association with Hiram's business. He added, "I wish you not to write to me again on this Bank subject, as I heard enough of such damned trash."[95] Calvin also ridiculed the suggestion by Hiram that he was planning to convert his Peppermint Bank under the new National Banking law, telling his nephew: "The time has passed for such a business."[96] Calvin died on June 28, 1866, and with him went any hope Hiram might have had of borrowing the bonds he would need to securitize a new banking venture. The Peppermint Bank carried on its business for another year, despite the devaluation of state banknotes caused by the implementation of the federal government's 10 percent tax. In January 1867, the Syracuse

Journal reprinted a story from the Lyons *Republican* stating the "rumor of the failure of H. G. Hotchkiss & Co.'s Bank of Lyons, which has found its way into some of the newspapers, has no foundation." The apparent cause of the rumor was that "for some reason the Metropolitan Bank of New York has latterly thrown out its notes, and that they are only taken at ten per cent discount on deposit at the banks." But that was only because all state bank notes were subject to a 10 percent tax, the newspaper assured its readers. Hotchkiss's notes "are, however, current about town at par, as heretofore, and are being redeemed in greenbacks at the Hotchkiss Bank."[97] It is unclear exactly when Hiram's Peppermint Bank shut its doors, but local histories record that its end corresponded with the destruction of state banking.

The elimination of state banking produced the rural problems the Banking Act's opponents had feared. Not only was there inadequate money in the hinterlands to support business growth, there simply were not enough banks. The number of national banks grew slowly: by 1890 there were fewer than thirty-five hundred.[98] By 1897, after thirty-three years of national banking, Midwestern businessmen attending the Indianapolis Monetary Convention complained about the lack of adequate banking facilities in their states and lobbied for decreases in the capital required to start a bank, as well as for the establishment of branch banks, which were illegal under federal law. Branch banking, which critics argued would increase the power of the central banks allowed to open branches, was not expanded. Instead, the demand for rural and small-town banking services was met by a new wave of free-banking laws passed by the states in the 1880s and 1890s. Like antebellum free-banking laws, they allowed new banks to be established without legislative charters; they also reduced the restrictions imposed by national banking regulations. The states set much lower capital requirements, allowed their banks to make mortgage loans on real estate restricted by national banking law, and established very low or nonexistent reserve requirements. By 1900, there were nearly forty-five hundred state-chartered banks, mostly serving rural hinterlands.[99]

Sociologists Bruce G. Carruthers and Sarah Babb have observed that "money works best when it can be taken for granted, when its value, negotiability, and neutrality can simply be assumed."[100] Their observation applies, ironically, to the historians studying money—especially those who focus on a period when the value, negotiability, and neutrality of currency was less stable than it is today. Banking historian Howard Bodenhorn has suggested, "To most historians, the lessons of free banking were clear. Banking, left to its own devices, was inherently unstable. Unless banks were closely supervised, banking and financial markets degenerated into chaos, causing substantial losses to the public, and eventually slowed real economic activity."[101] This is an incorrect assessment, Bodenhorn has argued, because both state banks and national banks habitually issued fewer notes than the market required for optimal growth. Ohio senator John Sherman had told the Senate in February 1865, "The national banks were intended to supersede the state banks. Both cannot exist together." He meant that the national banks would never survive while state banks were permitted to "carefully keep out their state circulation."[102] For the new federal currency and the banks using it to succeed, state banks and their circulating notes had to disappear. The tax on state banknotes enacted in 1865 drastically reduced the number of state banks but failed to eliminate them. Four years later, Chief Justice Chase read a Supreme Court opinion (*Veazie Bank v. Fenno*) acknowledging that the legislation had been designed to eliminate state banks. Although the Court's decision to uphold the tax on banknotes damaged the cause of free state banking, the banks could not be eliminated as long as they could fulfill the remaining function of banking in the postbellum era, deposit, the importance of which even Bodenhorn underestimated in his focus on banknotes.

The state bank that Hiram Hotchkiss owned, however, had always been more focused on financing his own business operations than on taking deposits and lending funds in the local market. Although frustrated by changing regulations, his adventure in banking ended with the death of his uncle Calvin, whose wealth had guaranteed Hiram's obligations in spite of extreme stresses that may have shortened Calvin's life (he died at the age of seventy-four). In later years, Hiram's financial woes increased. The approach Hiram had to financing, especially his belief that debt was negotiable, was increasingly unpopular in a period when businessmen sought to operate on more objective, rational terms. A comparison of R. G. Dun credit bureau reports on Hiram and on his brother, Leman, are revealing. The entry in the credit company's ledger begins in 1858, noting: "HG and LB Hotchkiss & Co. are not in partnership. LB resides at Vienna [Phelps] and is said to be well off. HG has a large amt of RE in his hands but I am informed he owes a good deal of money. He pays many of his debts at the end of execution. No one can tell me what he is worth."[103]

A few years later, another Dun entry on Hiram states: "Cannot say how good he is. Has large amt of property in his hands. Appears to owe considerable. Is sued quite frequently."[104] In 1869, the reporter commented: "Cannot say what his respons[ibility] is. He owes a great deal of money and has been sued a great many times and many executions have been returned unpaid and are still unpaid. He has considerable property in his hands but he never pays I believe until the end of an execution. Difficult to tell whether he is worth anything or not. I cannot say."[105] In 1873 another reporter added, "Has considerable property in his hands but very much encumbered, and doubt collection could be enforced vs. him. Is not regarded reliable and has no credit here."[106] In 1877, the reporter noted that Hiram had tried to divest himself of his property to avoid attachment: "The firm is now HG Hotchkiss and Sons. HGH swears that he has nothing . . . neither his word nor note passes current here. . . . All the RE is in the hands of Mrs. HGH and daughters." The reporter concluded, "[Hotchkiss] owes largely and would like to owe more, but he is too well known here."[107] A final entry at the end of 1889 concluded the story on a note altogether unlike the heroic tale told by local histories and Hotchkiss company memorials: "He declines to make any showing whatever. The firm is composed of Leman, Calvin, and Hiram G. Hotchkiss Jr., the three sons of Hiram G. Hotchkiss." The reporter notes that the sons had worked in the business since 1873, and that the business shipped peppermint and other essential oils worldwide, especially to London and Paris. Their reputation for quality peppermint oil was intact and the Hotchkiss company had won several prize medals; the family company's credit "standing however is at the lowest point. They have plenty of property however in the family but keep transferring it from one to another, so that it is utterly out of reach. As a firm [they] are considered thoroughly irresponsible, never known to pay anything they can get out of, will beat everyone they can, have absolutely no credit, and should be dealt with accordingly by outsiders. They are a hard lot, do not ever pay debts for living expenses around town, and are not trusted here out of sight."[108]

In contrast, Leman prospered, especially once he managed to break free of his brother. In 1867, Leman was reported in the R. G. Dun ledgers "to be good for anything he agrees to pay, and [says] that he pays a larger tax than any three men or firms in Phelps. Considered good."[109] Two years later, the reporter wrote: "Owns $100,000 or more RE in and around the village of Phelps, has $40,000 in the Air Cure at Clifton, has $50,000 in the bank, he is a shrewd and careful manager and deals largely in peppermint oil and makes money. He is considered very sound and all right."[110] In 1879, the reporter added: "Owns large amt RE and his children also have some inherited from their mother. This RE is free and clear. He has cash to purchase oil and is supposed to be worth $250 to $300,000."[111]

Hiram operated his business using a code of ethics that seemed disconnected from any moral norms. His treatment of partners, especially relatives such as Leman and Calvin, was deplorable. Cultural historian Warren Susman has noted that Ralph Waldo Emerson's seminal definition of character, "Moral order through the medium of individual nature," was challenged at the end of the nineteenth century by a growing interest in personality and performance.[112] The differences between the business practices of Hiram and those of his brother Leman and uncle Calvin may be an early example of a shift from character to personality as a determinant of success, as Susman has suggested. I consider these differences in more detail in the next chapter. Hiram's behavior was based not on ignorance but rather on early experience as a businessman in western New York. Hiram understood how business was traditionally conducted, but he felt free to bend or break the rules whenever it pleased him, relying on his charm and on personal relationships to win people to his point of view or retain their support in spite of his actions. He understood the principles of banking as they were developing during his lifetime but had no respect for them. He used his bank almost exclusively to finance his own business. He considered anybody who presented his notes at the counter of his bank for specie to be an adversary, and he developed strategies to delay payment or meet

demands for payment with new requests for credit. Ultimately, his interest in banking was completely subordinated to his obsession with being
the peppermint king. It is ironic that Hiram *is* remembered as the
peppermint king of western New York, while his brother, Leman, who
was ultimately much more successful and left a valuable inheritance to
his children—and who had probably sold as much peppermint oil as
Hiram in his lifetime—is all but forgotten.

S • E • V • E • N

The Dark Side of Family Business

Hiram G. Hotchkiss is remembered in Lyons as "a most interesting personality. He was a man of almost gigantic
stature, and in his youth was regarded as a remarkably
handsome man. He was most positive in his convictions
and when he had decided on a course never was swerved in the slightest
degree. He never forgave an injury nor forgot a favor." The account of
Hiram, printed across eight columns just a day after his death on October
27, 1897, from information undoubtedly supplied by his family, continued
by describing Hiram as "hospitality personified" and as a diligent businessman who "rarely left his home except to go back and forth to his
business, to which he attended with the greatest regularity up to almost
the very day of his death, and for occasional visits to New York or abroad."[1]
The obituary then repeated the inaccurate story mentioned earlier of
how Hiram had singlehandedly invented the peppermint oil business,
listed all the awards he had won for his peppermint oil, and claimed: "He
was just as cordial to his most inveterate business and political enemy as
to his friends."[2] Although the account went to great lengths to portray
Hiram as a benevolent, self-made entrepreneur who had always put the
needs of his family, friends, and community before his own, this was
not the case. In spite of the social mores of his time, and against the
repeated protests of business partners, friends, and family, he was a

monomaniacal autocrat who blustered and bullied his way toward a success that, despite his claims, he never really achieved.

The story of his business conduct illustrates the extent to which Hiram believed that the rules of society did not apply to him. It also suggests what those rules were, providing a clearer outline of social mores in nineteenth-century western New York. Loyalty, honor, and strong family ties supported business in positive ways in the story of the Ranneys. Hiram Hotchkiss's story is a counterpoint, illustrating the ways friendship and family loyalty could be betrayed and perverted to enable intolerable behavior. It is generally accepted by contemporary historians that kin networks and long-term friendships determined the flow of investment funds and products in nineteenth-century western New York and more broadly throughout American society. Historian Paul Johnson has observed that "individual fortunes were meshed with social networks . . . and entrepreneurial activity was typified by caution and cooperation, and not by ungoverned individual ambition," resulting in "a remarkably orderly and closed community of entrepreneurs."[3] Hiram's career offers a counterexample to Johnson's largely accurate narrative; reviewing Hiram's family interactions helps illustrate the boundaries of acceptable behavior by examining the actions of someone who habitually transgressed them.

As Hiram became increasingly successful as a miller and merchant, his behavior worsened over time as he gradually abandoned his inhibitions. When he began his career, he was a family man who seemed to appreciate the contributions others made to his success. As he began expanding his business to trade in New York City, he expressed his gratitude for the support of family and friends. In the spring of 1845, he wrote to his wife, Mary, from the city. Addressing her as "My dear dear dear wife," he described his trip down the Hudson River from Albany and the welcome he received in the household of his business associate, David Dows. Hiram confessed, "I have not yet succeeded in making sales of my oil but am in hopes soon to effect the sale so that I can come home. . . . I have since my return here from Albany been the most of my time engaged in putting up a small lot of oil to ship to England and Germany." Hiram closed by saying, "I fear you are out of money and I wrote Leman to go over to Lyons and see if you was right side up."[4] A few weeks later, he wrote to Mary again about their daughter: "Ellen seems perfectly delighted with her visit. She went with Sarah today to the museum. The fact is dear I am proud of our daughter Ellen."[5] In addition to demonstrating his warm feelings toward Mary and his children, the letters reveal that at the beginning of his career Hiram mixed friendship with business. He hosted his New York City partners in Lyons for summer holidays, and early letters about the joint ventures the brothers undertook with Dows and Cary in real estate and flour milling are often warm and personal.

The business relations Hiram had with his relatives also began well. Although they often disagreed, at the outset of their partnership Leman and Hiram were relatively tolerant of their differences. In August 1845, at the beginning of the peppermint harvest, Leman chided Hiram gently, "Now my dear Brother I am really surprised how you can work yourself up to such a pitch when you know I have no funds on hand. . . . However I have concluded to do the best I can."[6] A few weeks later, Leman wrote Hiram again, complaining: "It is very inconvenient for me to get along with our business without a horse & buggy. I was compelled to ride on horseback to subpoena witnesses 14 or 15 miles and it is not very pleasant in this hot weather."[7] Although the brothers were already involved in litigation against their neighbors (in this case, over the Auburn and Rochester Railroad), they were united by family loyalty against the outsiders. Hiram loaned Leman his buggy for the hottest weeks of the summer, and Leman was pleased. Later in 1845, Leman sent his brother a report on the progress of their railroad suit: "I have no doubt they will pay our $6000 judgment & buy our farm at a good round price & make Vienna [Phelps] the principal stopping place."[8]

But even when feelings of friendship existed with outside business partners, they were fragile and easily swept aside if Hiram felt he had been ill treated. At the end of 1845, the Hotchkiss brothers' relationship with David Dows exploded, when Hiram claimed Dows had skimmed profits on his flour sales. Hiram wrote an angry letter to Dows "setting forth his base conduct," which at the last minute he decided not to send. "You poor insignificant wretch, I wish to address you a few lines, to let you know that I know what a scoundrel you are." Hiram charged Dows with making sales of 1,105 barrels of Hotchkiss flour on his own account but then juggling his books to make it seem as if the flour had been sold when prices were lower, pocketing the difference. Hiram went on at length, finally asking: "Have you not made false charges of storage and insurance, cooperage and cartage, and that too against the person with whom you knew meant to deal fairly by you, your poor insignificant wretch."[9] Luckily, Hiram showed the letter to his brother Leman before mailing it to Dows.

Leman calmed his brother and convinced him to let Leman draft the letter the Hotshkisses ultimately sent to Dows and Cary. Unlike Hiram in his draft letter, Leman focused his remarks on the salient points of their disagreement and seemed genuinely interested in resolving those differences. "We regret to inform you," Leman began, "when your Mr. Cary was here last we informed him of our dissatisfaction in regards to your statements made to us as respects the sale and charges on the property which we have consigned to your house and which we believe was sold or great part of it at higher prices than those reported to us." Leman then gave a complete accounting of the situation as he understood it, citing dates, prices, and quantities. He closed by saying a complete reckoning of their account "would confer a great favor upon us. And when you take into account that a refusal on your part will be viewed as a very suspicious circumstance, we think you will do so without delay. Please let us hear from you at your earliest convenience on the subject."[10]

A lawsuit ensued that dragged on for more than a decade. The complaint in the suit was not, however, about shipments of flour sold at prices higher than reported. It was about 197 cans of peppermint oil, originally shipped to Dows and Cary but later repossessed by Hiram and transferred to George Morewood for shipment to England. At issue was the ownership of the oil when it was transferred to Morewood.[11] Hiram had tried to deflect attention from the fact he had broken his agency agreement with Dows and Cary by claiming that David Dows had betrayed him first.

Although the Hotchkiss brothers remained allies against the outside world, tensions rose and tempers occasionally flared. At the end of 1845, Leman warned Hiram: "I really hope you will not hereafter allow your ass to run away with your head. I suppose you are aware that we cannot loan money unless we pay interest on it."[12] Hiram had begun depending on his brother to finance both their flour-milling operation and Hiram's growing peppermint oil business. Leman often found himself riding from town to town to get promissory notes discounted. He grew frustrated when Hiram expected him to avoid payment and refinance the debts when they came due. Leman conformed to standard business practices and believed that the brothers should pay their debts rather than compounding them. After a decade of frustration, Hiram and Leman executed a contract that purported to be a settlement of their business affairs. The document included inventories, consignments of peppermint oil, notes and judgments, and even lists of the household items each brother planned to keep. According to the contract, "This is the basis agreed upon for a settlement between HG Hotchkiss and Leman B Hotchkiss in Lyons Nov 6th 1855." According to the settlement document, both parties "understood all old Claims, Debts, Judgments, Bonds, Mortgages & Notes not inventoried herein . . . belong to the firm of HG & LB Hotchkiss."[13] As mentioned earlier, Leman's thirty-one-year-old wife, Lucretia, had died in the summer, leaving him with five children to care for and a substantial inheritance of local Oaks Corner real estate to manage in trust for them. Hiram agreed to assume most of the outstanding debt, but in the following months and years the continued existence of the "HG & LB Hotchkiss" company mentioned in the document indicates the brothers had not actually severed their business ties, even though that was the story they told outsiders. It might have seemed to the brothers that an apparent separation from Hiram would improve Leman's ability to raise money. This was probably true, but agreeing to the ruse was a fateful mistake on Leman's part.

And the meaning of the 1855 settlement was ambiguous, even between the brothers. As part of their agreement, Hiram and Leman had split several debts and judgments, each agreeing to pay half. In February 1856, Leman forwarded Hiram a judgment in favor of David Dows, for which he had paid his share.[14] The next day, Leman sent another judgment on which he had paid his half, saying: "I want you to pay your part without making any words at all."[15] In March, only a few months after signing the contract, Leman wrote to Hiram: "I do not feel satisfied at all in your course about our money arrangements. I gave you my paper for

$3300 endorsed by Uncle Calvin and not one dollar as yet has been ap-
portioned to pay what was intended. Your financial skill is not at all
satisfactory and will not pay our debts <u>here</u>."[16] Their benefactor Calvin
Hotchkiss, whom the brothers had assured they had settled all their affairs together, wrote to Hiram: "I cannot see why you and Leman should
hold on so tenaciously on so much real estate when you could realize
50 pr cent more than it is actually worth. I would recommend to you to
calculate the difference between 7 pr cent income, & 7 pr cent outlay in
buildings & and other 7 pr cent in costs & taxes, and 25 pr cent loss in
credit. Not having much experience in the world," Calvin concluded
ironically, "I should like the advice of a <u>shrude practical financier</u> on this
subject."[17] Leman wrote a few weeks later, "I gave you my paper for $3300
to relieve me from all my liabilities at Lyons, and not for you to use in
your business at all, and when the paper is paid I want my liability to be
released, and I want no shuffling about it. . . . You do not seem to appreciate my situation at all, but keep constantly annoying me about
business <u>contrary</u> to our agreement."[18] Days later, Leman wrote again to
inform Hiram he was closing up his house in town, moving back to the
family homestead, and sending his children to live temporarily with
relatives. Leman complained, "Now Hiram I regret to be obliged to be
continually informing you of our agreement made between us on the
6th Nov last and you seem to be continually endeavoring to bring about
a state of things directly opposite to the agreement & understanding."
Leman said he was prepared to live up to the letter of the agreement and
conduct business with Hiram as he would with anyone else. "You do not
seem to realize my situation at all," Leman continued, "and I sometimes
think you dont care. I have five small children entirely dependent upon
me and together with my other business and perplexities I think I am
excusable in refusing entirely of being mixed up in <u>your</u> business." Leman concluded, "By Tuesday I shall be pretty well scattered and broken
up & I assure you this is a very unpleasant move."[19]

Hiram responded the following day: "Your meanness toward me is
perfectly shocking to my nerve. Your paper . . . has not thus far been
worth a 'tird' to me." Hiram insisted he had reduced Leman's liability by
increasing his own since the settlement. He complained, "[I] did not
expect to be treated in this contemptuous manner by you. I expected

you would be willing to 'help' meet or carry along these matters. I only agreed to assist in carrying along the 'thing' with a view only of being accommodating & <u>brotherly</u> to you. In return I only get <u>kicks</u>, and am accused by you of <u>shuffling</u>." Hiram attacked Leman's "intimation" that he was using his brother's funds to operate his business by admitting, "How in <u>Hell</u> did you suppose the liabilities could be met unless your paper could be made available for you know I had no money." Hiram closed by saying he expected Leman would also refuse to loan him four thousand dollars so he could pay another court judgment, which "would be all of a piece with your other <u>contemptible</u> treatment."[20]

The focus on his own interests by Hiram at the expense of his brother's did not go unnoticed. Their cousin William T. Hotchkiss wrote to implore, "Oh Hiram Hiram, be a man, give Leman your portion . . . and for the sake of the business reputation of the whole Hotchkiss family dont play baby and fool any more."[21] Calvin added his criticism, noting: "A distinction ought to be made between <u>business matters</u> and that of <u>joking</u>. . . . You claim to be a <u>business man</u> and <u>a great financier</u>, and as such, you never ought to suffer your paper to be dishonored or your endorsers Credit suffer by reason of any neglect."[22]

When Leman's health began to suffer, he attributed this to the breakup of his family and the stress of being forced to deal with Hiram's bad finances. He wrote to Hiram, "I have been a bed all day. . . . I feel quite strange and my powers of comprehension seems to be diminished." He continued: "You are too careless and negligent in your engagements to suit my constitution and I cannot stand it at all."[23] Leman wrote a few weeks later to see if Hiram had satisfied the judgment that he had relented and loaned his brother four thousand dollars to pay, mentioning: "My health is a little better but I feel satisfied that I cannot bear any perplexity at all. Since my apoplectic attack my nervous system seems to be in a very bad state."[24] The following week, Leman responded to the plaintiff's demand for satisfaction, assuring the man whom Hiram had not paid that his brother was good for the money, and asking: "At all events don't sue me. I would go to Lyons to attend to this business, but my health is so poor that I cannot under a few days."[25] The plaintiff responded that he planned to attach the assets of both the brothers, and Leman admonished Hiram to settle up so he would not be sued again.[26]

The brothers continued to market their International Prize Medal Oil of Peppermint and other essential oils under the HG & LB Hotchkiss brand, but Leman suspected Hiram had stopped regarding him as an equal partner. In the fall of 1856, Leman wrote to challenge Hiram: "Have you taken the Paris Prize Medal in your individual name? If you have, you have done wrong!"[27] Hiram assured his brother, "I have done nothing at Paris to undermine you & the sooner you get over such feelings the happier you will be."[28] Leman accepted his brother's explanation and reluctantly continued helping Hiram finance his peppermint oil business. In 1857, Leman wrote to Hiram to say he had paid an overdue note, saving his brother from another lawsuit. But he had been forced to pay in cash. The creditor had declined to take Leman's note in payment: "He felt very much dissatisfied after . . . giving us 2 years to pay he thought we ought to fulfill our promise." Leman again observed, "The fact is I have more trouble & perplexity on your business than I do on my own."[29]

The brothers' uncle William Hotchkiss, who had requested repayment of a loan he had made to Hiram, wrote: "Your conduct is inexcusable and is past endurance, your promises are mere trash and worthless." William had been coexecutor of their father's estate and did not care to be instructed in business by Hiram. "You talk that you 'must have capital in your business,' this is most insulting and you know it full well or ought to know it," William wrote. "Others require capital in their business as well as yourself."[30] Hiram's reputation continued to deteriorate. In early 1858, Leman informed Hiram that "it was currently reported between here & Lyons that you had failed." Leman said he had "heard it from 4 or 5 different sources." Leman was also losing patience: "What a splendid credit you maintain. I hope you will change your name to Goff at once expressly for my benefit. You pledged me your word that your note would be promptly met at maturity and if you fail to pay it, you can go to the devil hereafter for I will not allow you to prostrate my credit in this way."[31]

The growing tendency of Hiram to ignore the needs of even his family was again demonstrated in the spring of 1858. The brothers' mother, Chloe Hotchkiss, wished to move back to the area from New Haven, where she had been staying with relatives. Leman wrote, "Something has got to be done and I can see no other way, only for you to take

Ma in your charge."[32] Hiram felt he was too busy and suggested his brother should take care of the matter. Leman replied, "It is useless to multiply words abt my taking <u>Ma</u> in my house for I cannot do it and you ought to know that it would be impossible for me to do so. I have five small children and no one to oversee them but myself." Leman noted too that he had been contributing his share to their mother's upkeep, while Hiram had not. "You have paid Ma five dollars within the last five years and I have paid her over $800 in cash and you will please ponder over that."[33]

As protests for nonpayment and executions against Hiram increased, Leman again tried to separate himself from his brother's business. He wrote, "Now Hiram the only way I can see in order to save our selves from ruin & disgrace is to discontinue all business with you." Claiming to be really serious this time, Leman admonished his brother: "Now for god sake never ask me to negotiate any more of your paper."[34] A day later, he added: "I am not only compelled to pay your debts but I am compelled to run over to Lyons not only once but at least two or three times every time you have a debt falling due. I see plainly you are determined to ruin my credit if you can."[35] By late 1858, Calvin Hotchkiss too had lost patience with his nephew. Calvin wrote, "I once had confidence in your word as well as your Obligations, but as you pay no regard to either, of course my confidence is exhausted."[36]

When Hiram felt threatened, he often looked for distractions he could use to attack his antagonists. Leman tried to end his involvement in his brother's finances, and Hiram found a way to retaliate. In the fall of 1858 the brothers went to war over the quality of their respective brands of peppermint oil. Although they were both using a shared HG & LB Hotchkiss label, they were each producing their own peppermint oils in Phelps and Lyons. Reviving a perennial complaint he made against rivals, Hiram accused Leman of shipping adulterated oil, writing that he had tested a sample of peppermint oil that Leman had accepted, and had found it to be "adulterated" with wild pennyroyal growing in the mint fields. "How to protect myself from your consummate '<u>igno-rance</u>' and headstrong <u>belief</u> that you are a <u>judge</u> of Oil of Peppermint <u>I Know not</u>," Hiram raged. "I dare say you will still persist that the oil is pure, and that you will bottle it and stick to it that it is pure oil, and the brand will be completely <u>annihilated</u> and I reduced to <u>poverty</u> and <u>distress</u> by your <u>cursed</u> ignorance." Hiram told his brother, "You are no judge of oil of Peppt & what oil you purchase should be <u>packed here</u>" at Hiram's business in Lyons if Leman wanted to use the shared label. "I tell you once and for all that <u>I will not</u> be <u>identified</u> with your bottling this lot of oil," Hiram announced. Leman should send it into the wholesale market packed in tin and take a loss if necessary. Hiram insisted Leman had no right to associate the Hotchkiss name with an inferior lot of oil and demanded, "Let me hear from you <u>just</u> what you intend to do with <u>this lot</u> of oil & if you intend to <u>bottle</u> it. I have no patience with your performances . . . you are such an <u>ass</u> in your judgment of Peppt Oil."[37]

Leman responded to Hiram's disparagements of his peppermint oil: "I know it to be perfectly pure & as good as any oil ever made. You are at liberty to examine it and apply your test and if it does not come up to the quality of any Wayne County oil by <u>your own test</u>, I will give you a check on the Artisans Bank for $250, at sight." Leman said a customer had examined the oil "and he says it is very beautiful indeed. I will not nuckle to you in judging oil at all."[38] A few weeks later, Leman wrote that he could no longer do business because he was ill and had lost his sight.[39] Hiram responded, "Dear Brother, I am sorry you are troubled with your eyes and would like to see you if I could leave home," but things were quite busy in Lyons. He closed the letter by reminding Leman not to pack the oil they had argued over and asking him to renew another note.[40]

The illness was genuine, and Leman was forced to hire an assistant to handle his correspondence and business. A few days before Christmas, the assistant wrote to Hiram that "in consequence of the illness of LBH who has been confined to his room for five weeks nearly, it has been impossible for him to attend to business at all, being the greater part of the time in great pain and a portion of the time unable to stand." The assistant informed Hiram, "The doctors say that LBH has lost the sight of the left eye."[41] Hiram responded on Christmas Day: "I am absolutely obliged (for I cannot do any other way) to renew my note." Hiram appealed to Leman, "No bank can do anything for me & I have written to Uncle C that as soon as you are able to go that we must meet there and arrange our matters satisfactorily. I feel bad to hear that you are so afflicted with your eyes, & how to get along without your assistance I know not."[42] Leman's illness was inconvenient for Hiram, who could not continually refinance his debts without Leman's guarantee. The assistant informed Hiram in early 1859, "LBH has met with a great misfortune by the loss of the sight of one of his eyes." The assistant also announced that Leman was "expecting to go to Lewiston soon, where he will communicate your damnable conduct toward us to Uncle Calvin."[43] Leman decided he was too ill to make the trip to Lewiston, and wrote to Hiram: "I have repeatedly informed you of my health but you either do not believe or are determined not to understand that I am in a very bad situation. I am almost blind and therefore must not tax myself with writing a long letter to you. I want you to come here <u>alone</u> and have a personal interview with me."[44] Hearing of the ongoing disputes, Calvin reiterated: "It is highly necessary that you & Leman should settle your old copartnership business according to your former agreement. It is perfectly unwarrantable for such old matters to be delayed any longer."[45]

In spite of Leman's illness, Hiram continued to harass his brother about his peppermint oil. In February 1859, he wrote that he had discovered Leman had packed the disputed peppermint oil in glass and was preparing to sell it under their label. Hiram said, "I am perfectly astonished and I will never consent to your branding that trash. Your astonishing ignorance of the quality of oil Peppt perfectly astonishes me." Hiram complained that he was working hard to get himself out of the financial embarrassment he found himself in, but that if he failed it would be Leman's fault. He declared, "Altho my losses last year were considerable I live in hopes of doing something hereafter in Oil Peppt to extricate myself unless by your willfulness you destroy what little reputation I have acquired by packing adulterated oil Peppt." He concluded by threatening Leman: "I shall hold you responsible for all the damage you do me. <u>Take notice of what I say</u>. I have nothing further to say on this disagreeable subject."[46]

Leman responded, "I have made up my mind never to broach the subject of Oil Peppt to you again," but warned Hiram against bringing their uncle Calvin into the dispute. He reminded Hiram that he had offered him $250 to test the oil. "Your being a damned jackass I am not to blame for. I am not at all satisfied with your knowledge of the Michigan

& Indiana Oil, to pack it and brand it in my name and I shall hold you accountable for all the damage you do to me by doing so."[47] Calvin had no wish to be dragged into the argument, and wrote to Hiram: "I do consider it is a most disgraceful feature in both of you, to be <u>eternally quarrelling</u>, and hope you can reconcile all your difficulties between yourselves."[48] But the quarrel continued. A few days later, Leman informed Hiram he had received a letter from London saying "that [their] brand of oil was not in as good repute as it had been formerly." Leman also said it was becoming common knowledge in New York City that Hiram was buying peppermint oil from New York brokers, to "take it home and bottle it and then return it to New York and get a dollar a pound more for it." Leman said he refused to allow his reputation to be damaged by Hiram's cutting corners, advising him: "If you wish to purchase Michigan Oil buy it there, if you wish to purchase Indiana Oil buy it there . . . and for God sake keep out of the New York market in purchasing oil."[49]

Leman concluded, "I have always and do now uphold your brand and keep it up to the standard of mine, but if you continue this system you cannot expect me to uphold it any longer. In future please send me samples for inspection and I will aid you in selecting Pure Oil." A few weeks later, Leman wrote to inform Hiram he was no longer using the "HG & LB Hotchkiss" label but had begun packing oil solely under his own name. "My oil is packed under my own hand writing and my own <u>individual Label</u> and if it should not turn out equal in quality to yours you can readily see with half an eye that it would result in ruination of my brand and be a great benefit to you and your opinion to the contrary is <u>poppycock</u>. You say my oil is <u>bad bad bad</u>. I know that is a <u>lie lie lie</u>."[50]

Leman understood that his agreement to share responsibility for the debts of the partnership had been a grave mistake. In the summer of 1859, he wrote to Hiram: "You will please refer to our settlement papers of Nov 6th 1855 and not appear so ignorant as you pretend. I have paid my part and am released on the notes."[51] Although they had agreed to pool their resources and purchase western oil together, Hiram and Leman began competing with each other for Michigan peppermint oil, each sending agents into the field to buy directly from farmers. Hiram had ceased trying to remain polite in his letters to his brother, even when seeking favors. He wrote asking Leman to help him get extensions on three notes coming due, and concluded his letter, "<u>Do you still persist in packing that Ohio Oil in Glass ... you chuckle head</u>."[52] A week later, Hiram wrote demanding his half of a shipment of Michigan oil that Leman had purchased and for which Hiram had not paid his share. "You do not send that order for the Western Oil. You do not reply to my letter. Never could I have believed that you would have put yourself out & done what you have done for the last 2 months <u>to destroy my business</u>."[53] Hiram was beginning to believe that people who did not behave as he wished were either ignorant or willfully set on his destruction. The next day, he wrote again: "Indeed Leman since I have been on the stage of action I have never had anything <u>effect me</u> so than I have to see your determination to destroy my business. I have long felt that it was your intention to do so, but I could not have believed that you would resort to the <u>means</u> you have done to accomplish it. <u>I feel bad</u>."[54]

In spite of his claims of hurt feelings and the fact they were still nominally buying oil together, Hiram continued disparaging his brother's product. Leman responded, "I observe your remarks abt oil Peppt which is perfectly disgusting as has been the case for a long time & unless you discontinue your misrepresentations abt my oil I will never have any thing further to say to you on that subject." Leman again argued that if his own brand of peppermint oil turned out to be inferior, no one would benefit more than Hiram. He said he had checked with all his customers, and they were very pleased with his oil. "But on the contrary I hear some of your oil—I mean HG Hotchkiss <u>New Brand</u>—is not quite as good as formerly. This I have direct from the parties & I can prove it right to your face, and I challenge you to do the same by my brand which is easily distinguished by my individual label." Leman also responded to the charge that he was "injuring the price of oil" by shipping an inferior product and warned Hiram that if he wanted his half of the Michigan peppermint oil they had contracted for together, he needed to pay for it. "I am to forfeit the oil if I fail to pay for it on the <u>1st day</u> of February in Michigan. So be prepared on your part."[55]

Leman had denied Hiram's charge that he had injured the price of Hotchkiss peppermint oil by shipping an inferior product. It was probably truer that Hiram's profits had been eroded by the competition between the two for oil in Michigan, which had driven up the prices they paid to farmers. But responsibility for that price inflation was at least half Hiram's. In the summer, anger boiled over, and Leman wrote his to brother: "Your god darn ill treatment has got to be stopped for I will not stand your god darn ill treatment any longer."[56] Hiram responded, "Your contemptible letter is in my shit house," but in a typical display of audacity he included a new note in the letter that he asked Leman to take in place of one coming due.[57] Phillip Wells, Hiram's Michigan buyer, warned him: "If you and LBH are in competition the result will be that you will run the price up so that neither will make any money this fall in oil."[58] The difference between Leman and Hiram's buying trips to Michigan, however, was that Leman sent agents with fat packets of cash. Hiram couldn't always send cash, but he could send his Peppermint Bank's paper. Wells wrote to Hiram again: "Send me more of your certificates of deposit. They go first rate and will get a long circulation and it is the best kind of business for a bank."[59] Whether this was entirely true or was what Wells knew Hotchkiss wanted to hear, the Hotchkiss Peppermint Bank's engraved promissory notes were used in place of currency by many Michigan farmers, which helped Hiram compete with his much more solvent brother. Hiram sent packets of twenty-five-dollar certificates for distribution to the farmers and urged his agents to try to make small down payments with promises of full payment on delivery of the oil.[60] His policy of paying "the rise" in price between contract and delivery was to a great extent forced on Hiram by his inability to pay farmers in full up front, allowing other buyers to offer more for the yet-to-be-distilled oil.

In late summer 1860, Leman told Hiram through his assistant that he could not loan him two thousand dollars. Hiram responded, "You promised to let us have your draft on NY at 1/2 per ct prem for $2000 til abt middle or last part of Sept when our currency from the Bank department will be here & we can pay you out of it. Dont be afraid of your friends & send it along. Yours truly, HG Hotchkiss, Banker."[61] Leman wrote, "This institution is not in the habit of lending money without having something to show for it. If you wish to borrow $2000 till the 15th of Sept next with int at 7% send your certificate of deposit and we now think we can lend it to you."[62] Hiram replied the next day, "[We are sending] our man Jno Kraufman over to Vienna to get your sight draft on NY for $2000 as <u>promised</u> us. We can give you our currency for it within 20 or 30 days. We hand you a certificate of deposit for $2000 for dft & exchg. We have to pay for the balc of our State Stocks tomorrow & I am all ready if you let us have the $2000 as agreed. Now dont fail to send it to me."[63] Although Hiram was depending on his brother to help him buy securities to send to the state's Bank Department, he was also plotting against Leman in Michigan. Hiram received a letter the same day from his agent Phillip Wells, who informed him. "I shall pay out all the $500 tomorrow for oil and will ship it next day. It won't buy 300 pounds and then I will be out of money again. If Delemus [Latin for destroyer, one of their code names for Leman] comes on with money which he will he will sweep all the oil in spite of me." Wells reminded Hiram that he had been warning him since the previous season and that Hiram had assured him there would be plenty of money. If he had no competition, Wells wrote, "[I] could wiggle them along and accommodate you. But you do tie a man's hands and feet and throw him in the water and of course he will sink and I don't like to be made ass of." If Hiram could send five or six thousand dollars, Wells said, he could get the job done.[64]

Hiram responded, "How would HG Hotchkiss & Cos Bank certificates of deposit circulate in Michigan?" Hiram told Wells fifty thousand dollars of his newly engraved banknotes would be available from Albany within a few weeks. He added, "Lempus Oilutus [Leman] would be astonished if he knew how you was hustling in the oil. He dont know that King Philip is one of the wide-awake. We will learn him not to play grab as he did last fall."[65] A few weeks later, Hiram sent Wells "10 $50 Bank HG Hotchkiss & Co certificates at sight, or if they wish to hold them three months they get 5%, if six months 6%. The proprietors of this bank are worth $500,000 and Delemus dare not say otherwise."[66] Although he had boasted to Wells that fifty thousand dollars in currency would soon be available, Hiram sent only five hundred dollars in promissory notes. Hiram's boast counted his uncle's net worth in spite of Calvin insisting he did not want to be involved. He had urged his nephew to stick to the business he was good at: "My opinion is that, by mixing up all kinds of advertisements, on business Letters, such as Banking &c goes to show, You <u>are straining to catch a Lyon & only get a mouse</u>."[67] Hiram sent another packet of cash to Wells, writing: "I sent you in this mornings mail 20 HG Hotchkiss & Co Bank certificates amounting to $750 and now I hand you per express herewith the following: 20 $25 Cuyler Bank certificates of deposit, $500, 20 $25 HG Hotchkiss & Cos Bank certificates of deposit, $500." Hiram again sent certificates of deposit rather than small-denomination notes, and he concluded his letter by telling Wells, "N.B. If anybody refuses to take HG Hotchkiss & Cos bank certificates, I hope you will piss on them."

Hiram wrote to Wells again later in the day, sending another $750 of his paper and urging his agent to try to ensure that the certificates would not be returned quickly to the Peppermint Bank, explaining: "You see the certificates are payable at sight (for the law requires every bank certificate to be paid at sight) but if the holder sees fit to hold them three months they get 5% if six months 6%. Please circulate them to the very best advantage to this bank for they will find out by and by that this is an undoubted institution and no mistake."[68] Wells responded that the notes were "just as good here now as the Geneva banks," but he warned: "On the whole I would make them payable as sight as it will look a little like kiting." Wells also mentioned that he had seen Leman in Michigan: "Delemus said you gave him encouragement that you would go in and buy the oil together and when he found out you were fooling him . . . he feels like a dog with a sore head."[69] The following day, Wells reported: "Delemus acts perfectly rabid and crazy. He don't know what he is about now or care what he does or says."[70] But Leman had plentiful cash to pay the peppermint farmers, and a few days later Wells complained: "Your sweet Delemus is making a perfect ass of himself. He is around after my men that I have contracts with offering them 17/- [$2.125] per pound for their oil to get it away from me. Now I am afraid he will get some away from me if I don't get more money soon to take this oil. He tells them he has the money ready." Wells may have begun taking the competition personally, or he may have been saying what he knew Hiram wanted to hear when he wrote, "If they let him have the oil now and not I, I ought to give him a god damn pounding and if you say give him a flogging I will. He is a poor miserable lying underhanded scoundrel."[71] Wells promised to meet the higher prices Leman offered, but farmers were unsure he would have the money to pay them on delivery.

The next week, Hiram wrote to Wells: "I wish you would pay out the certificates in small parcels to the growers if you can and not in such chunks. $875 of HGH & Cos Bank certificates were presented and paid the day before yesterday. They kept out about 10 days and came I think from Kalamazoo."[72] As Hiram had explained, certificates had to be redeemed in specie when presented, which was the last thing Hiram wanted to do. He complained to Wells, "Oh Phillip how shamefully Leman uses me, my feelings cannot be described."[73] But a day later Hiram and Leman signed a contract stating that for the balance of the buying season "it is agreed between Hiram G Hotchkiss & Leman B Hotchkiss that all the oil of Peppermint remaining unsold from this day at noon and not delivered shall be purchased by them on joint account and to be equally divided between them each party paying for their half of the oil."[74]

A few days later Hiram wrote to Leman to say he would not be able to pay his notes coming due and complaining that Leman would not take his Peppermint Bank certificates to cover the debt and, he wrote, "circulate it as you agreed."[75] Leman responded, "All I can say is if your customers deal with you as you do with me I feel confidant that HG Hotchkiss & Co Bank is a short lived concern, at all events I cannot live under such treatment from you."[76] Leman added the next day, "Your note due the 14th discounted by Rochester Cty Bank will be protested as I cannot pay it. Self preservation is the first law of nature."[77]

The brothers agreed again the following year to buy western oil together, ostensibly to avoid inflating the price with their competition but probably because Hiram did not have the money to compete with his brother. At year's end, Leman told Hiram that he planned to go to Michigan to pay for peppermint oil and have it shipped to him in Phelps. "If you prefer," he wrote, "I will have the oil marked in your name but it must be shipped to me & remain in my possession until you pay for it, or rather your share."[78] Hiram responded, "I have acted in good faith with you and you are now pissing on me. I tried to get Chad [a cousin, working for Hiram] to go to Vienna yesterday & try & reason you out of your shitten position but he said it was no use."[79] Leman replied, "According to your own statements I have advanced on oil a much larger sum than you have. If you think such treatment is pissing on your agents—I hope you will never make another contract with me."[80] But, as usual, Leman relented and continued doing business with his brother. A month later they signed a new contract in which Leman agreed to buy two hundred cases of peppermint oil from Hiram for $2.60 per pound. The 4,725 pounds of peppermint oil was to be delivered in ninety days. Demand for Leman's peppermint oil was apparently quite strong.[81]

A few months later, Calvin Hotchkiss wrote to inform Hiram that his cousin William T. Hotchkiss had died. He chided Hiram for spending so much of his time in New York City, where Hiram had begun living in the Astor House for long periods to avoid his creditors in Lyons. "I should think it would be highly necessary for you to be at home in order to attend to the daily Protests on your Certificates of Deposit. I should like to know what object you have in view, in issuing Certificates, unless you have the means to meet them when presented."[82] In late 1864, Hiram wrote to his young cousin Chad, who was working for him full-time along with Hiram's sons while Hiram spent increasingly long periods at the Astor House. "I want you without fail to go to Rochester," Hiram wrote, to see his lawyers and "shew them the complaint of Calvin Hotchkiss against me to dissolve the partnership between Calvin Hotchkiss & myself. Have them prevent any default being taken against me," and "of course you must not let any one know any thing abt it at Lyons."[83]

Chad wrote to warn Hiram that his property was about to be seized and auctioned off by the sheriff, adding: "My opinion is not worth much but I think you had better get through with your business as soon as possible and come home."[84] Hiram answered, "I feel very bad to think I am again advertised by Sherriff Bennett & it astonishes me beyond measure that in my absence I must be kept in such a state of mind that I can hardly do my business here with any satisfaction." Hiram complained, "Uncle Calvin threatens to sell me out of Lyons if I do not remit some money this week. He keeps me in perfect Hell."[85] Hiram's wife, Mary, wrote to him in the city: "I think I never felt so angry and outraged in all my life as I have the last two days. Yesterday morning Bart Rogers, Bostwick Dickerson, and half a dozen others came here and took away my cows and sold the pigs." She said the authorities also took two loads of hay and a carriage and sleigh, and were selling their oxen. She wrote, "Old Bart sent in for the key to the smokehouse but I would like to see him get it out of my pocket. Now you come home if you don't stay but one day. It is dreadful to have to put up with such insults. Do pay up all such infernal scamps if you have to sell everything you have and live in Ashanti."[86] Although Mary had come from a respectable Lyons family, she had come to share her husband's belief that people who expected to be paid for products and services the Hotchkiss family consumed should be treated with contempt.

A few days later Hiram responded to Chad, "If ever I was annoyed & perplexed I am now by my 'Lyons friends.' You say my property is to be sold on Saturday next & that no postponement can be effected unless I pay $1100 <u>which I cannot do this week</u>." Hiram believed he was being persecuted by jealous neighbors and lamented, "By the <u>Eternal</u>, such treatment is enough to craze a saint. If you have not paid out the $1000 which I sent you day before yesterday hold onto it and bid my property in." Rather than pay the debts for which the property had been seized, Hiram instructed his nephew to bid on it at auction, which might allow him to buy it back for less than the debt owed. And in spite of the fact that his property was on the auction block, Hiram was even more agitated about buying peppermint oil before his brother got to it. He concluded, "<u>Secure</u> all the Wayne County oil you can for I do not believe we can get any from the West. Leman B is so <u>treacherous</u>."[87] What Hiram meant was that he was not going to be able to pay Leman for his share of the peppermint oil they bought together and doubted Leman would hand any over without payment. To compound his trouble paying his debts at home, Hiram was told by his Michigan oil buyer: "Now I wish you to send me $1000 currency—greenbacks if you can, as other currency don't go as well with us at present. Your currency is new and farmers don't know much about it, and are afraid of most any kind of currency except greenbacks."[88] Phillip Wells was also probably aware that the federal government was trying to tax state banknotes out of existence, and peppermint farmers would be unwilling to take Hotchkiss Peppermint Bank notes that were worth only 90 percent of their face values. Hiram disregarded Wells's request and wrote, "I send you $1000 of my <u>currency</u> which I presume will answer as well as greenbacks as it is <u>just as good</u>."[89]

At the end of 1864, Calvin Hotchkiss's farm and property were seized by the sheriff because Hiram had defaulted on a mortgage Calvin had allowed him to write on the property. Calvin threatened to withdraw the bonds he had loaned to Hiram for deposit with the state's Banking Department. Hiram asked Leman to intervene with their uncle, but Leman informed him: "I wrote to Uncle Calvin urging him to extend time for you, and he replied he would extend time if I would step in and be security for the money you owe him. What an idea this." Leman also mentioned, "[I] can't take your currency for I have no money in New York, I was compelled to buy a draft myself for $10,000 on Saturday to meet my paper."[90]

In summer 1866 Leman wrote to Chad, asking why Hiram was still in New York City. "Is he afraid of his creditors? or what is the matter?"[91] Hiram's wife, Mary, wrote of her own annoyance: "There were a half-dozen men here when I got your letter yesterday, waiting for money. O'Keefe keeps their time, so I gave him $20 to divide amongst them. I told him he would have to wait till you got home." Mary told Hiram her overseer had responded "[that] you were never coming, that everybody said that you owed so much money you dare not come home. Mrs. Hotchkiss, you need not look for him, he will never come to Lyons anymore, and I must have my money right away." Mary concluded: "If you do not want to have me mobbed, I hope you will send some money to pay him."[92]

A few weeks later, Mary wrote again, complaining: "You seem to think that we do not use the money you send home in your business, but we certainly do except what we must have for the necessities of life. Our pork barrel is empty, ditto the beef, and our hams are all gone, and take it all in all we are about as poverty-stricken as anyone you'd wish to see." Mary remarked that she had been surprised how much money it took to run the peppermint oil business. "I can't see where the profit comes from. I was in hopes to take in some money for pasture to help out but that is out of the question. Every man that has applied has the same answer, I have an account against Mr. H and if he can't take my cow he must pay the money and of course there is nothing more to be said."[93] Mary wrote again, wondering: "Oh what is the pleasure of calling these broad acres and stately buildings ours when we know they are not. It is very poor comfort for me, I believe I am getting blue so I will stop."[94] Mary and Hiram's sons bore the brunt of the anger felt by local farmers and merchants Hiram neglected to pay. Despite her low opinion of the neighbors, the family was united in their agreement that this was no way to do business, Mary informed Hiram. "But what is the use of fretting? You never will see things or do things like other people. You seem to have a mania for doing things against your own interest. Is there nothing that will ever bring you to your senses?"[95]

As Hiram spent more of his time living at the Astor House and doing deals in New York City, his behavior became even more erratic. In early 1874, he received an angry letter from the New York City peppermint oil brokers Horner and Quetting: "Your childish and not businesslike letter of 23d to hand. We can but believe you are in your dotage and you have told us so many lies about our present transaction that we concluded to have no more business transactions with you until this is finished. We mean what we say as our name is not Hotchkiss," the brokers continued, threatening to go to Lyons and seize Hiram's property. "The meanest rascal and lowest thief would not be guilty of the miserable, dirty lying trickery which you have practiced on us since the commencing of this bottling," they continued, "and be assured Mr. Hotchkiss, if we have to come to Lyons again, we will make it very unpleasant for you and perhaps for both of us. We are utterly disgusted with you and wish you to beware how you drive a desperate man to the wall." Horner and Quetting reminded Hiram they had once been "your best friends and staunchest supporters. Your whole behavior is really disgusting," they concluded, "and we would rather break stones on the highway than make our living dealing with such a man as you are."[96]

Hiram's brother Leman made regular trips to the city throughout his career, but spent no more time there than business demanded. He wrote to Hiram, "It seems strange to me that you can spend so much time in New York and not have time to attend to your own business at home and leave your endorsers in the lurch. I don't think you will make anything in the end by this course."[97] When his brother finally refused to bail him out, Hiram tried to get Leman's son Thaddeus to endorse his notes, but his nephew was less willing than Leman had been to let the bonds of blood pull him into the financial drama. Leman wrote, "You god darn scoundrel. Thad says he will not endorse any mans note that pays so little regard to protect his endorsers & gives them so much trouble as you do. I suppose it would be your highest ambition to get all of my children involved with you, but I don't think you will be able to accomplish it."[98] As for the note, Leman declared: "You will have to pay it or be shoved into bankruptcy."[99]

As months passed without Hiram's return, his son Calvin wrote: "Everyone seems to think around here you are in Wall Street and anything I can say will not make them believe different."[100] Protesting the claim that Hiram needed to stay in New York until the price of peppermint oil rose, his son Leman wrote: "Now do take some advice and sell and come home for you are losing at least $4000 by neglecting your farm. Don't be foolish and hang onto your oil any longer for it has reached the top notch, it will go no higher and unless you sell you will be very sorry." Calvin urged his father, "Sell sell sell at all hazards for it is going a good deal lower and you are making a good thing at the present price and you will lose if you hold it."[101] Hiram's son wrote again the next week, "There seems to be no doubt in the minds of Lyons people that you are losing all your profits in stocks and I assure you your family are very uncomfortable on that account for your creditors are all out of patience with you."[102] In order to avoid having property seized, Hiram's other son, Leman, said his mother, Mary, had transferred the deeds to all the family's land holdings to his sister Emma. A few days later, the younger Leman wrote again: "Mother wants you to send money enough to pay the Maki execution as the sheriff holds an order of arrest against her and he says they are pressing him very hard. The amount is $175."[103]

Hiram tried to make other arrangements to avoid Mary's incarceration, but his creditors were out of patience. Mary sent a telegram, "Mr. Williams refuses. Send money tomorrow. Answer or I go."[104] A few weeks later, Hiram invited Mary and their daughter to visit him in New York. Leman wrote his father, "Mother feels quite hard about this and is quite mad over it. She says that instead of inviting her and Alice to watering places you might better take the money it cost and pay up some of these matters. These things are working on Mother very much. She feels them worse than I ever knew her to before and I do hope you will attend [to] this at once."[105] Leman wrote a couple of days later, "Mother is very anxious about the mortgage on this house. Wilson wrote that he would commence foreclosure unless interest was paid this week. Have you paid it? I do not see how you are going to get out of your difficulties."[106] Hiram wrote that his feelings were hurt by Mary's selfish refusal to vacation with him, and his wife replied: "Will you please inform me for what you claim my sympathy? You seem to be having a good time spending the summer at the best hotels and watering places, leaving me here with all the care of everything, and your creditors to contend with." Mary, who over the course of the marriage had borne twelve children and managed the household during Hiram's long absences, challenged her husband: "And I would like to know in what my selfishness consists? Is it because I ask you to pay your honest debts? I'm sure I can't think of any other favor I have asked of you, I think the selfishness is on the other side.[107]

In the fall of 1874, when Hiram sent Chad to Michigan to compete against his brother Leman for peppermint oil, Chad informed his uncle: "I must have money. You must be crazy to think I can compete with men with plenty of money. If you were here trying to buy oil with drafts people that had oil would laugh at you."[108] Chad reported that Leman had partnered with Horner and Quetting to buy oil, and Hiram replied: "Head off the shit ass. Keep good natured with him & maybe he will leave soon. Now let LB and Horner paddle their own canoe & we will paddle ours. Keep your eye on both of these gay deceivers."[109] Chad responded, "Now if you dont send some funds I shall not try to do business any longer. You speak about everything in your letters but sending home funds to do your business with."[110]

After the failure of his bank, Hiram's finances continued to deteriorate. To escape his creditors, in 1877 Hiram transferred his peppermint oil business to his sons. The R. G. Dun credit reporter wrote: "The firm is now HG Hotchkiss & Sons. HGH swears that he has nothing and stated that he was out of the firm on account of judgments."[111] Hiram continued spending most of his time in New York City, where he acted as the company's salesman. As before, he wrote to his sons regularly with instructions and often made commitments on behalf of the company. Occasionally, the sons objected. In spring 1877 they wrote complaining of another deal Hiram had done with their rivals Horner and Quetting: "You did this business contrary to our wishes and against our judgment. We told you how to do it and avoid trouble. But no, you must have your own way as you always do in the end and now you can fix this matter as we shall have nothing more to do with it."[112] Later in the year, one of Hiram's sons wrote: "We hope you will see the folly of buying tin oil hereafter." They reminded Hiram, "[We] advised you very strongly and we had some very hot words about your buying this oil at any price. But you was determined to buy it and now we have it on hand and will probably be obliged to hold it over another year and then in all probability we will take not to exceed 12 shillings [$1.50] per pound for it. Again I must say that the blockheads are right and you are wrong."[113]

Hiram's sons continued running the business from Lyons, while Hiram visited customers in the city. Without the support of the senior Calvin Hotchkiss, who had died in 1866, or their uncle Leman, who died in 1884, Hiram's sons were unable to prosper. In spite of the fact that H. G. Hotchkiss and Sons essential oils were a premium brand with an international market, Hiram's sons lost money. In 1887, the R. G. Dun credit reporter noted a change in the company's situation: "Hiram Hotchkiss Jr., Leman Hotchkiss, Calvin Hotchkiss . . . the above comprises the firm of HG Hotchkiss & Sons, but the business is carried on entirely by the senior HGH." The reporter explained that years before Hiram had "got buried in debt so deeply that he was obliged to do business in the sons names. After a time he got the boys in so deeply that he was obliged to do business in the name of his wife and daughters. And of late many of the old judgments against him have outlawed and he is now on deck again and the boys under."[114] Hiram had waited out the statute of limitations on judgments, but that did not clear the ledger as far as the neighbors he had swindled were concerned.

Hiram took control of the company back from his sons. He continued sending them daily letters of instruction, scrawled on the letterhead of his hotel in New York or of the offices of whichever broker he favored at the time. His sons gave up trying to wrest control from Hiram, who continued to believe in his own invincible authority as peppermint king. In 1888, he bragged: "I told one of Horner's brokers, Mr. Downer today, that Horner did not amount to a fart in the peppermint business now, and presume he told Horner what I said."[115] In 1889, the Dun report was updated, and the sons were declared "Worthless. Can't collect a dollar of them, and they will not pay debts for living expenses about town. Their father, HG Hotchkiss does all the business now and HGH & Sons do nothing in their own name. They work for the old man and they are a hard lot, and will beat anyone they can."[116] The bitterness of Hiram's sons is understandable. They remained under his thumb for the rest of his life. Hiram finally moved back to Lyons, incorporated his company in 1894, and remained in complete control until his death. In 1895 he wrote to his son Calvin from his home a few blocks from the company's offices: "You annoy me very much by not coming here and let me know what is going on." Hiram demanded to know whether a shipment of peppermint oil had arrived from Michigan and gave his son instructions on how to make an offer for oil. He closed with: "Send me oil paint and drug reports."[117]

When Hiram Hotchkiss died on October 27, 1897, he was memorialized in the eight-column article mentioned earlier and remembered fondly in a three-column obituary in another local newspaper as "the Peppermint Oil King and the best known essential oil man in America or Europe." The obituary went on to claim, "In the course of his dealings he has paid to Wayne County farmers millions of dollars; has enabled many a man to pay for his farm; has assisted thousands of men in raising mortgages and has done more for the poor man than any other person who has ever lived in this community." The article spoke of "men unnumbered" who would regret his sad end and enjoy memories of pleasant friendship. Like the longer article, the obituary stressed his hospitality and claimed Hiram was a man of "sympathy, kindness of heart, and genuine love for his household and their friends." The article, almost certainly written by a family member to repair the damage Hiram had done over the years to his own reputation, concluded: "No man was ever kinder, few more charming, none more indulgent."[118]

These memorials, published under the supervision of his family, described the man they wished Hiram had been. The memorials became local history, and he is now remembered as a groundbreaking entrepreneur and a great benefactor of Wayne County. The heroic image of him portrayed in local histories conforms with the social norms of the era, stressing traits like fairness, charm, and geniality, in spite of the fact that Hiram called attention to many of the norms of nineteenth-century business culture and society by continually breaking them. He took unfair advantage of business partners, friends, and relatives, whom he often treated quite brutally. He was unable to understand any point of view but his own and attributed malicious intent to anyone who failed to do what he wanted. He used the bonds of friendship and especially of family to cajole people to help and support him, even when it was clearly not in their best interests. He was a bully who browbeat his opponents into submission and avoided his obligations until many creditors simply gave up and wrote off his debts. But in spite of his faults, Hiram Hotchkiss is remembered as a successful businessman of great charisma and jovial good nature. Lyons still celebrates an annual Peppermint Days summer festival, which for years was funded by the company that his heirs ran until 1982, when the firm was sold to the William Leman Company of Indiana. In 2003, the Leman Company was purchased by Essex Labs of Salem, Oregon. Essex still sells Hotchkiss peppermint oil, which it calls "the oldest trademarked and continually produced essential mint oil recipe in the USA."[119]

Crystal White

Albert May Todd was born in June 1850 at the homestead of William Alfred and Mary May Todd in Nottawa, Michigan. The Todds had arrived in Nottawa in 1836, less than a year before Michigan statehood and the resulting flood of land purchases by new settlers like the Ranneys and speculators like the Hotch-kisses. Nottawa is slightly less than forty miles west of the region around Allen where the Ranney brothers settled and a similar distance south of Kalamazoo. Alfred and Mary Todd had met and married in Marcellus, New York, about forty-four miles east of Phelps and Lyons. Albert was the youngest of ten children, and although the family was not exception-ally prosperous, his mother had received an unusually thorough education in the classics and tried to provide her children with an exposure to the arts and humanities like her own. Albert was remembered in the records of the local Union School as an apt pupil who added his own interest in science to his mother's love of literature and art.

As a boy, Albert became familiar with the peppermint plants local farmers grew and with the stills they used to process mint hay into oil. He amused himself by tinkering with the stills to try to improve their yields and the quality of oil they produced. In the mid-1840s, after the advent of steam engines, Michigan farmers had begun steam-distilling peppermint, substituting large wooden vats with steam-tight covers for the copper kettles traditionally used to boil peppermint leaves. Super-heated steam passed through the dried peppermint hay in these vats, carrying the essential oil away to condense in copper worm tubes.[1] This innovation allowed steam boilers to be kept at full heat while "charges" of mint hay were packed into the vats and removed, resulting in much faster and more efficient distilling. Albert improved the placement of the steam jets to such a degree that he was later able to file a patent for his improvement.

In 1866, the Michigan peppermint harvest was half its normal level due to winterkilled roots, driving up prices.[2] Recognizing an opportunity, in 1868 Albert and his older brother, Oliver, planted their first field of peppermint, at the same time the Michigan Ranney brothers and their friends such as H. H. Lawrence were shipping peppermint oil to Henry Ranney and his customers in New York and Boston, and the Hotchkiss brothers were competing with each other to buy Michigan oil for their own brands. The Hotchkisses' ongoing battles over the quality of peppermint oil induced Leman Hotchkiss to begin advertising in the 1860s that he had developed a "process of rectifying this oil unknown to any other person."[3] Although this claim may have been greatly exaggerated or even untrue, Leman's claim to have found a way to improve on the raw oil supplied by peppermint farmers may have stimulated Albert Todd's interest in distilling and chemistry.

Albert extended his education beyond the homeschooling he received from his mother by attending the newly built Union High School in nearby Sturgis. The only member of his family to attend the school, located about ten miles from the family farm, Albert graduated first in his class in 1873 at the age of twenty-three and enrolled in Northwestern University to study chemistry the following fall. He self-financed his college attendance with the money he and Oliver shared from their peppermint oil earnings. Todd family tradition describes Albert as essentially a self-made man, paying his own way in college, his travels in Europe, and his subsequent business ventures. The evidence seems to support this portrayal, since Albert's parents and siblings were never remarkable financially. The only Todd sibling who did moderately well financially was Albert's partner in the early peppermint oil business, Oliver, who later moved to Kansas, Idaho, and Oregon, where he grew peppermint and distilled oil that Albert bought from him.[4] Other evidence of Albert's self-reliance includes the numerous intricately detailed ledger books he left, which document his rapid rise from small-scale peppermint farmer to local merchant, icehouse operator, peppermint oil broker, and ultimately the peppermint king he became.

Albert managed to complete two years of college work in a single year, but his health suffered, and so he left the university and used the money he had saved for tuition to fill a backpack and do a walking tour of Europe and England. He later recalled, "The foundation of my art collection ... was made when during my first trip to Europe I undertook to obtain copies of the old masters."[5] He bought reproductions of famous artwork painted by gallery-certified copyists to begin his art collection. He also visited the peppermint fields of Mitcham, England, where he discovered peppermint farmers planting a superior variety of *Mentha piperita* called Black Mitcham.

After a summer abroad, Albert returned refreshed and healthy and immediately set to work on a number of projects. He partnered with Albert Drake, one of the officers of Sturgis's Union School, in a dry goods mercantile business. Drake was an established merchant in Sturgis, and his esteem for Todd probably opened doors to business opportunities and credit. In spite of a decade-long recession in the 1870s, Todd expanded his ventures beyond peppermint distilling and dry goods. He built icehouses and cut ice on nearby ponds, which he sold to railroads for chilling meat and produce. He bought out his brother Oliver, who had decided to move westward, and opened the Steam Refined Essential Oil Works in Nottawa. Albert began buying oil from local farmers and redistilling it using a new steam process he had developed. Although only twenty-five years old, he had an edge on eastern businessmen such as Ranney, Hotchkiss, and Wells, who were the peppermint farmers' previous customers. Albert was a local grower himself, and he was well known among the members of the local business community. Without a family fortune to fall back on, he seems to have rapidly expanded his enterprises through hard work, scrupulous attention to the details of his business, and possibly using capital provided by local businessmen and the good will of farmers who were eager to work with a trusted local rather than an increasingly unpleasant cohort of easterners, dominated in the 1870s by the constantly warring Hotchkiss brothers. Equally important, Albert had a technological advantage. He discovered that the yellow or light amber color of most American peppermint oil was caused by resins that damaged the oil's flavor, and he developed a proprietary method to remove them. In 1875, he began marketing his Crystal White brand of peppermint oil and menthol crystals, identifying himself on the product labels as Albert M. Todd, Distilling Chemist.[6] He bottled his oil in clear glass, to emphasize its unique purity.

The year 1876 was a busy and eventful one for Albert. In January, he married Augusta Mary Allman in Sturgis. He continued selling ice to the railroads and dry goods with Drake. In the summer and fall, he handled eleven thousand pounds of peppermint oil, which he estimated was "about half the crops of Mich and Indiana entire."[7] After the harvest, he spent ten weeks at the Centennial Exposition in Philadelphia, where he won a gold medal for Crystal White Peppermint Oil. He visited New York City after the exposition and met with Hiram Hotchkiss. Hiram wrote to his sons that he had "a long interview with Todd today who has returned from Philadelphia. He wants us to make him an offer for 2000 pounds oil of peppermint subject to approval." Hiram instructed his sons to "telegraph me on Monday morning your best offer and I am to meet him at noon Monday. He says he is offered $2.50 and that he made some small sales in Philadelphia at $2.60. Don't know whether he lies or not."[8] Hiram had trouble trusting anyone and tended to think anyone beside himself who did well in the peppermint oil business must be cheating. On Monday he wrote to his sons again, expressing his impression of his young rival: "I do not think Todd adulterates oil but I do think he is a poor judge of quality."[9] For his part, Albert was more generous with his assessment. He wrote his brother Oliver in January 1877 with a copy of his new business card and news of his activities, saying: "Of course you all know I was in Philada. Spent 10 weeks there and after a hard fought battle, was victorious." Albert mentioned that he met Ohio governor Rutherford B. Hayes at the Exhibition and "had a pleasant chat with him. Enjoyed the Ex very much." He told his brother he had begun shipping Crystal White peppermint oil to Europe. He said, "I am doing well but I tell you I haven't left a stone unturned to push business to a successful issue. I have to fight men of ability—and experience,

and withstand the assaults of jealousy." Apparently Hiram Hotchkiss
was not very good at hiding his feelings. Albert then turned away from
the peppermint oil business and concluded, "I have made some fine ad-
ditions to my library but do not have much leisure for improving myself
mentally and I am afraid I do not improve morally or religiously as
much as I ought. In the course of a couple months I hope to have some
leisure for study and physical exercise."[10]

Before returning home to Michigan, Albert visited Hiram Hotchkiss's sons in Lyons in January, but they were away when he called.[11] He
also called on the essential oil dealers Hale and Parshall in nearby Alloway and sold them a thousand pounds of peppermint oil.[12] He sold
some spearmint oil to the Hotchkisses, since very little (if any) spearmint was grown in western New York.[13] Along with peppermint, spearmint oil would later become a very important product for the A. M.
Todd Company.

Albert's proprietary peppermint oil distilling and refining processes attracted attention, some of it unwelcome. In 1878, Albert wrote to an
employee, instructing him to investigate a dealer named H. D. Cushman
in Three Rivers, Michigan, who he discovered had "stolen and [is] using
my crystalizing process . . . and is putting up a building for doing it more
extensively." Albert said Cushman had developed a glass bottle called a
"menthol inhaler," an innovation he thought was "all right, but I shall
stop him from making any of the crystals themselves for I cannot give
them what has cost me years of care and expense for nothing." Albert
wrote, "They have not yet I think got on to my refiners so I will get them
patented & now instruct you to let no one in the refining room, nor give
any one any information as to any parts of my business or apparatus
either refiners or otherwise." He remarked, "They are tenfold more vigi-
lant & careful than we have been, and we will have to keep our business
closer or it is lost."[14] He had been naïve and had not protected his innovations, but he learned this lesson well.

In 1880, Albert received a patent for his "Crystal White Steam Rectified" process for distilling peppermint oil. The process and the hard-
ware he also patented became centerpieces of his essential oil business.
Four decades later, a description of the still-unrivaled process continued
to appear on the labels of A. M. Todd Company's peppermint oil: "The

'Crystal White Steam Rectified' Oil of Peppermint is distilled from the finest plants of Mentha Piperita (when in full bloom), which are cultivated with scrupulous care in a soil and climate peculiarly adapted to their most perfect development." The label then described the patented process: "The oil, after having been distilled from the plants by improved steam processes, is placed in a specially designed receptacle, and steam, which has passed through a second quantity of fresh Peppermint Leaves, is conveyed to the oil in a long pipe and blown through it by means of curiously constructed perforated cylinders and accessories invented especially for the purpose." The label explained that only the best components of the oil were evaporated in the second refining process, while "the inferior parts, which in natural oil cause bitterness and rancidity, are separated and cast away. To make certain Absolute Perfection, this process is repeated." The quality of Todd's oil was thus based on a particular chemical process, rather than on the luck of finding an attractive blend of all the peppermint oils that brands like Hotchkiss and Todd were now understood to be buying from farmers in New York, Michigan, and elsewhere. Hiram Hotchkiss had claimed to be the ultimate judge of peppermint oil's purity and quality and had further claimed there was something particularly special about Wayne County, New York, oil, even when most of his supply came from Michigan. Albert claimed also that in his patented process none of the peppermint oil's "vitality is impaired, since steam heat only is applied; while under the usual process by direct heat, much of the vitality is lost." Finally, like the Hotchkiss brothers, "To prevent adulteration, the Manufacturer places his Copyright Label upon each bottle and can, and over the cork, his seal; and all orders should be sent him directly at his factory."[15]

In addition to his focus on the chemistry of essential oils, Albert wanted to improve peppermint plants. Growing up in the peppermint country of southwestern Michigan, he understood the agricultural challenges facing peppermint farmers. In 1880, he imported a large supply of the Black Mitcham peppermint roots he had seen in England.[16] He planted the new crop in Nottawa, and when local peppermint farmers saw the improved yields and quality of the oil they produced, he began selling peppermint roots. Hiram Hotchkiss had imported a shipment of Mitcham roots in 1845, but at the time he and E. C. Patterson had been more interested in reducing the planting of peppermint to try to corner the peppermint oil market than in shifting to a better peppermint plant. And unlike Hiram, Albert was a peppermint farmer as well as a processor and distributor. By 1900, Black Mitcham was the dominant commercial peppermint plant in the United States.[17] In March 1884, Albert received another patent, for "An Improvement in Process of Producing Crystals from Oil of True Peppermint."[18] And in September 1884, he received a trademark for the term "Crystal White" in the category of "Essential and Volatile Vegetable Oils and their Products."[19] To emphasize the transparency of his oils, he continued packaging them in clear glass bottles. Menthol crystals never became as big a part of his business as oils. This may have been due to others figuring out his process before Albert could protect it but was probably mostly because menthol could be made much more easily and economically from a cheaper, lower-quality mint called *Mentha arvensis,* or Japanese mint.

In 1886, ten years after he made his name at the Centennial Exhibition, Albert published an article in the *Proceedings of the American Pharmaceutical Association* entitled "The Oil of Peppermint." He traced the history of the herb and its uses from ancient times and discussed current conditions in the peppermint oil industry. He mentioned that he had managed to get yields as high as eighteen pounds of oil per ton of mint straw but had also seen poor cuttings yield as little as 1.5 pounds per ton.[20] He included historical details made available by his growing library of antiquarian texts, including many alchemical and natural history volumes that described the earliest medical uses of mint plants and the discovery of peppermint in seventeenth-century England. His article combined history with cutting-edge science, establishing Albert as one of the foremost authorities on the subject.

His focus on the scientific growing and distilling of essential oils was not merely a marketing technique. Albert had begun his peppermint career tinkering with stills to improve their efficiency. His interest in peppermint oil led him to study chemistry at Northwestern, and he called himself a manufacturing chemist. He pioneered the use of fractional distillation to separate the various constituents of peppermint oil, which gave him the unique ability to vary the blend of these constituents based on the flavor profile desired by a customer. The A. M. Todd

Company retained this strategic edge into the twenty-first century and based its success on a technical ability pioneered by Albert to produce blends that met clients' subjective tastes by manipulating the objective properties of natural oils.

In 1891, Albert bought a large house in an affluent neighborhood in Kalamazoo and moved his family there. Albert and Augusta had five children, William Alfred, Albert James, Paul Harold, Allman Avon, and Ethel May. According to newspaper reports announcing his move, Albert controlled half the American essential oil business and was beginning to be called the new peppermint king. After a few months operating in rented space, he moved into a building he built downtown, on the corner of Kalamazoo Avenue and North Rose Street. The four-story, twenty-four-room brick structure was the Todd Company's headquarters until 1929 and stood until 1971, when it was torn down to make room for a new Kalamazoo County Administration Building. The sign above the company building's front entrance read "A. M. Todd, Mfg. Chemist."

In 1893, Albert's peppermint oil won a prize medal in Chicago, and the Todd letterhead began to carry a notice in red at the top, announcing: "Five Highest Awards—Medals and Diplomas—World's Columbian Exposition, for Finest Essential Oils; Distilling Apparatus; Essential Oil Plants; Fine Chemicals; Chemical Library; Etc."[21] In 1893, a forty-three-year-old Albert Todd entered politics with an unsuccessful run for mayor of Kalamazoo. He was elected to Congress in 1896, a topic explored in detail in the next chapter.

Unlike the Hotchkiss brothers, who devoted little of their energy to actually farming peppermint, Albert was extremely interested in improving peppermint culture and agriculture in general. In 1895, he purchased a large peppermint farm in the marshy mucklands of Allegan County, near the town of Fennville. He set to work improving the farm he renamed Campania, directing the digging of more than ten miles of drainage ditches and straightening the stream that flowed across the property.[22] He established a second plantation he called Mentha in Van Buren County, west of Kalamazoo. He installed fifteen miles of ditches at Mentha, connected to a four-mile-long main ditch. Although he continued to buy and redistill the peppermint oils of an increasing number of farmers, his own farms were a vital source of both peppermint and spearmint oil, as well as being the sites of botanical as well as social experiments. Unlike Hiram Hotchkiss, who left his family in rural western New York in later life and resided in a posh New York City hotel, Albert lived with his family in a small Midwestern city and remained intimately connected with rural life on his several farms.

Throughout his life, Albert kept extensive handwritten records in a series of ledger books. In 1897, his annual balance sheet for his operation showed assets of $134,119 and liabilities of $56,589. The net value of the A. M. Todd Company was $75,529.[23] Albert's success sparked some jealous reactions. A neighboring oil dealer allied with the Hotchkiss operation wrote to Hiram's sons, "Todd came back from New York City and says he will buy 10,000 pounds next week and 10,000 the week after and pay a good big price for it, so he says to farmers around here."[24] And an employee, Felton D. Garrison, quit Albert's company, stole the names of Albert's farmers and customers, and tried to go into business for himself. In March 1897, Garrison began writing to everyone on Albert's customer list. "I have been in the Crystal White Works for about 5 years," he said, "and know that I can give you just as high quality of oil as that brand at a lower price than you paid for the last you bought." Garrison offered sample bottles at $2.50 per pound and assured Albert's customers, "My brand will be known as Dew Drop and will be made only from the purest oil that I can find." Garrison also wrote to peppermint farmers, saying: "The prices are near $1.00 per pound yet and if your oil is Prime American I might better this a trifle."[25] He worked furiously, sending handwritten letters to Albert's entire client list in just a few weeks. He shipped samples to many, but it is unclear whether his oil posed a credible threat to the Todd Company. If he infringed on Todd's patents, Garrison would presumably have been stopped; but there was not enough time to find out. Felton Garrison died of tuberculosis a year later, and his Dew Drop brand disappeared.

Although Albert spent quite a bit of 1897, 1898, and early 1899 in Washington as a member of the 55th Congress, leaving the business in the hands of sons whose judgment he trusted, he remained involved and took the time to respond to business issues. In early 1899, he responded to a letter from his brother James, who lived in nearby Burr Oak, Mich-

igan, and raised peppermint there. Albert wrote in answer to his brother's inquiry regarding peppermint oil, "I have not bo't any for about a
month, as I have all I can use for 3 or 4 months unless trade improves. I
think 80¢ is all that could be obtained now in New York after paying
shipping expenses, for prime quality, and I would pay you this if you
wish to send it here."[26] Later in the summer, when he had returned from
Washington and resumed the day-to-day running of his business, Albert
discovered his yields had been reduced. "The mint crop this year will be
a small one, owing to the devastation of the cut worm. I have lost 200
acres myself," he told the Grand Rapids *Herald*, "and the yield of the
other land will be much reduced." But, he added, "this will not affect us
so much, since the price of peppermint is now down below the cost of
production. It has driven the small growers out of the business, and the
large growers will produce much less mint in hope that the restricted
production will cause a raise in prices."[27]

Albert exhibited his peppermint oil at the Exposition Universelle
in Paris in 1900 and won another gold medal. The Paris Exposition was
the event historian Daniel Rodgers described to open his 1998 history of
transatlantic Progressive thought, *Atlantic Crossings*. Rodgers mentioned that the Socialist International convened in Paris in 1900 and that
Albert Todd's acquaintance Jane Addams was "drawn to Paris as a
delegate to the international women's congress and a juror for the 'social
economy' section of the fair." Todd, like Addams, would have been
attracted by the socialists' examination of what Rodgers called the
"painfully disruptive revolution in human relations" triggered by the
intersection of technological change and the "social ethics of the marketplace."[28] Although Todd did not write anything that survives regarding this aspect of the exposition, it is probable that like Addams, Todd
was aware of and influenced by the fair's social pavilion. Albert Todd's
politics are examined in greater detail in the next chapter.

Crystal White Oil of Peppermint won first prize again the following
year, at the Pan-American Exposition in Buffalo, New York. With Hiram
Hotchkiss's death in 1897, control over New York's H. G. Hotchkiss and
Sons essential oil company passed to Calvin Hotchkiss and then to H. G.
Hotchkiss Jr. Although the Hotchkiss brand remained powerful, western
New York peppermint oil production fell behind that of Michigan and

Indiana, and even the Hotchkisses depended almost entirely on western farmers for their oils. Using hardier, higher-yielding Black Mitcham plants, Michigan farmers produced more than a hundred thousand pounds of oil annually throughout the 1890s and in the peak years of 1894 and 1897 placed 175,000 and 172,000 pounds of oil on the market, respectively.[29] As Albert observed in the Grand Rapids *Herald* and mentioned to his brother, the oversupply caused peppermint oil prices to fall from $2.84 per pound in 1892 to less than a dollar per pound in 1899. Depressed commodity prices were a common problem for farmers during the economic recession of the 1890s. But Albert was also aware that low prices were encouraging some farmers to turn away from peppermint and to grow other crops like celery, which became an important cash crop for muck farmers around Kalamazoo. Albert knew that in spite of low prices caused by oversupply and the deepening depression of the 1890s, in the long run reduced supplies of oil would ultimately drive up prices.

On December 31, 1901, the A. M. Todd Company Ltd. was formed as a "partnership association," capitalized at a hundred thousand dollars. A thousand one-hundred-dollar shares were issued and distributed to family members. Albert took 850 shares and gave fifty shares each to his wife, Augusta, and his sons William and Albert James. William became secretary of the company, and "Bert" became treasurer. Among the company's assets were listed Campania Farm (1,640 acres), "Lands in Van Buren County," which became Mentha Farm (1,850 acres), Sylvania Ranch (seven thousand acres), and the headquarters building in Kalamazoo. Also listed were 350 cattle, thirty-two horses, machinery patents, and label trademarks.[30] In 1902, a local newspaper announced: "Todd puts his business on a profit-sharing plan."[31] The plan consisted of paying very low monthly salaries to the company's principal shareholders, Albert and his family, and instead basing most of their compensation on profits. His ongoing focus on the company's profitability insured that Albert and his descendants would continue to develop innovative solutions to the changing markets they served.

Also around 1902, posters were put up in Chicago calling for "Farm Workers for A. M. Todd Co.'s Mint Farm, 60¢ per hour—10 hours per day. No Lost Time. Good Board $1.05 per day, Free Room with Plenty of Showers and Laundry Facilities. Free transportation—No Fees. Leave

Chicago Grand Central Station 11 a.m. daily except Saturday and Sunday."[32] Although it seems unimpressive today, sixty cents per hour was a very substantial wage at this time. Farm labor paid an average of fifty cents *per day* at the turn of the twentieth century, net of room and board. Even ironworkers, the highest-paid manufacturing workers, received wages of only $2.03 per day, which did not include their housing and food expenses.[33] The opportunity to earn nearly five dollars per day after room and board was unprecedented. Albert traveled to Chicago regularly to meet with customers such as William Wrigley, who had begun packaging chewing gum in addition to his main business, baking powder, in 1892. Albert also maintained political connections in Chicago, including with Jane Addams, who had cofounded Hull House with her partner, Ellen Gates Starr, in 1889.

After lower prices drove farmers out of peppermint production, prices rose again as Albert had expected. The surplus oil the company was holding in its warehouses began to appreciate in value. In the fall of 1902, newspapers across the nation carried stories claiming "Todd has a corner on mint oil, holding 95 per cent. of mint and essential oils of the world." According to the Michigan *Telegram*, "The price of peppermint oil, which a month ago was $2.50 a pound, is now $5. As the total crop this year is about 190,000 pounds, the total value will be $900,000, and the advance amounts to nearly half a million." The article blamed New York speculators for depressing peppermint oil prices and reported Albert's prediction that "under the new arrangement the growers will reap profits. The crop of the present season is only two-thirds as large as usual. The heavy rainfall has produced the smallest crop in ten years."[34] Aside from pointing out that higher prices benefited peppermint farmers, Albert did not address the claim that he had cornered the market. He sent an "Outlook" letter to his customers and the press, explaining the situation. "The total American crop is the smallest for many years, not exceeding 130,000 lbs.," he wrote, "which is less than one-third of the crop of 1896, and practically only one-half of the world's annual consumption (250,000 lbs.)." He explained that from 1895 to 1898, surplus peppermint oil production drove the market price below the cost of production, "resulting in the abandonment of the industry by many growers who plowed up their fields and allowed their distilleries to rust and decay." More recently, due to an unusually wet season, "many farms were inundated since low lands are now almost exclusively used, the result being that the crop obtained is still smaller. In many cases it was impossible to cultivate with horses at all (which is the usual manner), requiring the work to be done by hand at far greater cost per acre, while the yield was much less than ordinary." As an example, Albert described the situation at one of his own farms, on which he had made "an investment of over $50,000, and where we should have secured over 5,000 lbs. Oil, only 600 lbs. was obtained, costing over $6.00 per lb." Another grower, he said, who usually produced 10,000 pounds of peppermint oil from his 350-acre planting, had distilled only 1,800 pounds. "At Decatur, where 130,000 lbs. were produced in 1896, but 19,000 lbs. were obtained this year."[35] Albert had command of the facts, and most of his readers were convinced that higher peppermint oil prices were not due to the A. M. Todd Company cornering the market.

Albert followed up his outlook with a warning to his customers to be wary of dealers selling oil of questionable "QUALITY. Owing to scarcity and consequent higher value, the temptation to adulteration which has always been practiced more or less, will be increased." Albert reported that his chemists had analyzed samples "sold as 'Prime,' containing over 40% adulteration, some adulterants costing not over 10c per lb. so that the mixture is sold at a large profit materially below the cost of pure quality." He mentioned that in the past one of these adulterants had been "Japanese Mint," which he explained "is no true peppermint (_Mentha Piperita_) but [is] (_Mentha Arvensis_), having many of the characteristics of pennyroyal."[36] Since _arvensis_ oil was a more abundant source of menthol than the more valuable peppermint oil, it was used primarily to produce the menthol crystals used in medical formulas by manufacturers such as the Vick Chemical Company. But after the menthol had been removed, Japanese oil was frequently used as an adulterant to stretch peppermint oil and reduce its cost. Albert had warned against this adulteration as early as the 1890s, but the problem persisted, and _arvensis_ use spiked whenever scarcity pushed up the price of genuine peppermint oil. His passion for keeping "Japanese Mint" away from his peppermint was carried on by his heirs. In 2010 his grandson and his brother-in-law, both officers of the firm, remarked they would be damned if they'd ever let *arvensis* get through the company's doors.[37]

To emphasize his concern, Albert sent a second letter to customers and journalists in 1902, entitled "Pure vs. Adulterated Oil Peppermint." He called attention to the fact that due to current scarcity, lower-quality "resinous, weedy, and adulterated Oil Peppermint, which accumulated during the period of overproduction from 1897 to 1900," was entering the market. He offered an example of the economics of adulteration, explaining that five pounds of pure peppermint oil costing $1.80 per pound could be sold to customers for ten dollars, returning a profit of twenty cents per pound, or one dollar. But if an unscrupulous dealer bought four pounds of pure peppermint oil at the regular cost of $7.20 and then added a pound of adulterant worth ten cents, his cost on the five pounds would be $7.30. The dealer could then sell adulterated oil to customers for $1.80 per pound, the cost of pure peppermint oil, and make $1.70 in profit. Albert explained, "Everything of value in this (4 lbs. pure @ $2.00 per lb.) would have cost the consumer only $8.00, so, in buying the 'cheaper' oil, he is paying $1.00 for 1 lb. of injurious substance costing 10¢." He concluded that even if the adulterant was only a dilutant and did not compromise the quality of the oil, buyers would still have been better off "to obtain their supplies direct from actual producers of established reputation."[38]

By late 1902, the price of peppermint oil had risen significantly. A. M. Todd Co. Ltd.'s Price List of Essential Oils, dated October 23, 1902, listed two varieties of peppermint oil. Crystal White Double Distilled was priced at $3.50 per pound and Super-Extra Natural at $3.15. The form also left blank space for handwritten quotes of "Production of other growers." Crystal White Double Distilled was Todd's rectified peppermint oil, described as "produced from the finest cultivated plants of True Peppermint (*Mentha Piperita*) grown and distilled by us in the most perfect manner with approved appliances, and is not only GUARANTEED ABSOLUTELY PURE, but also UNEQUALLED IN FLAVOR, STRENGTH, SOLUBILITY, WHITENESS, etc., and is recognized throughout the world as the HIGHEST STANDARD OF QUALITY." Super-Extra Natural was a lower-priced unrectified oil produced on Todd's own farms, described as "the finest oil possible to produce, as above, from select cultivated plants of True Peppermint, but is not submitted to a double distillation. It is ABSOLUTELY PURE and EXTRA CHOICE IN EVERY RESPECT, and is unsurpassed by the highest quality of any other producer."

In addition to being a peppermint farmer and controlling a patented processing technology, Albert wanted to be known as a *local* producer who was in touch with growing conditions and able to provide detailed, timely information on Midwestern mint oil production. "Regarding the production of other growers," the price sheet continued, "we would state that being situated in the center of the producing district, and being able to personally inspect all fields of growing plants, etc., we are able to purchase with better discrimination than would otherwise be possible, and can supply the trade on the most advantageous terms." In addition to peppermint oil, the price list included Spearmint Oil ($5.00), Wintergreen Oil ($2.10), Wormwood Oil ($5.50), Tansy Oil ($5.00), Sassafras Oil (.75), and True Fireweed Oil ($2.50). The payment terms Todd offered were net thirty days, with a discount of ½ percent for payment in less than ten days from invoice.[39]

Unlike Hiram Hotchkiss, who had considered his ability to distinguish quality a unique talent, Albert Todd tried to establish his reputation as an authority on scientific measurements of purity and quality. In 1903 he sent out another letter to customers and the trade press regarding adulteration. He quoted extensively from a recent report in Britain's *Chemist and Druggist:* "It has been recently shown by the British Chemist, E. J. Barry, B.Sc., F.I.C. that nearly every sample of Oil Peppermint coming under his observation recently is impure." He quoted an excerpt, listing the specific gravities and optical rotation results of ten samples of peppermint oil. He noted the chemist's conclusion that all ten specific gravity results were "too low for perfectly pure Oil of Peppermint . . . and that the optical rotation in every sample is less than that required for pure quality." The British chemist had concluded, "Under these extraordinary circumstances consumers will do well to scrutinize the quality of their purchases with the utmost care, and in the case of doubt . . . to employ an expert chemist to verify the quality."[40] Of course Albert Todd, in bringing this information to the public, was also establishing his bona fides as the type of expert chemist customers needed on their side. In contrast to Hiram Hotchkiss, who had simply declared himself an expert judge of quality and purity, Albert Todd claimed there were objective, scientific standards of quality and that he had the credentials to ensure they were met.

Albert diligently positioned himself as a reliable conduit of information from peppermint oil producers to essential oil consumers. By the beginning of the twentieth century, more than 90 percent of America's peppermint crop was grown within a hundred miles of Kalamazoo, so he was well situated to gather intelligence for his customers. In May 1903, he wrote to his customers to advise them that the shortage of peppermint oil might continue. Higher prices had caused growers to try to increase their plantings, he wrote. "The month of March, however, opened extremely warm, causing the roots to sprout, and was followed in April by one of the most severe blizzards ever known in that month, extending over the entire Peppermint producing district with a fall of snow averaging about twelve inches."[41] The snow had been followed by heavy rains that had prevented many farmers from planting new roots. In the fall, Albert wrote to his brother James in Burr Oak, who had offered to gather statistics from farmers in his area. Albert sent a printed form and asked James to note "their names, the Post Office address, the number of acres planted this year, with the amount of oil produced, and the total number of acres which they distilled this year including old and new, and the total amount of oil produced; and you may also note down any remarks regarding the crop and its quality, etc. so far as you should happen to learn." Albert cautioned that James might find some of the peppermint farmers "rather reticent about giving information" and instructed him not to push too hard for answers. Albert also said James could convey the A. M. Todd Company's interest in buying the oil, but not make any commitments regarding prices and quantities. Albert was aware the growers were hoping for price rises: "They are generally holding at from $2.25 to $3.00, and in some cases as high as $4.00; but there is no prospect at present of these higher prices being reached." Albert also asked his brother, "Whenever any of the buyers come into that territory you perhaps better 'phone us to let us know what they do. ... We have the 'Bell' telephone both in our office and home." He reminded James that if he called after 6 P.M. the rates would be less and that he could of course reverse the charges.[42]

In March 1904, Albert wrote to inform his customers that planting was slow and that due to snowmelt "a great many of the fields have been completely covered with water for ten days to a depth of eighteen inches, and unless this can be promptly carried off a large proportion of the roots will doubtless be drowned out, as they have been much weakened by the extreme winter."[43] In September the Todd Company sent a follow-up letter noting, "Distillation of the new crop of Oil Peppermint is now practically completed and results prove that our predictions for a small production made some time ago were correct." Albert reported that the peppermint oil supply reaching the market would be "about thirty-five thousand pounds smaller than last year's, and less than two-thirds of a normal yield." He went on to caution that prices were rising. "There is however some rejected adulterated stock on the market, which will again probably be offered under changed labels. As these oils consist largely of adulterants costing from 5¢ to 10¢ per pound an enormous profit is made whenever a sale can be effected even at the lower prices. It is needless to state that the consumption of such oil is ruinous to manufacturers of fine confectionary and pharmaceuticals."[44] Any deal that seemed too good to be true, Albert reminded his customers, really was.

The A. M. Todd Company continued working on innovations that would improve peppermint distilling and farming. In early 1906, the company hired a Kalamazoo patent attorney to research mechanical root planters. The lawyer's search returned three designs similar to the planter the company had designed, but different enough to enable the filing to go forward.[45] In November 1907, Todd employee John Shirley received a patent for his invention, which he immediately assigned to Albert James Todd (Bert), company treasurer. In October 1908, a Kalamazoo paper printed news of a visit to the region by the president of the H. G. Hotchkiss Essential Oil Company, Calvin Hotchkiss. Michigan's peppermint crop yields, Hotchkiss estimated, were 50 percent to 60 percent of normal. He estimated that a hundred and fifty thousand pounds of new peppermint oil would be supplemented by about seventy-five thousand pounds of oil held over from the previous year. He also reported that in Wayne County, New York, "the planting was about one-third of the previous season's extent, but with the yield favorable, the aggregate of the new crop and undisposed stocks from the former production will reach the fairly normal quantity of 30,000 pounds."[46]

While the Todds took business very seriously, unlike the contentious Hotchkisses they remained a very close family and retained their sense of humor. In June 1909, Albert wrote to his son Paul, who was completing his course in botany at the University of Michigan at Ann Arbor. Paul wanted to take a summer capstone course in plant hybridizing, but his father was not convinced it would be valuable enough and suggested that Paul either take the time either to relax before coming to work during the stilling season or to take a tour. Albert wrote two pages about the pros and cons of different tours Paul could take of regions where the company had business interests. Then, closing his letter, Albert remarked: "I had momentarily forgotten that sometimes other equally strong attractions (or 'attachments') are found in Universities, especially where Co-eds participate. I am willing to presume that it is purely plant breeding that you had in mind, and shall not intrude into any of your secrets, but if it really is some fair Co-ed, just tell me whether she is a blonde or brunette!!"[47] The available records do not provide an answer to Albert's question, but presumably his son saw the humor in the exchange. Not long afterward, in January 1910, the Todd family celebrated the wedding of the youngest child, Ethel May Todd, to Edwin LeGrand Woodhams, an Englishman who was overseer of the Mentha plantation.

As the first decade of the twentieth century ended, the A. M. Todd Company's preeminence in the essential oil business was becoming apparent. In 1908, the company's balance sheet showed assets valued at $346,935, of which $225,722 consisted of the company's farms and headquarters.[48] The following year, merchandise inventories of $104,836 boosted the bottom line to $478,049.[49] Not only was the A. M. Todd Company beginning to dominate the wholesale domestic and export businesses Hotchkiss had pioneered, it had discovered new markets that had not existed when the Ranneys and Hotchkisses had dominated the peppermint oil business, which would soon overshadow exports, confectioners, and druggists. Tooth powders based on soap, chalk, and charcoal evolved into toothpaste when Colgate first mass-produced jars of the new product in 1873 and began manufacturing tubes of toothpaste in 1890.[50] Firms like Colgate, Pepsodent, and Kolynos began to use large quantities of peppermint and spearmint oils to flavor their toothpastes.[51] Gum chewing began in colonial America using the resins exuded by native trees such as spruce and balsam. Products based on tree resins led the market until the 1870s, when they were overtaken by paraffin-based gums made from by-products of Pennsylvania's new oil industry.[52] By the 1890s, gums based on chicle, the sap of the Central American sapodilla tree, were gaining in popularity. An 1895 news report stated that 90 percent of the gum consumed in America was made from chicle, of which four million pounds was imported annually.[53] Observing that earlier chewing gums had been attacked as dangerous and foul-tasting, manufacturers flavored their chicle-based gums with peppermint, spearmint, and wintergreen. Taking advantage of the traditional medicinal legacies of these herbs, advertisements for the new chewing gums claimed they aided digestion, perfumed the breath, cleared the voice, and offered a healthy alternative to chewing tobacco and a breath freshener after smoking newly popular cigarettes.[54] In addition to William Wrigley, who began shipping chewing gum in 1892, other companies such as Beech Nut, Fleer, Sen Sen, Beemans, Zeno, and American Chicle had entered the rapidly growing gum business. In March 1910, Albert Todd wrote to his son Paul from New York: "I am glad to tell you I succeeded in contracting to American Chicle Co. 10,000# Natural Peppt @ 2.00 tho they had just bot 7000 of Rudd @ 1.90 & wanted me to sell at $1.75."[55] On the strength of its new business supplying peppermint and spearmint oils to gum manufacturers, the Todd Company was incorporated in 1911. And on January 1, 1912, the company's $130,847 worth of merchandise and $285,400 worth of real estate contributed to a total value of $543,052.

Unlike Hiram Hotchkiss, who had both micromanaged and belittled his sons, Albert Todd had enough confidence in his children that in 1912 and 1913 he and Augusta spent fourteen months in Europe. He vacationed, added to his art collection and library, and studied the public-utilities systems of Austria, Bavaria, Belgium, Denmark, Egypt, England, France, Greece, Holland, Italy, Norway, Prussia, Saxony, Scotland, Sweden, and Switzerland. He collected documents and reports and took more than five hundred photographs of public utilities. The children kept their father apprised of major business developments, and Albert offered them occasional advice. In January 1913, Albert James Todd (Bert) wrote to his parents. "Our higher priced Wrigley contract starts," he said, "and we will avoid many of the delays we were obliged to encounter last year so unless something unforeseen happens I think we will have the best year on the farms we have ever had." Bert provided some of the details that inspired his confidence and concluded, "I think our total profits will be in excess of what they have ever been before by fully twenty thousand dollars unless conditions should again be awry and we unable to exercise any control over them."[56] In March Albert senior wrote to his children from Berlin, about business. He suggested furnishing a social hall above the general store in their farm community, Mentha. "The hall above the store is an unusually beautiful and well-lighted room and is suitable for social amenities for the employees and such others as might be invited, while at the same time the walls afford excellent opportunity for attractive pictures, which I will be glad to personally furnish as well as what furniture and so forth may be necessary." Just as he had arranged to pay his farmworkers more than any comparable labor force in America, Albert wanted Mentha to be an actual community. He continued, "Such a place would I think add largely to the morale as well as the happiness of the employees, and thus also add incidentally to the stability of the building and the pleasure of all the members of the community."[57]

Albert Todd's farms, Mentha and Campania, were the largest peppermint-growing operations in the nation, and they produced most of the spearmint oil on the American market. Between 1911 and 1928, Mentha produced 361,870 pounds of spearmint oil and 84,163 pounds of peppermint.[58] Yields averaged about thirty pounds of oil per acre, and Albert used the two farms' production to make his Crystal White and Super Extra Natural oils. He applied for a trademark on the "Super-Extra-Natural" name, but the regulators considered it too descriptive.[59] In spite of this setback, he continued working to differentiate his products on the basis of objective, scientific measures. In 1915, he received a reply to a letter he had written to Dr. C. Kleber at Clifton Chemical Laboratory in Passaic, New Jersey, regarding U.S. Pharmacopeia specifications for rectified peppermint oil. Kleber agreed with specifications

that required "rectified Oils of Peppermint from which the first frac-
tions (containing sulphides and lower aldehydes) and also the tarry
residue have been removed as these have a bad odor and irritating properties." Kleber believed, however, that the U.S.P. standard really only applied to oils used for medicinal purposes, and that commercial users
ought to be able to make up their own minds. Kleber also stated, "Regarding the content of Di-methyl sulphide it seems to me that all Peppermint plants grown for some time on American soil produce this very
undesirable substance, that Mitcham plants are generally free from it,
but will gradually assume under the influence of American soil and climate the character of the American plants with production of sulphides."[60] Albert had improved the quality of American oils by importing
Black Mitcham roots from England, but he continued experimenting in
his laboratory and at Mentha to produce a better peppermint.

The continual effort of Albert to improve his plants paid off very
quickly in spearmint. As the close relative of peppermint became more
popular with chewing gum and toothpaste manufacturers, he introduced a new variety of Scotch spearmint (*Mentha cardiaca* G.) that one
of his suppliers had found in a Wisconsin garden. Scotch spearmint was
hardier than native spearmint and produced as much as 50 percent
more oil. Albert planted Scotch spearmint at Mentha, and it quickly became the standard plant for producing spearmint oil.[61] The Todd Company's balance sheet for 1917 included $243,010 in merchandise (mostly
peppermint and spearmint oils held at Kalamazoo) and $411,000 in real
estate at Mentha, Campania, Kalamazoo, and Sylvania, for a total value
of $775,343.[62]

While Michigan and Indiana gained ground each year as the centers of peppermint production, the Todd family also helped introduce
peppermint to the Pacific Northwest. Albert's older brother, Oliver, had
moved west from Michigan in 1873, when he had sold his stake in the
Nottawa partnership to Albert. Oliver settled first in Kansas and then in
Idaho, where he planted a little peppermint. When he began making
plans to grow peppermint in higher volume in 1912, Oliver decided to
try the lowlands beside the Willamette River in Oregon. In December
1916 the *Pacific Drug Review* reprinted an article from the *Oregonian*
about "Oregonians Distilling Peppermint." The article announced,

"Four thousand pounds of peppermint oil, distilled from plants in the upper Willamette Valley . . . is being shipped by O. H. Todd, of Eugene, the brother of A. M. Todd." The oil was distilled in Albany, Oregon, "where for four years a number of farmers have been growing mint very successfully and where there are approximately 250 acres planted to peppermint."[63] Washington, Idaho, and the Willamette Valley in Oregon are still important peppermint-growing regions today.

By 1920, the A. M. Todd Company was the acknowledged leader in the essential oil market, and Albert was known as the peppermint king or sometimes simply as "Peppermint Todd." Over the years, Albert had educated his customers and the industry press on how to accurately measure the purity and quality of essential oils. One of his letters to his customers included detailed descriptions of twelve scientific tests they could use to measure the purity and quality of peppermint oil. Taking advantage of this increased knowledge, Todd's labels carried detailed specifications: "The Sp. Gr. of the Crystal White Oil Peppermint at 15°c is never below .903 and never above .913," and included a space where the results of a polarity test on each can's contents could be penciled in.[64] Another notice in red stated, "This can is sealed with a Metallic Cap, impressed with the manufacturer's name, secured by a Protective Strip bearing his Guarantee of purity and quality, with signature. Refuse any package not corresponding to the tests and specifications hereon, and advise the manufacturer, giving date and number on label, with particulars."[65] Albert used security devices developed by the Hotchkisses, but the products his seals and signatures protected were validated not merely by the authority of his name and reputation as a judge of subjective oil quality but also by scientific measurements of the specific, objective chemical properties of the oil he sold.

As Albert aged, he began turning over responsibility for the family business to his children. Although he still held most of the company's stock, the list of shareholders grew to include his younger children, Paul, Allman, and Ethel, and Ethel's husband, LeGrand. The children took control when Albert turned his attention to politics or traveled. Including his fourteen-month trip in 1912–13, Albert visited Europe eight times between 1907 and 1923. During that time, he shipped home twenty-six cases of art objects weighing more than thirty thousand pounds.[66] When his children wrote him to get his counsel, he gave his opinion but left most decisions to them. In March 1920, for example, the children wrote to their father in Los Angeles for advice regarding a large land purchase they were contemplating, to expand the peppermint farm at Mentha. Albert wrote a four-page explanation of why he wouldn't buy the land, if it were up to him. He admitted, "You will probably think I am holding a pessimistic view or at least an ultra-conservative one, and you are tolerably right in so assuming." He went on, "I have no doubt but that were I twenty years younger I would feel much more optimistic, so I do not feel that you should be held back by my timidity." He concluded that the children were going to have to live with the results of their decisions and told them they had his permission, "since you are young and will have to shoulder the responsibility, to do as the majority of you think best."[67] He wrote again a few days later, reiterating that he was against the purchase but would go along if they really wanted to buy the land. He advised them not to pay more than fifty thousand dollars, but "I should leave this to you," he said, "for as the care and responsibility will rest with you, I think you should have the right to decide whether it should be bought or not."[68]

His confidence in his children paid off. In the 1920s, while Paul Todd was managing Mentha, he worked with operators there to design a new still that would recover the small quantity of peppermint oil left in the distillate waste water. Their new processing plant recovered an extra 26,273 pounds of oil in its first eight years of operation, from water that would otherwise have been discarded.[69] And Albert's sons took over major accounts like Wrigley, with whom they developed an innovative new relationship. In 1919–20, Wrigley bought fifty-five thousand pounds of peppermint oil from the A. M. Todd Company. In the summer of 1920, before the buying season commenced, company treasurer Bert Todd wrote a new contract with Wrigley, for whom the company would "act as your buying agents for Oil of Peppermint and are to supply you with 50% of our purchases from this date until we have furnished you 40,000 lbs. Natural quality." Wrigley agreed to pay a fixed markup of sixty cents over whatever best cost the A. M. Todd Company could negotiate for their joint purchases, which would guarantee the company a fee of at least twenty-four thousand dollars but ensure there would be complete transparency regarding prices paid to the farmers. The contract also specified the shipping terms for the drums of oil the company would provide, and that the Wrigley Company "are also to provide the money with which to pay for these purchases as rapidly as we advise you the purchases have been made and the Oil ready for delivery to us."[70]

The A. M. Todd Company's role in this agreement was that of a purchaser, on its own behalf and for Wrigley. Rather than trying to guess what the price of oil might be, the Todd Company promised to make the same efforts it would make on its own account, and share evenly the oil it bought. The Todds predicted they would probably be able to buy oil at $4.50 per pound but promised to advise Wrigley immediately of changes in the market. Wrigley agreed to the deal, and the Todd Company ultimately delivered fifty-five thousand pounds of peppermint oil for a total price of $311,362.34 (about $5.66 per pound), plus a fee of thirty-three thousand dollars. In 1921, the price of peppermint oil had declined substantially, and Wrigley offered to buy thirty-five thousand pounds at $1.65 to $1.75, including a fee for the Todd Company of thirty-five cents per pound. Bert Todd responded that the prices he was currently paying farmers were between $1.50 and $1.60, so if he agreed to $1.75 including his fee, he would be selling the oil for $1.40 per pound, below his cost.[71] The transparency of the arrangement gave the A. M. Todd Company much more leverage than it would have had if the prices it had paid farmers had been invisible to the customer. The Wrigley Company ultimately paid more than it wanted to pay, but it could be confident that it had paid market prices rather than an arbitrary, negotiated price. The arrangement worked, and in 1921 the Todd Company balance sheet included $351,112 in merchandise and $595,939 in real estate. The company's total value was $1,071,659.[72]

The Wrigley purchasing-agent agreement was only one of several creative marketing arrangements Albert Todd and his sons tried in the 1920s. In 1923, The A. M. Todd Company contracted with the Wrigley Company to sell it between twenty-five thousand and sixty thousand pounds of spearmint oil annually for five years, for the fixed price of three dollars a pound.[73] Unlike peppermint oil, which it bought from farmers at market prices, much of the spearmint oil the Todd Company would need to fill the Wrigley contract was produced at Mentha. For the rest, the company signed a contract with George Wattles in Colon, Michigan, to plant 150 acres of spearmint in 1923 and two hundred acres in 1924 and to sell the spearmint oil to the Todd Company for $2.25 per pound. The company agreed to advance Wattles five dollars per acre in May and five dollars per acre in June against the proceeds of the oil sales in the fall.[74] George Wattles was the general organizer of the American Society for Equity's Essential Oil and Mint Grower's Branch, which was organized in 1906 to fight "speculators from the east as well as the west [who] depressed the market."[75] Apparently the fixed-price deal gave the activist confidence he was being treated fairly by the company he had once suspected of cornering the essential oil market.

In 1927, an assessment entitled "The Mint Industry in the United States" reported that Michigan and Indiana produced 450,000 pounds of peppermint oil annually, which accounted for 85 to 90 percent of all the peppermint oil distilled in America.[76] The article listed the main uses of peppermint oil in their order of importance: "1st chewing gum, 2nd dental creams, 3rd confections, 4th medicinal purposes." The article noted that after the first distillation the water "which flows from these receivers is conducted to a special building where the patented Todd equipment for removing the oil from distillate water is in operation. This equipment the writer was not permitted to see, and in fact no mention was made of it by the officials who explained the operation of the still." The authors were impressed with the size and efficiency of the distilling operation. "The Todd still is equipped with six 200 horsepower boilers of which five are in operation when the distilling equipment is used to its fullest capacity." The article also stated that there was nearly no remaining peppermint production in western New York. After price increases in 1925 and 1926, a few New York farmers had ordered roots from Indiana to replant, but even so "while 50 acres was set as the maximum it is likely that the actual average is much less," and only six growers had reported any plantings. The article mentioned that the Hotchkiss Company of Lyons depended entirely on oil from Michigan and Indiana, although the author noted that the western oil was probably rectified and blended to make it fit the flavor profile expected of Wayne County oils.[77] Of course, since peppermint oil was rarely kept more than a few years, it is impossible to know how the Hotchkiss oil of the 1920s compared to the Hotchkiss oil of the 1850s. The flavors of A. M. Todd's essential oils also probably changed over time, but at least Todd's oils had been subjected to thorough chemical analyses that helped ensure recipes for clients like Wrigley and Colgate would remain as consistent as possible.

Albert May Todd retired from the peppermint oil business in 1928, when the company moved from the four-story brick building he had built in downtown Kalamazoo to its newly built headquarters on Douglas Avenue north of the city. In a sixty-year career, Albert had helped establish Michigan as the center of both the peppermint and the spearmint oil businesses. He had invented new technologies and pioneered agricultural processes that improved the yield and quality of essential oil production. Although a strong salesman and a charismatic leader, he deliberately established his business on a scientific basis and promoted objective standards of purity and quality. And he treated his family, workers, and business associates fairly and with respect.

Albert educated and prepared his children to succeed him in his business and then gave them the opportunity to run it without interference. They were remarkably effective, improving the company's performance during his lifetime and continuing it successfully after his death. The A. M. Todd Company remained a privately held corporation throughout the twentieth century, always headed by a member of the Todd family. The company remained the world leader in peppermint and spearmint oil and continued its strong relationships with manufactures like Wrigley and Colgate. In 2010, the company for the first time appointed a chief executive who was not a family member. In 2011, the A. M. Todd name and the company's product portfolio and intellectual property were sold to WILD Flavors, a German firm that had invented the Capri Sun fruit drink in 1969. WILD GmbH is now owned by the global conglomerate Archer Daniels Midland.

Socialist Capitalist

lbert May Todd grew up in rural Michigan. His home state is remembered as both a Grange and a Greenback region, but also for the founding of the Republican Party in 1854. Part of the Northwest Territory and settled largely by Yankee and Yorker farmers from New England and western New York like the Ranneys and their neighbors, the state inherited a northeastern sensibility that placed a high value on education.[1] Michigan's public school system had been established in its 1835 territorial constitution and in legislative acts passed in 1837 when the territory achieved statehood. According to Michigan historian Roy Strickland, education was so important to the residents of the new state that a school was "often the first institution . . . in a newly settled community of the state. The school embodied a confident vision of the future for its citizens."[2] As communities grew and enrollment in the ungraded schoolhouses established with each new township increased, the state built union schools in towns and cities. Like the earlier one-room schoolhouses, union schools housed all the region's students in a single building. But they contained separate rooms for the various grades.

Albert grew up surrounded by the Free-Soil principles that would help define the early Republican Party but that would in the long run be overshadowed by the Whig priorities of strong central government and spending on internal improvements. Later in life, Albert told a story of the party's beginnings, to chastise Republicans in Congress. The party had begun, he said, in Jackson, Michigan, on July 6, 1854, at a convention that attacked slavery and resolved to defend "the first principles of the republican government and against the schemes of aristocracy. After reading this patriotic declaration of principles," he commented in 1899, "is it to be wondered at that those who founded the Republican party, seeing that corporate greed had seized its control for the purpose of destroying its splendid early history, should be forced to find another political home where they could still serve the cause of human liberty?"[3] Unlike the Republican Party, his political journey did not stray from the interest in social justice Albert acquired in rural Michigan.

After a childhood spent following news of the Civil War and studying at home with his liberally educated mother, Albert attended the Sturgis Union School, where he concentrated on the classics.[4] In 1874, after a year of college, he took a backpacking trip across Europe and England, visiting museums and galleries and absorbing the culture and politics of the Continent and Britain. Early exposure to education, art, foreign cultures, and politics broadened his horizons and opened his mind to new ideas. Travel to Europe and England, and later to Philadelphia, Chicago, and New York City as a young businessman, gave Albert a cosmopolitan perspective. All these experiences propelled him toward public service and into a much more egalitarian style of politics than might have been expected for an affluent businessman from the Midwest. Cultural historian Daniel T. Rodgers described the creation of a transatlantic Progressive movement as a relatively urban intellectual development. Albert's political career suggests Rodgers's depiction may have missed an important rural element in the transfer of European ideas into American politics.

Histories of the people and ideas that catalyzed the Progressive movement tend to focus on urban reformers like Jane Addams or national politicians like William Jennings Bryan. These people and their ideas are important, but they don't tell the entire story of political change in America. For example, when Rodgers described the creation of the Public Ownership League of America, he mentioned three of the league's urban intellectual vice presidents, Frederic Howe, Edward

Dunne, and Jane Addams, but not its rural founder and president, Albert May Todd. The transatlantic transference of social experience and policy models Rodgers described in *Atlantic Crossings* seems heavily weighted toward academic and urban contributors to the dialogue of cultures in the Atlantic world. Even when he discussed agrarian movements, Rodgers remarked: "In a spectrum framed by the issues of the urban, industrial cores, the farmers' parties occupied no stable, predictable place," despite the fact that, during much of the period he described, farming was the occupation of the majority of working Americans and more than half the population lived in rural settings.[5] Perhaps Rodgers focused on urban academic sources because there truly were very few rural people with Progressive ideas. But Albert Todd, like Robert La Follette, attacked the railroads in Congress. And, like William Jennings Bryan, he visited Europe and returned "enthusiastic about the idea of municipal ownership."[6] In a book that discusses municipal ownership at length in more than a dozen lengthy passages, Albert Todd is not mentioned. Perhaps rural Progressives like him are not found because they are not looked for.

Albert first ran for office in the Kalamazoo mayoral race of 1893. He ran as a Prohibition candidate and polled only 193 votes. Although he revered the egalitarian impulse that had helped found the Republican Party, he had no illusions about the party's transformation during the Gilded Age.[7] The following year, he ran for mayor again and received 192 votes, probably from the same core constituency of local prohibition activists. This was too narrow a base of support, so when he decided to run for Congress in 1895, he ran as a fusion candidate. Fusion, defined by political historian Peter H. Argersinger as "electoral support of a single set of candidates by two or more parties, constituted a significant feature of late nineteenth-century politics, particularly in the Midwest and West, where full or partial fusion occurred in nearly every election."[8] Although Democrats were still discredited nationally by Republicans as the party of slavery, their success in fusing with Populists, Free Silver advocates, and others elicited a Republican program of electoral reform in the Midwest in the 1890s that "involved a conscious effort to shape the political arena by disrupting opposition parties, revising traditional campaign and voting practices, and ensuring Republican hegemony—

all under the mild cover of procedural reform." By the early 1890s, Michigan Republicans had experienced more consistent fusion opposition than any other state, and in 1893 a new Republican legislature decided to "purify elections and prevent fraud" by outlawing fusion. As one Republican legislator candidly explained, "We don't propose to allow the Democrats to make allies of the Populists, Prohibitionists, or any other party, and get up combination tickets against us."[9]

Albert ran for Congress in defiance of the new Republican law, on a fusion ticket including endorsements from the Democratic Party, the People's Party, the Free Silver Party, and Prohibition. He had grown up during a period when the Democratic Party was considered by most Michigan residents to be the party of slavery. But he entered politics at a time when the Republican Party had abandoned the Free-Soil ideals that had helped create it.[10] Outsider movements like Prohibition, Free Silver, and especially Populism appealed to his sense of justice and rural self-determination. His electoral defeat was announced by Kalamazoo newspapers that assumed only his Democratic voters would be counted. But Albert challenged the constitutionality of the anti-fusion law and sued for a mandamus ruling that would require the election committee to count all his votes. In March 1895 regional newspapers and even the *New York Times* ran a story announcing "Michigan's Anti-Fusion Law is Upheld—It Compels a Candidate to Elect on Which Ticket He Will Run." The Michigan Supreme Court validated the Anti-Fusion Act passed by the legislature "but held that, as the time limit under which Todd could have made his selection expired without giving him an opportunity of electing on which ticket he should run, the mandamus prayed for in his case was granted."[11] He entered Congress as a nominal Democrat—the first to represent Michigan's Third District since the Civil War.

Todd wrote to his "Friends and Patrons" informing them that he had been elected a member of Congress but assuring them, "My business will be carried on without interruption, under the management of my sons, who will also refer to me promptly all questions needing my personal attention, so I trust we may continue to receive your confidence and patronage."[12] Todd also offered to assist his customers and supporters with any concerns they might wish him to call to the national legislature's attention. At least one of his important customers took Todd up on his offer, and on March 23, 1897, Todd presented Congress with "Memorial of William Wrigley Jr. & Co., of Chicago, protesting against the proposed duty on gum chicle—to the Committee on Ways and Means."[13] But most of the issues he championed for his constituents were classic Populist causes. Among the many petitions he presented to the clerk of the House was an April 1897 petition from the city councilors of Detroit and the Detroit branch of the United Garment Workers Union (although Detroit was well outside his congressional district), protesting the passage of a bill restricting the sale of railroad tickets.[14] The so-called anti-scalping bill was of great concern to many of his constituents and would consume much of his energy over the next few years. Although Todd regularly presented protests and petitions from his constituents on issues such as pensions for veterans and cigarette and liquor sales, he spent most of his time fighting what he called "the money power."

Early in the first session of Congress, Todd spoke against the Dingley tariff bill, saying it had been sponsored by "great corporate interests who seek protection from foreign competition, that they may combine among themselves, crush out small producers, and exact unjust tribute from the great mass of people who are the consumers and purchasers." Instead of raising rates higher even than the 1890 tariff, Todd proposed: "So far as the collection of the Government revenues is concerned, we should stop, for once and forever, this present system of taxing the necessities of life for the encouragement of trusts, and we should maintain our National Government, as we do our State and municipal governments, by direct taxation of all wealth, that of the rich and poor alike, according to that which they possess."[15] Todd was proposing not only an income tax but a tax on wealth. State and local property taxes, he reasoned, taxed the principal wealth of average people, their homes or farms. But no taxes on greater fortunes had ever been attempted, and during the Gilded Age such greater fortunes had begun to capture an increasing percentage of national wealth. His suggestion was seen by some as a betrayal of his class, but Todd did not consider himself a member of the class into which his success in the peppermint oil business had propelled him. Unfortunately, his suggestion went nowhere. The Dingley bill had the support of Congress's Republican majority and

active cooperation from President William McKinley, who had preceded
Maine congressman Nelson Dingley Jr. as chairman of the Ways and
Means Committee and had introduced the previous 1890 tariff that bore
his name. The Dingley tariff act became law in July 1897 and became the
longest-lasting tariff with the highest rates (52 percent) in U.S. history.[16]
Todd rebuked House Republicans in a speech on the floor: "You of the
majority have, many of you, voted to pass this bill against your better
judgment, and against the judgment and protest of those overtaxed and
overburdened people whom you represent, because your leaders sold
the influence of your once glorious party to the usurers and trusts who
now dictate its policy; and under the party lash and the rule of your
caucus you have been driven, at the loss of your independence and manhood, like lambs to the slaughter for the banquet of princes."[17]

Todd's speech covered twenty pages of the appendix to the *Congressional Record*, and it ranged from opposition to the tariff to the case
for bimetallism and a warning against the trusts and plutocrats Todd
believed were taking control of the nation. If the plutocrats were not
stopped, he said, "it requires no prophetic eye to discern the consolidation of political power following hard after the consolidation of wealth."
And if government failed to check the excesses of business and was re-
vealed to be merely a tool of the wealthy, "then the masses in the cities
will become the hotbeds of sedition, and the masses in the country will
subside into a peasantry without hope." Although, unlike Hotchkiss,
Todd never overextended his credit or complained of problems with
banks in his own business operations, he objected to concentration of
power in the hands of Wall Street bankers. He supported bimetallism
and Populist proposals to reorganize banking and the money supply on
a more democratic basis. The fact that he was a successful businessman
helps highlight an aspect of rural Populism that is not widely noticed.
Unlike many of the portrayals of Populists, he was an opponent not of
business but of monopoly and oligopoly. This may also have been true
of many more of the people who supported the People's Party and its
platform.

In addition to opposing the tariff, Todd called for an income tax,
saying that the recently passed Wilson-Gorman Tariff Act of 1894 imposing a 2 percent tax on incomes of more than four thousand dollars

had "rested on the simple principle that the opulent ought to be taxed as well as the poor . . . whose wages and modest profits derived from daily toil."[18] He supported a tax on incomes like his own but said, "Against this principle the money power arrayed itself in solid phalanx. Plutocracy filled all the trenches with its mercenaries for the defense of its citadel." The law, which had attempted to reduce the rates set by the McKinley tariff and make up the deficit with an income tax, had been struck down in 1895 as unconstitutional in the Supreme Court decision in *Pollock v. Farmers' Loan and Trust Co.* Todd called the decision "an example of what the Supreme Court could do in shoring up and fortifying the system of human bondage." It would take the 1913 passage of the Sixteenth Amendment to establish an income tax in the United States. Many manufacturers took positions on issues such as tariffs based on the effect they would have on either competing imports or their own exports. By the 1890s, the A. M. Todd Company was a leading exporter of peppermint oil, and Todd was always concerned about the introduction of low-quality imports, especially "Japanese" oil made from *Mentha arvensis*. He believed, however, that he was able to deal with these challenges in the market rather than by recourse to government action. He considered tariffs a direct tax on working people who were the consumers of protected products, for the benefit of large corporations that did not care to improve the competitiveness of those products.

Todd passed his distaste for tariffs on to his children. Even after he had handed over control of his company to his sons, the A. M. Todd Company relied on its ability to outcompete its rivals in the market. In 1922, during a period of rapidly rising peppermint oil prices, the protective tariff on imported essential oils was raised from twenty-five cents per pound to 25 percent of the oil's value. Indiana peppermint growers, suspecting a foreign conspiracy to regulate American exports for the benefit of the Japanese oil producers, lobbied their congressman to raise the tariff rate on Japanese oil to 100 percent. The A. M. Todd Company did not support the tariff, and the bill failed to pass the House; but like other peppermint oil producers, the Todds were concerned about the introduction of lower-quality Japanese mint into the U.S. market. They were willing to compete in the market, but wanted the playing field to be fair. The A. M. Todd Company got the relief it sought in 1923 when the

U.S. Department of Agriculture ruled under the statutes of the Pure Food and Drug Act that any product labeled "mint" or "mint flavored" had to contain natural peppermint oil (*Mentha piperita*) and could not be flavored with Japanese mint (*Mentha arvensis*). Strict labeling of mint products to prevent fraud was an approach that better fitted the Todd attitude toward competition and the role of government than tariffs. Peppermint was further protected under the *United States Pharmacopeia*, which specifically designated that any medicinal product compounded from natural peppermint oil had to use material distilled solely from *Mentha piperita*.[19]

Although Todd was already a successful businessman in the 1890s when he entered Congress, many of his ideals closely matched those detailed in the People's Party platform of 1892. He was a lifelong resident of Michigan, which shows Populism addressed concerns held by rural people outside the South and West, as typically portrayed. In addition, the fact that a prosperous capitalist was an opponent of railroads and monopolists and a supporter of Populist ideals suggests the traditional historical understanding of Populism as a resistance movement of down-and-out farmers is flawed. Populism made sense to a successful Midwestern entrepreneur, but both contemporary and historical descriptions of the movement may have failed to appreciate this because they misunderstood the nature of American business. The American people, Todd said, had been tricked into thinking that the nation's business interests were the interests of the money power. It was more than a mistake to believe that the interests of most businessmen were aligned with those of Wall Street financiers and monopolists: it was a misunderstanding that served the agenda of the money power. Business, Todd declared, included "all the honest and rational industries of the people, applied first to the soil, secondly to the shops, thirdly to the stores and streets; last of all and highest of all, to the intellectual and moral resources of the nation." It did not belong to the plutocrats, Todd argued in a speech in Congress. "The idea that business is that high-up, occult, and shadowy fact that we see in spectral outline behind the bond, behind the stock exchange, behind the secret conclave of millionaires banqueting at night is one of the false and pernicious aphorisms which the enemies of public liberty have promulgated by a subsidized press to delude the people and lead them to their own destruction."[20]

As an independent businessman who had made his own fortune in a competitive market, Albert Todd was a living example of rural entrepreneurship that shared the values of rural Populists. He was not a paternalistic patron of rural voters, pandering to their concerns to garner votes. Nor was he beholden to wealthy sponsors rather than the voters of Michigan's Third District. He felt completely free to fight for values he shared with his constituents and to attack fraud and corruption when he saw it. On February 5, 1898, he made a speech about an armament appropriations bill (H.R. 7441), attacking the Carnegie Steel Company. "If there is any one thing that should fill the American people with amazement and alarm," he said, "it is the unblushing effrontery with which powerful corporations that have for years plundered the nation ask and receive from Congress the privilege to dictate the laws upon our statute books and continue their system of spoliation." Todd argued the effect of the appropriations bill would not only be to squander "fabulous sums"; Congress would be authorizing purchases from "disloyal and dishonest corporations . . . at extravagant prices." He elaborated, listing the "stupendous frauds recently perpetrated upon the Government by the corporation in whose interests these measures are to be passed."[21]

Todd reviewed evidence described in a report presented to the Fifty-third Congress, which established that Carnegie Steel had a few years earlier supplied the navy with 8,958 tons of armor plate costing nearly $5.5 million. Carnegie had charged the U.S. Navy more than six hundred dollars per ton for this armor, more than twice the rate most other nations paid for comparable plate, Todd said. But the company had delivered "worthless armor plates . . . containing 'blowholes' over 18 inches long [that] were filled with shavings. The opening was then plugged, and the surface was afterwards planed and covered with dust to hide the defects." To make matters worse, Carnegie Steel had both hidden these defects and lied to the navy about them. Todd said, "False sets of books . . . were kept for the use of the Government inspectors, and another set showing the actual defects were kept by the company in secret." The nine-hundred-page report, which Todd quoted extensively, also concluded that Carnegie employees had manipulated testing machinery and armor plates to improve test results and increase the apparent tensile strength of the armor. Todd, tying Carnegie Steel's fraud to the tariff he had recently spoken against, went on: "It is well known that since the enactment of the Dingley law the trusts have become more solidly allied for the purpose of controlling the production and advancing the price of everything which the nation will need in time of war. These trusts have the nation by the throat." He accused the Carnegie Steel Company of having "practical control" of a trust controlling capital of nearly a hundred million dollars. He concluded his argument by suggesting, "Surely the evidence of its treason is such as alone to demand that the Government cease from further patronizing it." Instead, he said, Congress should ensure the nation's safety by funding "the erection of Government works for manufacturing armor plate, ammunition, and arms."[22] His suggestion regarding a government-owned munition works was an opening remark for his ongoing advocacy of public ownership. In ironic confirmation of his warnings about the trust, about two years after his speech Wall Street financier J. P. Morgan merged Carnegie Steel with several other companies to create U.S. Steel, the world's first billion-dollar corporation.

A few weeks later, in February 1898, Todd proposed an amendment to a bill (H.R. 6358) authorizing the Nebraska, Kansas, and Gulf Railway Company to build and operate a line through the Indian Territory. The amendment would have prohibited the railroad from offering free passes to politicians, issuing stock or bonds exceeding the actual cost of the line, or purchasing mines or other properties unrelated to operating the line as a common carrier. But the key feature of the amendment would have given the government a ten-year option to buy the railroad from the Gulf Railway Company for 10 percent over the cost of construction. A point of order was raised, and Todd's discussion of government ownership of the line was ruled not germane to the bill in question. Todd responded to the objection by admitting he had nothing in particular against the company under discussion but thought a public-ownership provision should be added whenever new railway projects were authorized.[23]

Todd was a dues-paying member of the Academy of Political Science, the American Political Science Association, the American Social Society, the American Economic Association, the American Association for the Advancement of Science, the Stable Money League, the Fabian

Society, the American Academy of Social and Political Science, the Proportional Representation League, and the National Municipal League. He also contributed regularly to Kalamazoo's Cooperative Society.[24] He had a large library and read widely but was not easily tempted by the more utopian strains of contemporary social thought. As the owner of several large properties, including the multithousand-acre farms Mentha and Campania, he was not an advocate for public ownership of all land, as suggested by Progressive economist Henry George. And as the president of a thriving business, Todd did not favor state ownership of all industry as proposed by the Nationalist Clubs extending the ideas of Edward Bellamy. On the other hand, Todd's opposition to the abuses of workers and customers and the defrauding of the government by railroad corporations and monopolies made him a natural ally of Eugene V. Debs. Todd sent contributions to the Debs brothers and to Eugene Debs's defense committee during Debs's incarceration. Todd did not despise business; he objected strenuously to monopoly and the abuse of power enabled by concentrated wealth. This is a distinction that he was well aware of, based on his arguments in Congress, but one that many historians of the Populist era have lost sight of. It is a distinction that could be useful today.

Todd took advantage of his business background, which included extensive experience shipping and receiving freight via American railroads, to cut through what he considered the absurdity of Congress's subservience to wealth. In March 1898, he commented on a proposed amendment to a bill regarding fees paid to the railroads for transporting U.S. mail. "It has been repeatedly shown from undisputed and official authorities that the service for which the Government pays the railroads $8 per 100 pounds for a distance less than a 500-mile basis the railroads obtain for 40 cents per 100 pounds." Todd criticized the additional annual fee of three million dollars the railroads charged the government for "car service" and asked, "What would an individual shipper, a business firm, or a corporation say if, after paying simply the regular tariff rates for freight, the railroads were to demand more under the claim of 'car rental'? The railroads would not dare suggest it." The Republicans, Todd continued, said they supported "a 'business Administration.' Here, gentlemen, is an opportunity to prove your sincerity. Let us apply in the administration of the public business the same care, common sense, and honesty we apply in private business."[25]

His opposition to a military-industrial money power dominated by companies like Carnegie Steel did not make Todd a pacifist, however. On March 30, 1898, he introduced "a joint resolution (H. Res. 209) declaring war between the United States and the Kingdom of Spain and recognizing the independence of the Republic of Cuba."[26] But if the United States was going to war, Albert Todd expected American businesses to pitch in—or at the very least to refrain from profiteering. On May 2, 1898, he called the House's attention to the fact that the presidents of the Pennsylvania Railroad and the Central Traffic Association had been appointed as heads of a national transportation authority to coordinate war shipping. He charged that under the new system "no competition will be allowed for the Government business, and . . . there is no one to represent the interests of the Government." The result, he said, would be "wholesale plunder of the Treasury and the money needed to carry the war to a successful conclusion."[27] To protect the war effort, he introduced a joint resolution (H. Res. 254) of inquiry, directed to the secretary of war, "requesting information regarding the rates paid the railroads for transportation of troops and Government supplies; whether competition exists; and how the public welfare is affected by the appointment of a railroad president and other railroad officials to assume official control of Government transportation."[28]

Todd also made a speech in May 1898 supporting another plank from the People's Party platform of 1892, a constitutional amendment mandating the direct election of senators. He elaborated, suggesting that in addition to direct election, America should consider direct legislation through initiatives and referenda. He gave the example of the recent purchase by Switzerland of its national rail system for 1.2 billion francs in February 1898, following a referendum that passed with more than a two-to-one majority. The first result of direct legislation in Switzerland, he said, "was the total abolishment of the lobby, 'the third house.' The bribers gone, the professional politician soon became unknown as such, and then in turn political parties were dissolved, and now partisanship never warps the judgment of the voter. . . . To-day Switzerland is a model republic."[29] Todd concluded by introducing "a bill to purify the public service, and to prevent unjust discriminations by corporations against citizens of the United States." He attached an appendix to the record, including an article describing the Swiss railroad initiative in detail and the constitution of the Direct Legislation League of Philadelphia.

In May 1898 Todd also returned to the anti-scalping issue had had raised earlier in the session, presenting sixty-five petitions from Michigan unions and organizations "protesting against the passage of the bill forbidding railroad ticket brokerage."[30] The anti-scalping bill, introduced by New York Republican James Sherman, was seen by Todd and the unions as class legislation. Although Sherman had claimed that the bill "had been repeatedly recommended by the Interstate Commerce committee, that it had support of newspapers and commercial bodies, and that over 3,000 petitions in its favor had been presented to the House," organizations such as the National Building Trades Council and the American Federation of Labor opposed it.[31] During congressional hearings, a representative of Samuel Gompers declared the bill was written in the interest of the railroads. "It is not in our interest, we believe. It is legislation which proposes to restrict the privileges of the citizen." Speaking for Gompers, the union representative said the bill was "more reaching in its vicious spirit than the proposed attempt to make more moral, more honest, the ticket broker," as its proponents claimed.[32] The point was that the railroads claimed the right to prevent the buyer of a ticket from disposing of it as the buyer chose, because that choice might include giving or selling the ticket to a third party. Although the financial issue for railroad corporations might be large-scale ticket brokers, the issues for individual ticket buyers were convenience, the principle of ownership, and the fact that restricting ticket resale would lead to higher ticket prices.

On the bill's final day of debate, during a four-hour session, Todd made a long speech defending an amendment he proposed, which would have eviscerated the bill by prohibiting the railroads from imposing "any restrictions or limitations as to when or by whom any ticket may be used after having once been purchased from the common carrier issuing the same or any legally authorized agent."[33] The point of the amendment was to ensure, as the union representative had suggested, that any ticket holder would be able to use, give away, or sell a rail ticket in the same way he or she could any other personal property. Although the bill was ostensibly directed at ticket brokers, Todd said the true "object of the bill is, by making it a crime to buy and sell railroad tickets except through the men whom the railroads appoint, to entrench the railroad pool behind another bulwark of law and enable them to advance and maintain rates already oppressive." As an example of the wickedness of railroads, he spoke at length about the Crédit Mobilier scandal of 1873, which he said had been systematically erased from public memory. The House Committee report on the subject "is extremely difficult to procure, copies having been destroyed as far as possible to remove from public view the great crime committed." Todd connected the suppression of the report with the nomination of James Garfield, who had been a key figure in the scandal: "Within less than an hour after Mr. Garfield's nomination to the Presidency nearly every copy had been sequestered from the Capitol, he being among the number implicated." Todd digressed to discuss the Standard Oil Company's collusion with the railroads in a section of his speech entitled "The History of a Corporate Crime." He then quoted extensively from the 1887 Pattison report on the Crédit Mobilier scandal. Todd remarked he was adding all this material into the record "for the purpose of placing in the debates of Congress for the use of the future historian who shall write 'The History of the Rise of Corporate Imperialism.'" Todd's amendment was defeated, the bill passed the House 119–101, and Todd's colleagues voted to have his speech stricken from the *Congressional Record*. It was printed instead in the appendix, where it has been very useful to future historians.

Todd did not win reelection to Congress. In November 1898, he was narrowly defeated by Michigan's secretary of state, Republican Washington Gardner, by 21,182 votes to 19,864.[34] The close vote, in spite of the defeat of fusion tickets and the Republican Party's decision to run a heavyweight candidate in Michigan's small Third District, suggests that his political ideas had a widespread following among his constituents. Todd spent the final months of the Fifty-fifth Congress arguing against government waste and corruption. In the summer of 1898, he proposed an amendment to a naval appropriation bill (H.R. 3483) for the war in Cuba, suggesting a decrease in the amount budgeted for transportation over the next six months from $44 million to $20 million. He cited several examples of railroads grossly overcharging the military, even in excess of the rates they charged the general public, which he suggested were already abusive. The amendment failed.[35] On January 28, 1899, Todd spoke against a bill to increase the size of the standing army in peacetime. He offered an amendment: "The Army of the United States shall in time of peace consist of the same numbers as the peace footing authorized by existing law." The amendment also directed the president "to recall the military and naval forces of the United States from the islands of the Philippines whenever the United States Government shall have evidence of the formation of a stable and independent government in those islands by the inhabitants thereof." Todd argued that the Filipinos "have already adopted a republican government of their own."[36] This amendment also failed.

Finally, in February 1899, before the new Congress began in March, Todd offered another amendment attempting to lower the appropriation for troop transportation. He argued that the railroads were gouging the government and remarked, "Whenever I have had the honor to address Congress or to offer amendments for the protection of the public from the avarice of trusts, gentlemen on the other side, who are the agents and attorneys of these trusts, have endeavored by disorder, ridicule, or sneers to prevent a fair hearing." Todd complained that in an effort to silence him, " 'points of order' would be raised, it being well understood that whatever is opposed to the onward march of the trusts is subject to a 'point of order.' I have," he said, "always considered it an honor to be opposed by such influences, and believe that he whose work here has not earned the antagonism of the opposition has not merited the approval of his conscience or the public."[37]

His final amendment of course failed, but Todd left Congress undeterred. In September 1899 newspapers across the nation ran stories about a large antitrust conference held in Chicago. Todd was a member of the executive committee of the new organization, which was reported to be "national in scope and non-partisan in character, and is to be amalgamated finally with the National Anti-Trust League."[38] In 1900, he ran for mayor of Kalamazoo but was defeated by Republican judge A. J. Mills. Todd decided not to run for Congress in 1900, and a Grand Rapids newspaper remarked, "This is something to be sincerely regretted. . . . It was Mr. Todd who brought the prohibitionists, democrats, populists, silver republicans, and socialists together in one grand combine." The paper concluded that the state was unfortunate that "no other man in all Michigan could engineer the formation of such a political trust."[39] After the passage of the anti-fusion law, Todd would not have been able to achieve the same upset victory he had managed in 1896. But he had almost won reelection as a Democrat in 1898, suggesting that many of his supporters in the other parties were prepared to vote for him regardless of the ticket he ran on.

Being out of office did not keep Albert Todd out of the national spotlight. He made the news again in 1900, when newspapers everywhere ran a story entitled "Socialists to Start a College." The papers declared that after being "forced out of the colleges and universities endowed by the rich, several leaders of socialistic thought in the United States and England have determined to organize educational institutions of their own." Supporters of a school "where the believers in the ideas of socialism may make their homes" were several business leaders and politicians, including "Mayor Samuel Jones of Toledo, N. O. Nelson, the St. Louis manufacturer, Mrs. E. D. Rand, who endowed the chair formerly held by Prof. Herron at Iowa College, and A. M. Todd, 'The Peppermint King,' of Kalamazoo, Mich."[40] The school would come to be known as the Rand School of Social Science, after its main benefactor, Mrs. Rand. Caroline Amanda Sherfey Rand was the daughter of a Burlington, Iowa, merchant and the widow of Elbridge Dexter Rand, a wealthy livestock and lumber baron. Mrs. Rand's daughter, also named Caroline, married Christian socialist George Davis Herron, who along with Eugene V. Debs, Jane Addams, and Annie Diggs had founded the Social Reform Union.[41] When Mrs. Rand died in 1905, she left two hundred thousand dollars to establish a school for socialist education, naming her daughter and Professor Herron as trustees. The school opened in 1906 in New York City, where it held classes and ran a summer camp in the Poconos for fifty years.

Todd remained a strong supporter of the Rand School for the rest of his life. And in 1903 he put some of his social idealism on display. An advertising supplement he had printed in London's *Chemist and*

Druggist for January 1903 included quotes from an article on Campania, entitled "The Largest Mint Farm," that praised the peppermint farm's efficiency. The article described Campania as being "operated on the principle of avoiding every unnecessary waste. And this principle is extended to the management and welfare of the employees. They are paid something higher than usual wages, and a higher standard of efficiency is accordingly expected and realized from them." Todd and his managers, the article continued, "evidently believe it is good economy to greet their men cordially whenever they meet them at their work or elsewhere. They are treated as *men*, not merely as 'hands,' and consequently have every inducement to improve their efficiency in the work."[42]

Todd entered local politics again in 1907, when he proposed at a hearing convened to consider amending the city of Kalamazoo's charter that the city should bar officials of local corporations from holding office. The proposal was not adopted, but Todd remained interested in both local and national political issues. He continued to send contributions to the Debs brothers and supported Eugene V. Debs in his political campaigns. In the fall of 1913, after Albert and Augusta Todd's fourteen-month visit to Europe, the Wilkes-Barre *Times* ran an article entitled "Todd's Little Ticket." It described the National Popular Government League's convention in Washington and told the story of a rail ticket Todd had bought in Switzerland. "Todd was over studying the initiative and referendum. Todd wanted to travel throughout the cantons; to go by rail and also by boat. He wanted to be spared the bother of buying a new ticket every time he started for the next place." He asked the state rail service to sell him a single ticket for his entire forty-two-day stay in Switzerland, and it obliged him. Although the Swiss rail system was "the costliest-per-mile roadbed in the world—costliest because of two great tunnels driven through the granite heart of the Alps," the government-owned system sold Todd a twenty-seven-dollar ticket that allowed him unlimited travel for his entire stay. The article concluded, "The Swiss railroads are good roads. They give a good service. They also give a cheap service. And they serve the public first—no banker management, no underwriting graft; no inside ring buying up scrap-iron feeders and selling it at big profit to themselves as officers and directors; and, naturally, no doubtful securities or trouble to get funds when the road needs fixing up."[43] The railroad corporations of the United States, which had received massive gifts of government funding and 175 million acres of land grants (an area larger than the state of Texas), could make none of these claims.

Using information he had accumulated in his travels to advance his long-held interest public ownership, Todd brought together four like-minded Kalamazoo residents to form a local Municipal Ownership League in August 1914. The league's first order of business was to advocate that the city of Kalamazoo should take over its gas supply. In March 1915, the league hired a British expert to write a detailed assessment of the current gas company and propose an alternative plan for a public gasworks. The expert concluded that the public project could provide gas to consumers for seventy-five cents per thousand cubic feet at a profit that would pay for the project in less than twenty years, versus the current private rate of $1.25. The expert concluded that even if it decided against undertaking a municipal project, the city ought to renew the private franchise at a rate of seventy-five cents, which he calculated would still be profitable for the contractor. At the lower rate, he predicted, gas consumption in Kalamazoo would rise significantly. A referendum vote in September 1915 failed to return the three-fifths majority needed to create a municipal gasworks. Todd attributed the loss to "lavish expenditure of money on the part of the [private] gas company [that] so influenced public opinion through the press and widespread misrepresentation of facts by means of cunningly-worded literature."[44] A few months later, Todd became founding president of the Public Ownership League of America. Other officers of the new national organization included Jane Addams, vice president, and New Jersey manufacturer Charles H. Ingersoll, treasurer.

By the 1910s, the A. M. Todd Company dominated the peppermint oil and general essential oil markets, and Albert Todd's children were largely responsible for the daily running of it. Todd received regular profit-sharing dividends on his company shares, in addition to a modest $416 monthly salary. He had abundant money and time to devote to his political passions. He opened an office for the Public Ownership League in Washington, D.C., and increased his support of the Rand School, which had its own page in Todd's ledger book. In August 1917, Todd recorded a contribution of five thousand dollars to the Society of the Commonwealth Center. In parentheses he added, "I have written to the Society that if they are able to reduce their indebted to $50,000 by Sept. 1, 1918, the $5,000 is to be made a gift to them, & the bonds returned to them marked 'Canceled and paid.' I offered as per letter enclosing checks, to return the stock canceled if total debt is reduced to $50,000 in one year."[45] The Society of the Commonwealth Center was the leaseholder of the "People's House," a six-story building purchased from the YWCA that became the Rand School's new headquarters in the fall of 1917. And Todd subsidized the Public Ownership League's printing office, which published a series of booklets, several written by Todd himself. One of these was a 122-page booklet entitled *Municipal Ownership with a Special Survey of Municipal Gas Plants in America and Europe*.[46]

Todd introduced the subject of public ownership by saying that because of the "intimate relations early in life with the railroads, telegraph and other public utilities" he had experienced as a merchant and peppermint oil dealer in rural Michigan, "the conviction came to [him] that the corporations operating them were not only usurping functions that rightly belonged to the government, but were rapidly becoming so rich and powerful as to be a serious menace to liberty, justice and democracy, in defiance of which, private monopoly ever sought to control the making and administration of law." He explained how coal gas was made and gave an overview of the history of the gas industry and its present scope. He then devoted individual chapters to the municipal gas works of Virginia, Minnesota, Indianapolis, Germany, and Great Britain, and to "The Fight for Municipal Gas in Kalamazoo with an Investigation of Costs and Profits." In his discussion of the Kalamazoo situation, he noted: "All of the public utilities of Kalamazoo, Michigan, with the exception of the electric lighting of the streets and the operation of the public water plant are under the control of a single monopoly directed from 14 Wall Street, New York City, which corporation also controls the public utilities of many of the other cities of Michigan as well as those of other states." Number 14 Wall Street was the address of the newly built Bankers Trust skyscraper. The tower's entire thirty-first floor was occupied by an apartment belonging to banking mogul J. P. Morgan.

In late 1918 the *Washington Times* carried an article entitled "The Public Ownership League of America," written by the league's secretary, Carl D. Thompson. "The people," Thompson wrote, "want the Government to *keep* the railroads and the wire systems now that it has 'taken them over.' And especially since hundreds of millions of dollars of the people's money is being put into the roads to repair them and bring them up to standard." The takeover Thompson referred to was Woodrow Wilson's wartime nationalization of the American rail system in December 1918. Since public money was being spent to renovate the national rail system, Thompson argued, the time had come to make public ownership of the rail system permanent. The article featured a list of the league's officers, including its president, Albert M. Todd, and vice presidents, Jane Addams of Hull House, former Illinois governor Edward F. Dunne, chairman of the War Labor Board Frank P. Walsh, and president of the United Mineworkers Union Frank Hawes.[47]

On February 21, 1919, Todd gave testimony as president of the league, advocating for public ownership of the railroads at hearings held by the Interstate Commerce Commission. The league, he said, "does not advocate Government ownership of private industries, but is largely devoted to studying and applying the practical problems of democratic government in a broad and impartial manner, and sending its findings to all parts of the country." Demonstrating his thorough understanding of the economic principles involved, he continued: "It [the league] is especially interested in promoting Government ownership of those resources and agencies which are natural monopolies and which the Government can own and manage better for the general public welfare than they can be owned and managed by private interests."[48] Natural monopolies are defined by economists as situations where the most efficient number of firms in a market is one, generally because only one is needed. Many Americans accepted the observation that railroads were a natural monopoly, because of the excessive cost of laying competing tracks side by side simply to create price competition. The issue was how to reduce prices without competition, and the answer to that was public ownership. Woodrow Wilson had nationalized the American rail system in December 1918, and Todd wanted government ownership to continue after the war under the provisions of a bill (H.R. 10550) introduced by Wisconsin congressman William J. Cary. "The railroads," Todd said, "are a natural monopoly, and a private monopoly is abhorrent to democracy."[49]

Todd observed that ineffective government regulation of privately owned railroads "has made 'looting' of the roads and public possible. Why not remove the loot and secure public ownership of the railways at the same time, since they inevitably and naturally go together?" Todd concluded by suggesting that although it might take five or ten years after nationalizing the railroads for them to pay for themselves, "the period in which the Government has been in control and facing a world war and the most adverse obstacles of all kinds here at home, has been quite sufficient to demonstrate both to unbiased experts and to millions of our people, railroad employees almost universally, and many others, that Government control must be continued."[50] The Interstate Commerce Commission ignored Todd's testimony and the league's proposal, and the railroads were returned to private control in March 1920, under the Esch-Cummins Act. Although rail workers had won an eight-hour workday during the war years, in 1922 they faced a 12 percent wage cut. Four hundred thousand workers walked off the job, beginning the largest rail strike since Eugene V. Debs's Pullman Strike of 1894.

In addition to supporting American corporations, Wilson's wartime government suppressed dissent. The Red Scare and wartime attacks on the civil rights of American citizens also affected the Rand School, which was raided and prosecuted under the Espionage Act of 1917. In an attempt to explain that it was not a training school for spies, the Rand's administrators published a booklet in the school's defense, declaring: "The Rand School of Social Science last year had 5,000 students. Rand students, when they finish their training, go out to be lecturers, street speakers, teachers and organizers in the labor movement." The school, they said, prepared its students with social theory to make sense of the experiences they had as workers. "They become leading spirits among their fellows, for they have supplemented their toil-won knowledge of present social and industrial evils with an intelligent, constructive idealism that builds in a new and better way where the present system fails and collapses." This knowledge and the activism that resulted was designed to be a force for positive change rather than an attack on America. The school claimed that its students had "created a high and unique function for itself . . . whose energies are dedicated to the cause of political freedom and economic justice."[51] His ledger page for the school lists a number of contributions Todd made to its defense fund and to the personal defense fund of the school's publication editor, Algernon Lee.

In July 1918, Todd presented an essay to the Academy of Political Science at its National Conference on the War Economy. His "Relation of Public Ownership to Democracy and Social Justice" summarized his thinking on the subject and was reprinted by a variety of public-affairs periodicals and by the Public Ownership League. Todd framed his argument with an affirmation that "democracy is the greatest thing in the world," and by pointing out the extreme sacrifices people had just made in the world war to "make the world safe" for it. He then quoted Lincoln, suggesting that securing democracy was the "unfinished work which they who have fought here have thus far so nobly advanced . . . that government of the people, by the people, for the people, shall not perish from the earth."[52] The challenge to democracy, Todd continued, was "special privilege." He again quoted Lincoln, saying that "as a result of the war, corporations have been enthroned, and an era of corruption in high places will follow." Todd continued, "His prophecy already has been in part fulfilled, because special privilege has been permitted to secure the control of our great public functions. To restore Democracy, by nationalizing our great public utilities in the interest of the public good, is the great work now before us."[53] To Albert Todd, advocacy of public ownership had become a fight to restore democracy to a nation overrun by corporate power. He framed his argument in his interpretation of America's founding principles, learned in his youth on the Michigan prairie.

Todd claimed that in order to avoid what Jefferson had called the "aristocracy of our moneyed corporations," the public should own and the government should operate all "utilities and services which are of universal need . . . and especially those which either by nature or by law are monopolies." Specifically, he proposed to nationalize railroads, telegraph and telephone services, and municipal services such as street railways and gas and electricity utilities. Drawing on his travels in Europe and his study of other nations such as Russia, Japan, Australia, Mexico, and China, Todd observed: "*The United States of America is the only nation in the world which does not publicly own and operate its telephone and telegraph systems as government functions*" (original emphasis).[54] He claimed that contrary to a public opinion beguiled by the corporate-controlled press, European public utilities were operated economically. "All these public utilities were efficiently administered and gave a profit to the government." And "strikes and labor trouble of any kind are so extremely rare as to be almost unknown under public ownership, for the public has no interest nor desire to treat its 'citizen employees' otherwise than with generosity and justice."[55]

Todd never expressed his opinion regarding the Federal Reserve System, established in 1914. It is possible he viewed it as an attempt to restrict the influence of the money power as it was expressed in financial institutions such as J. P. Morgan's Wall Street bank, which had presided over the creation of the trusts and monopolies Todd had consistently opposed. To the extent that J. P. Morgan and Company seemed to oppose the government intervention in banking undertaken with the Federal Reserve, Todd may have considered the central bank a positive change.

Todd continued with a detailed description of the Swiss railway system, which had begun under private ownership but had been purchased by the government and been nationalized after a public referendum in 1898. He observed that although the mountainous terrain of Switzerland made railway construction about five times as expensive as it was in the United States, Swiss fares were substantially lower than those in America. He then reviewed the history of the Pacific Railroad construction and the Crédit Mobilier's bribery of politicians before moving on to more recent history. Between 1912 and 1915, he said, the Interstate Commerce Commission had investigated five railway systems that accounted for one-third of the nation's rail miles. "The evidence secured by the commission shows that *every railroad company investigated knowingly falsified its accounts*, partly in order to hide expenditures of large sums for controlling politics and elections and influencing legislation and the administration of laws."[56] In the case of one railroad, the report had found "more than 300 subsidiary corporations in a web of entangling alliances with each other, many of which are seemingly planned, created, and manipulated by lawyers expressly retained for the purpose of concealment or deception." This railroad, the report continued, was plagued by "the most glaring instances of maladministration," and the problems railroads faced were caused by their own mismanagement and not at all by government regulation, which was a frequent excuse. In fact, Todd said, a railroad corporation's "greatest losses and most costly blunders were made in attempting to circumvent governmental regulation and to extend its domination beyond the limits fixed by law."[57] He closed by reiterating, "Government ownership of railroads is desirable; it is practicable; it is the only democratic and just solution of the railway problem, the great emergency of American reconstruction."[58]

Todd invited Jane Addams of Hull House in Chicago to visit him in Kalamazoo in May 1921. Addams was a vice president of Todd's Public Ownership League, and the two reformers had traveled in roughly the same circles for decades but may not have met more than briefly. Todd said he had been to Hull House, "but unfortunately on occasions when you were not present." He wrote to Addams in early May in response to a letter from her, to say he would be happy to be her host in Kalamazoo, as she had apparently suggested, or, he said, "[If] circumstances make it inconvenient for you to come I shall be delighted to call upon you when I am in Chicago, (where I go quite frequently)."[59] He also responded to her inquiry about his interest in starting a school of social science like the Rand School in Chicago. He said he had made some "preliminary surveys" but had become concerned that recently "the forces of special privilege and those who have grown rich through war, realizing the injustice of their acts, have decided to eliminate from our schools the teachings of fundamental justice." He noted that a bill had recently reached its third reading in the New York legislature "compelling every teacher to affirm under oath that he or she does not believe in a 'change of government' by force or otherwise." If such laws passed, he said, "a school such as I had in mind might be compelled to close. It is, of course, possible that the character and courage of the American people will not permit this." A few weeks later, again responding to a letter from Addams, Todd asked her for the name and address of a man who had written to him on Hull House stationery to discuss starting a school of social science in Chicago. Todd said he had misplaced the letter and asked her to "express to him my apology" and to "transmit my views of the situation as expressed to you. I greatly regret the apparent discourtesy arising from the mislaying of his letter."[60]

In 1922, Todd retired as president of the league and was replaced by Willis J. Spaulding, the public-utilities commissioner of Springfield, Illinois. Spaulding was twenty years younger than the seventy-two-year-old Todd and was later instrumental in establishing public water and electrical services in Springfield and building Lake Springfield. Todd retained the title of honorary president but began spending more time at home with his books and artworks. In the eight trips he had made to Europe between 1907 and 1923, he had acquired and shipped home more than thirty thousand pounds of art objects. At the end of his life, he accelerated the process of giving his art away. Other wealthy art collectors such as J. P. Morgan admitted to the press that they had failed to "make some suitable disposition" of their collections "which would render them permanently available for the instruction and pleasure of the American people."[61] Todd began giving his art collection away during his lifetime. He provided paintings to decorate the walls of the social hall in his farm community at Mentha and of the public schools of Kalamazoo. He loaned a large part of his collection to Kalamazoo College and the University of Michigan at Ann Arbor, which later became permanent gifts. His only stipulation in these gifts was that the recipients had to display the art where the public would be able to see it.

Albert Todd's gifts of art had a profound social goal in addition to aesthetic appreciation. Todd told a reporter from the Detroit News, "I am buying pictures that will make man more human to his brother." But the aesthetic goal was also profound in his mind, and he continued, "But also that will strike at the roots of all exploitation by developing the general appreciation of beauty. If the world saw beauty, it would abolish the wrongs of economic injustice; it would open the door of equal opportunity for all."[62] Although he apparently considered himself a religious man, Todd never explained any of his actions in terms of his faith. His personal beliefs seem to have provided him with a moral compass rather than with specific rules for action.[63] In this sense of secular morality, Todd was not too different from the previous peppermint-oil-producing family descended from the explicitly materialist Samuel Ranney. All told, Todd gave away more than four hundred paintings during his lifetime. He told another reporter, "It is as important to lift the hearts of men by beauty as it is to challenge their thought by pointing out social misery and wrong." People needed a belief in the goodness of humanity and the world to challenge injustice and hope for change, Todd thought. And, he said, "I am having a good time buying what I don't need and never can use. But people can use them, get joy and inspiration from them." Todd replied to the reporter's final question: "No, I've never figured the money I've spent for paintings. If I did, I might get scared and quit."[64] When Albert May Todd died at the age of eighty-one on October 6, 1931, his family continued his policy of sharing his collection. In November, paintings worth sixty thousand dollars were given to the city's public schools, again with the single stipulation that they be kept on display in classrooms and public spaces. A month later, twenty-nine more art objects from the Todd collection were given to Kalamazoo College.

Todd grew up in rural Michigan and lived in the small city of Kalamazoo. He traveled extensively for business and pleasure and was an avid student of European culture, politics, and economics. He was a very successful capitalist who by the end of his career was credited with (or accused of) single-handedly controlling the American peppermint oil markets. But he achieved his success in a competitive marketplace and consistently opposed monopolies built on government-granted privileges or protection. His rural background and Midwestern experience drew his political ideals toward populism and democratic socialism. But Todd was far from the stereotypical populist or socialist. In *The Populist Vision*, historian Charles Postel examined the ways "Americans responded to the traumas of technological innovation, expansion of corporate power, and commercial and cultural globalization" at the end of the nineteenth century.[65] Postel told a story of how "Populists were influenced by modernity," but not all Populists were *victims* of modernity. Albert Todd was a technological innovator and the leader of a corporation with an international clientele that was occasionally suspected of seeking to monopolize the essential oil business. His populism was not characterized by rural anxiety over the baffling complexity of new urban commercial and financial centers. Todd was one of the populists Postel described who "sought to reshape government as an agency of the majority rather than of the corporate and wealthy minority." But Todd wished to use government as an agent of democracy not from a generalized dread of plutocracy enflamed by muckraking media but because he had precise personal knowledge of the excesses and corruption of an economy run for the benefit of the money power.[66] Similarly, he supported socialists and their organizations throughout his life but never advocated the elimination of capitalist competition and collective ownership of all of the means of production. It may be significant this was the single plank of the Socialist Labor Party's platform that the populists had rejected when formulating their 1892 party platform.[67] Todd's example of a successful businessman supporting Populist ideals suggests the standard portrayal of the People's Party may be incomplete. Like many populists, Todd had no interest in nationalizing everything. He sought public ownership of natural monopolies and government action to break trusts and combinations that prevented competition. And he fought to eliminate tariffs that supported wealthy corporations at the expense of poor, often rural consumers. Ultimately, he believed in people. He advocated for democratic reforms because he trusted regular people like himself to make better decisions than plutocrats. And he gave his artworks to public institutions to "lift the hearts" of his neighbors and help them believe in a brighter future.

Global Peppermint

P eppermint began its history in North America when roots of the recently discovered hybrid were imported to newly independent British colonies at the start of the nineteenth century. The Ranney family concentrated on bringing medicinal peppermint essence to American consumers, and the Hotchkiss brothers and Albert May Todd and his children exported large quantities of peppermint oil back to Great Britain and to Europe. Peppermint has been an item of international commerce from its earliest days. As markets consolidated and integrated in the second half of the twentieth century and the beginning of the twenty-first, peppermint has remained a global commodity. When Albert Todd retired from the peppermint oil business in 1928, his company dominated the essential oil market. Directed by his descendants, the A. M. Todd Company continued to lead the industry in sales of peppermint and spearmint oils, in research and technology, and in expanding peppermint production to the Pacific Northwest and ultimately to India after it achieved independence from Britain following World War II. In 2011, the company became a subsidiary of a German firm. But before we examine the national and international scope of the peppermint oil industry in the recent past, it is important to recall that growing peppermint and distilling oil was a personal, day-to-day activity that changed the lives of many individual American farmers.

Among the farmers whose personal stories included peppermint oil was Mary Clark of Galien, Michigan. Mary was first noticed by the *Detroit Free Press* in a 1905 article entitled "Woman Farmer's Success— Miss Mary Clark of Michigan Does All the Work on 80 Acres." The article began with the news that Mary Clark "was paying girls a dollar a day and their dinners" to work on her farm.[1] As word of the high wage Clark offered spread, the article reported, "the story stirred up the sluggish imagination of half the wage earners of Berrien county, where flesh and blood are cheap—where women pick berries in the broiling sun for twenty-five cents a crate; where they toil week days and Sundays for the same pitiful sum and work in the kitchen for a dollar and a half a week." The women who went to work for Mary Clark did not earn as much as Albert Todd's farm workers, but they did much better than they would have otherwise. But the "fortunate few" whom Clark hired to tend her peppermint fields worked for their money, because "they literally worked shoulder to shoulder with the most indefatigable woman in the country—a woman noted for her tremendous capacity for work, and whose endurance is the marvel of men where brawn is the common heritage."

The article described how Clark had taken over running her widowed mother's farm at the age of sixteen and bought an additional forty acres next door. "She cuts and rakes twenty tons of hay," the author of the article marveled, "milks ten cows night and morning, and once a week sends half a ton of milk eight miles to the creamery, where her checks average $50 a month." Returning to the women earning a dollar a day and their meals on Clark's farm, the article explained: "This is the basis on which these unusual wages were paid—the workers must keep abreast of their leader, like a regiment of soldiers, to get their dollar and their dinner. To their credit be it recorded, not one went hungry and every girl had her shining piece of silver when the day was done." The following year, the *Kansas City Star* too ran a story about Clark, entitled "Girl Runs Peppermint Farm," remarking: "She made a study of the chemistry of the soil and of the rotation in crops. With this knowledge she made the ordinary crop growing a secondary consideration, and went into the raising of peppermint and the distilling of peppermint oil."[2] The article noted that the peppermint farmer made her own decisions, which did not always conform with the accepted wisdom of

peppermint culture. "Miss Clark has adopted a system of autumn planting, which is contrary to established rules," the article remarked, and the
region's peppermint farmers predicted disaster. "But the innovation was
a success, and is now heartily endorsed by farmers, as the cost of planting
is doubled in the spring, it being hard to get hands at any price to work in
muck soil in the wet season." The article concluded, "Miss Clark employed fifteen women in the weeding season, paying those who worked
shoulder to shoulder with her $1 a day and their dinners. However, she
says women cannot stand the hard work in the peppermint field, and
she has decided to employ men for this work hereafter."

   This last comment attributed to Clark was apparently a bit of fic-
tion, because several years later year in 1912 the *Philadelphia Inquirer* ran
a half-page feature entitled "Wealth for Women on Peppermint Farms."
The article described her success as a peppermint farmer, naming Clark
"the 'Peppermint Queen,' as her achievements in the cultivation of peppermint may well prove an inspiration to other women farmers to spe-
cialize on some one crop and make its cultivation a rousing success."[3]
Peppermint farming, the article claimed, was becoming increasingly
popular with women farmers in Michigan because it was "an ideal occupation for feminine bread winners and one in which the profits [were]
practically assured." The article included a long passage in which Clark
told her own story. She had been fourteen, she said, when she took over
the farm. Friends advised her to sell it and open a boarding house in
town. She had begun with two acres of peppermint and had added two
acres each year. But she rotated fields out of peppermint after five years,
because, she said, "after that time the crop became less remunerative and
my profits faded." She rejected the claim that she had shifted to employ-
ing men: "I employ as many half-grown boys and girls on my farm as I
can get. Mint setting is not heavy work, and besides, the stooping makes
it especially adapted to people with young, supple backs ... weeding
must be done by hand, and for that purpose again I prefer women and
children. They are lighter on their feet and more nimble with their fingers, and, if painstaking, do as clean work, covering more ground than
men." She concluded, "We make a good income and we now have a
high-priced farm, free from debt, but both of us, my mother and I, have
had to work for it. Every year that passes we are thankful that we stuck

to our land and didn't try boarders and the shop." In a period when Progressive reformers were beginning to address the "Country Life Problem" and women were beginning to chafe at the limitations imposed by patriarchal society, Mary Clark's peppermint farm offered a valuable example for women and for farmers eager to take charge of their own rural destinies.[4]

Prices for peppermint oil reached twenty-eight dollars a pound in 1925, encouraging many growers to plant more roots. A farmer named John Irmer in California's San Joaquin Valley planted sixteen acres of peppermint, and over the next few years peppermint fields were planted up and down California's Central Valley.[5] Unfortunately, California peppermint oil never achieved a strong reputation for quality, perhaps due to weediness. The low prices they received for their inferior oil and the high cost of production relative to alternative crops convinced most California growers to abandon peppermint, and by 1939 only a single farm, near Stockton, remained in production.[6]

During the Great Depression of the 1930s, peppermint production held relatively constant, at about a million pounds of peppermint oil annually. Prices averaged in the $1.70s. For many farmers, these prices were painfully close to their cost of production. Many continued producing peppermint oil only because mint was part of a crop rotation plan, or because they were heavily invested in expensive distilling equipment. Luckily for American peppermint farmers, worldwide production declined, and exports increased from about two hundred thousand pounds in 1927 to 386,000 pounds in 1936. By 1939, nearly half the peppermint oil produced in America went to the export market.[7]

In October 1935, the *Oil Paint and Drug Reporter* ran a report from Washington, D.C., that a Michigan representative named Fred Lewis Crawford had asked the Federal Trade Commission to investigate rumors of a monopoly. The report related that the congressman had said he "had been given information indicating that one firm, which he did not name, maintains a monopoly on the purchase of peppermint oil, and that, while the market price is around $2.50 per pound, the farmers are unable to get more than $1.25 per pound in selling their oil."[8] The unnamed firm was of course the A. M. Todd Company, and the real issue soon became clear, when investigators discovered the complaint had originated with growers who were unhappy that company buyers had judged their oil to be inferior, resulting in them being offered lower-than-market prices. In 1936, an internal company memo summarized a conversation between Bert Todd and the FTC investigator. The investigator, Bert said, had asked "whether there was any agreement between Colgate, Beech-nut and Wrigley with respect to prices. I told him that there was not, that we canvassed the situation and recommended to these three firms a price that we thought should be paid for choice oil and to this price was to be added the differential we receive for buying." The investigator was satisfied with Bert's explanation and "stated that so far as he was concerned the investigation was closed."[9]

Congressman Crawford and some of the Michigan growers were unsatisfied with the results of the investigation, so 150 mint farmers met at Saint Johns in April 1936 to form the Michigan Peppermint Growers Association. The group's purpose was "to promote the marketing of peppermint and spearmint grown by members and the collective purchasing for the members of the commodities used in the growing and distilling of peppermint."[10] This mission was similar to that of many agricultural cooperatives. The key difference for the peppermint growers was that, unlike the value of other commodities such as wheat, corn, or milk, which was fairly uniform, the value of essential oils depended on purity and quality, which varied widely. Many producers of high-quality peppermint oil were afraid that cooperative marketing would hurt their chances of selling their oil at a good price. They felt the co-op benefited producers of poor peppermint oil more than it did themselves. The association tried to reassure its members: "Remember, THIS IS NOT A POOL—Oil placed in the association warehouse will be tested, tagged and labeled for you and may be taken out and sold at any time you choose."[11] If that was the case, wondered many farmers, wouldn't the co-op be better off sticking to pools for equipment purchase and education?

As the Great Depression dragged on, peppermint farming remained a viable business in a depressed agricultural sector. In October 1937, the New York Times ran a story entitled "Peppermint Fields Offer Jobs." The article, filed from Kalama, Washington, described peppermint farming in the Columbia River Valley and encouraged workers to come west for jobs or to try peppermint farming on their own.[12] In 1938,

Bert Todd visited London, where the British *Manufacturing Perfumer* published a notice announcing his arrival and mentioned that Great Britain had purchased 185,323 pounds of peppermint oil exported from America, most of it from the A. M. Todd Company.[13] The outbreak of World War II in late 1939 had a substantial effect on essential oil markets. Uncertainty drove peppermint oil prices up to about four dollars a pound.[14] The Japanese attack on Pearl Harbor drove prices higher still. In December 1941, the *Wall Street Journal* announced: "Peppermint Oil Prices Jump $1 a Pound Here." The article explained that "dealers attributed the sharp increase to the cessation of menthol imports from Japan, the principal source of supply." The article also commented, "Some dealers believe the increase represented a purely speculative move on the part of the growers. They seem to be holding stocks, perhaps remembering the first World War when peppermint oil values advanced from $3.25 a pound to $28."[15] A few months later, a March 1942 *Wall Street Journal* article reported that due to the absence of Japanese mint oil in the market, the Vick Chemical Company had placed an order with "an essential oil refiner" for menthol extracted from peppermint oil.[16] Since Albert Todd had patented the process for extracting menthol crystals, it is likely the A. M. Todd Company was the source of Vick's wartime menthol.

Once the United States entered the war, peppermint oil was requisitioned for military use and for export in the Lend-Lease program. Lend-Lease allowed the United States to transfer arms and other defense materials to Britain without the immediate payment required under the Neutrality Act of 1939, and peppermint oil was designated a war material. Chewing gum and toothpaste were both components of the soldiers' rations, so there was substantial allied demand even before the United States entered the war in December 1941. Peppermint oil also came under the control of the Office of Price Administration (O.P.A.), which instituted price ceilings, and the War Food Administration (W.F.A.), which set quotas. When prices rose to more than seven dollars a pound in early 1942, the O.P.A. set price ceilings for dealers of six dollars a pound for natural oil and $6.35 for redistilled oil.[17] The price ceiling for growers was fifty cents less, which caused some dealers to complain that their profit margins were too thin. The Todd Company had already become well accustomed to buying peppermint oil for customers such as Wrigley on a cost-plus-commission basis, so the price controls were not that unusual, and the company was able to sell its refined Crystal White oil at the higher price point. In 1943, the British government requested two hundred thousand pounds of peppermint oil under the Lend-Lease program. The W.F.A. issued a Food Distribution Order in September 1943, freezing the entire national supply of peppermint oil. The W.F.A. stated it had "acted to assure the equitable distribution of oil of peppermint—an essential oil now limited in supply but important in both food preparations and pharmaceutical uses—by reserving all such oil for Government action."[18] In April 1944 the O.P.A. raised the price ceiling to $7.50 for natural peppermint oil and to $8.05 for redistilled oil.[19] While the price delta between the growers' ceiling and the dealers' remained fifty cents, the premium for redistilled oil increased, benefiting dealers like the A. M. Todd Company who were actually adding value by refining their peppermint oil. And the higher price allowed to growers encouraged new farmers to try their hand at raising peppermint.

In 1950, the journal *Economic Botany* published an article entitled "Domestic Production of Essential Oils of Peppermint and Spearmint"; U.S. production had grown to an average of 1,410,000 pounds annually from 1940 to 1950.[20] "The production of peppermint and spearmint oils in the United States is second only to that of turpentine in the volatile-oil industry," the article reported, of which "five percent is employed in pharmaceutical preparations, 15 percent in miscellaneous flavorings, 15 percent in dentifrices, 15 percent in confections and about 50 percent in chewing gum." The article identified that three varieties of peppermint, "called 'black,' 'American,' and 'white,' are reported to occur in commercial areas. The black mint, sometimes called 'Black Mitcham' or 'English mint,' is by far the most extensively grown of the three, although some American mint can be found in certain areas. It is doubtful that any of the white mint, sometimes called 'white Mitcham,' is now grown commercially."[21] American mint was in the process of being phased out in favor of the higher-yielding, hardier black. The white mint, which was "reputed to produce a higher grade oil," was not grown, "because it is not hardy and yields less oil."

Academic interest in peppermint production accelerated in the late 1940s. In 1947, two Mint Research Conferences were sponsored by

the Beech-Nut Company, which led to the establishment of a permanent program of assistantships and fellowships for mint research at
Purdue University, Michigan State, Oregon State, Washington State,
Rochester University, and the University of Washington.[22] Much of the
early research focused on combating pests and Verticillium wilt, which
had been discovered in 1924 on Albert Todd's Mentha plantation. The
wilt was caused by a soil fungus, *Verticillium dahliae*, that caused peppermint plants to dwarf, twist, curl, blanch, and lose leaves. Cankers
grew on roots, making them less likely to winter successfully, and of
course the leaf damage reduced yields tremendously. There was no
known chemical control for the fungus, and once introduced to fields
on infected roots, it persisted in soils indefinitely.[23] In the early 1940s,
Michigan acreage began to decrease steadily, as farmers planted infected
fields with crops unaffected by the wilt and as new, uncultivated mucklands became scarcer.

By the early 1950s, the problem of Verticillium wilt had become
severe in both Michigan and Indiana.[24] Although many farmers were
turning away from peppermint to grow other muckland crops like cel-
ery, some were reluctant to write off their investments in specialized
tools and distilleries. But in spite of the persistence of some Midwestern
farmers, the Pacific Northwest region where Oliver Todd had introduced
peppermint culture took over as the region of greatest production, with
seventy-five hundred acres in Washington and fifteen thousand in Oregon planted with peppermint. And the western region's average yield
of 58.5 pounds of oil per acre was more than double the average of
26.25 pounds produced in the peppermint fields of Michigan and Indiana. As a result, in 1952 western production was more than twice that of
the Midwest.

Higher western peppermint oil yields were partly attributable to
newer plantings, more technology, and freedom from wilt. Another
western innovation was the use of geese to weed peppermint fields. The
geese ate grass and weeds but left peppermint plants alone. A Washington goose-grower's guide remarked, "It has been estimated that twelve
young weeder geese, properly managed, will replace the work of one
man and hoe."[25] The guide outlined the savings of keeping geese versus
hiring labor and reminded farmers that at the end of the growing season

"returns from marketing the geese should be deducted which will make the actual cost far less." But these innovations did not tell the whole story. Oil yields had been higher in the Pacific Northwest ever since Oliver Todd had first planted peppermint there in 1912. In the 1940s, studies by agricultural experiment stations found that day-length, or "photoperiod," was a critical factor in the oil production of peppermint plants. Researchers discovered that peppermint is a long-day plant that produces its greatest yields in geographical zones with a photoperiod of sixteen to eighteen hours. This high-light requirement suggested much higher ideal latitudes for peppermint growing than those of the mucklands of Michigan and Indiana, but winter temperatures and the Canadian border were a barrier to an ideal situation.[26] Although it was also south of the ideal location, the Pacific Northwest was several degrees north of the Midwestern mucklands, the climate was milder, and western fields received an hour extra of sunlight, on average. In 1960, Purdue researcher N. K. Ellis observed that "little oil will be produced in a 14 hour day length, and for economical production, the day length must approach 16 hours." Ellis added, "This is still not the whole story, for there is a great difference in the intensity of sunlight between the two areas with the midwest running from 450 to 550 langley units . . . in Indiana, while eastern Washington may get as much as 700 langley units."[27] He concluded that peppermint plants metabolized nitrogen into a variety of different compounds, depending on day length. Some of the compounds produced in western peppermint were liabilities, but the West's greater yields were impossible to ignore. As a result of the Pacific Northwest's solar advantage, in 1955 there were 7,005.5 acres of peppermint planted in Michigan and 9,659 acres in Indiana, while Washington farmers planted 7,761 acres of higher-yielding peppermint, and Oregon had 13,410 acres. In contrast, Michigan farmers planted 7,906.5 acres of spearmint, which was less affected by day length and was immune to Verticillium wilt, and Indiana had 6,976; Washington had 1,599 and Oregon only twenty-five acres of spearmint. And when another study suggested that cooler nighttime temperatures encouraged oil development in peppermint plants, the A. M. Todd Company began a search for new producing areas that led to the development of the Madras district of central Oregon.[28]

In the late 1950s and early 1960s, the Midwest produced an average of 467,000 pounds of peppermint oil annually. Indiana led in production, followed by Wisconsin, where fields planted during the price rise of World War II produced more than double the oil distilled in Michigan. Oregon and Washington together produced 1,996,000 pounds of peppermint oil, with Washington's total slightly ahead of Oregon's.[29] A new development that helped widen the West's lead was portable irrigation equipment, which not only increased yields but also helped mitigate the effects of Verticillium wilt when it struck. By 1959, supplemental irrigation was being used on nearly all of Oregon's peppermint farms but on nearly none of Indiana's.[30] In 1959, domestic peppermint oil production reached 2,388,000 pounds, and Indiana peppermint acreage diminished to forty-seven hundred acres.[31]

A mint industry research fund was established in the late 1950s, financed by users such as Wrigley, Beech-Nut, Colgate-Palmolive, American Chicle, and Proctor and Gamble and by dealers such as the A. M. Todd Company and William Leman and Company.[32] The fund sponsored research programs focusing on Verticillium wilt, insect and weed control, and plant breeding. In his review of peppermint and spearmint production, N. K. Ellis had observed: "*Mentha piperita* L. 'Mitchum' [*sic*] is thought to be a naturally occurring hybrid. It has been postulated that ... *M. piperita* is really a three way cross involving *M. aquatica*, *M. sylvestris*, and *M. rotundifolia*. I might say, however, that although considerable work has been done in breeding for mint resistance to the current diseases, geneticists have not been able to reconstruct this cross and come up with the quality oil which comes from this naturally-occurring hybrid."[33] Developing new peppermint varieties is difficult because commercial peppermint is a hybrid, which renders the plant sterile. Traditional crossbreeding can only be done using a plant's seeds, which in the case of peppermint are not viable. Michigan State University's plant breeder Ray Nelson reported that in one sample of eighteen thousand peppermint flower spikes he recovered 2,888,000 ovules containing just fifty-five seeds, and only five of them germinated.[34] When hybrids do set seeds, the resulting plants are usually not "true" to the traits of the parents. Peppermint plants resulting from Nelson's and Todd employee Merritt J. Murray's breeding experiments differed from their parent plants and represented mutations that occasionally introduced subtle new flavors and scents. Murray, who worked as a plant breeder for the A. M. Todd Company from 1947 to the late 1970s, recognized the possibility that these hybrids could become valuable in the aromatic trade, rather than in the company's traditional flavoring business.

In addition to developing hybrids with novel flavor profiles, Murray spent decades working on the problem of resistance to Verticillium wilt. In the 1960s he took tens of thousands of peppermint roots to Brookhaven Laboratory in New York, where he had the roots irradiated. Although mutation by radiation was a hot research topic at the time, progress was slow. Nearly fifty years after Murray's experiments began, only two successful cultivars, Todd's Mitcham and Murray Mitcham, have been developed using irradiation breeding. While these hybrids have become commercially successful, some farmers have resisted adopting the new cultivars due to unfavorable mutations. More recently, researchers have taken advantage of new scientific techniques to explore direct genetic manipulation through in vitro shoot regeneration.[35]

By the mid-1960s, Midwestern peppermint oil production had decreased to an average of 403,000 pounds annually. Indiana led the region, followed by Wisconsin, which produced three times as much oil as Michigan. The West produced 2,167,000 pounds of peppermint oil, with Washington's total slightly ahead of Oregon's.[36] Agricultural technology continued to improve, and most peppermint farmers began using combines that cut the mint hay and deposited it in hoppers with built-in distilling capabilities. Rather than loading and unloading mint hay into tanks connected to steam boilers, the new harvest hoppers could be directly connected to a steam source and a condenser. Spent hay could then be driven back to the fields and spread as mulch or dried and used as livestock fodder.

A 1972 U.S. Department of Agriculture pamphlet on American mint oil and European markets found that due to significant increases in Wisconsin peppermint production, Midwestern oil production had increased to 598,000 pounds, with Wisconsin dominating the region. Washington peppermint production was down substantially, and Oregon produced 75 percent of the West's 2,798,000 pounds of oil.[37] Washington farmers had replaced a great deal of their peppermint plantings with spearmint and produced 80 percent of the national total of just under a million pounds. Reflecting on foreign markets, the article also mentioned that only sixty to eighty acres of mint were grown in England.[38] The practical elimination of mint culture in Britain was probably due to high land costs associated with the encroachment of Greater London onto Mitcham.

Reflecting new discoveries in the science of volatile oils, the article discussed the chemical properties of the peppermint oil that was exported. A large percentage of oil exports were of a variety called Yakima oil, for the region in Washington State where it was produced. The soil, water, and sunlight conditions there produced a biting flavor profile disliked by the chewing gum and toothpaste industries. "However, the U.S. confectionary industry reportedly uses this oil because of its strong flavor burst, necessary in candy products."[39] Yakima oil was described as containing 52.5 percent total menthol, 8.5 percent menthylesters, 19.9 percent menthone, and 8.6 percent menthofuran. This was a higher-than-average percentage of menthofuran, which imparts a musty flavor and is regarded as one of the least desirable components of peppermint oil. The ability to separate these components using fractional distillation techniques pioneered by Albert Todd allowed dealers like the A. M. Todd Company to customize their flavor profiles to client needs, blend the oils of different regions, and deliver a standardized product to their customers regardless of annual fluctuations in the peppermint crop.

The Todd Company's success tailoring its services to the needs of its clients frustrated some of its rivals. In the late 1980s, the company found itself at the center of an antitrust lawsuit alleging that the company had conspired with major clients like Wrigley and Colgate to fix prices and restrain trade. An investigation was conducted, based largely on an inaccurate portrayal of the A. M. Todd Company presented in historical geographer James E. Landing's 1969 book, *American Essence: A History of the Peppermint and Spearmint Industry in the United States.* The book, which ironically had been published by the Kalamazoo Public Museum with a grant from the Todd Foundation, used imprecise business terminology that allowed the nature of the A. M. Todd Company's relationship with Wrigley and other large companies to be mischaracterized in the lawsuit. In the end, the charges were proven to be as baseless as the suspicions that had led to the Crawford Federal Trade Commission investigation of 1936. But the episode was not without its detrimental effects. Winship Todd, the company president who had defended the family business during the investigation and lawsuit, recalled the period as the worst five years of his life.[40] And many of the documents and archival materials that Landing was given access to in researching *American Essence* were lost during the investigation or discarded in frustration during its aftermath.

Peppermint acreage in the United States peaked in 1995 at 149,000 acres. Over the next ten years, acreage decreased to less than eighty thousand acres in 2005.[41] Meanwhile peppermint acreage in India, where land and labor are significantly less expensive, doubled over the same period. U.S. production shifted from Oregon to south-central Washington and western Idaho, where yields were higher. To offset the decreasing acreage, peppermint oil yields have increased from an average of about sixty pounds per acre in the 1960s to nearly 110 pounds per acre today. The A. M. Todd Company, still the world leader in peppermint and spearmint oils, opened a production center in Mumbai. Although Indian peppermint is grown at latitudes around 28° north, the lower oil yields and quality differences of Indian peppermint are mitigated by dramatically lower production costs.

At the turn of the twenty-first century, the A. M. Todd Company found itself under pressure from cost-conscious customers, which encouraged them to seek new markets for flavoring products. A 1999 article in *Business Economics* featuring the company observed, "Plant-derived chemicals . . . represent a vast range of materials of limitless variety and containing a richness and complexity that is nearly impossible to duplicate artificially."[42] The author noted that while the "complexity of composition gave essential oils a significant advantage over synthetics . . . the science of analyzing and identifying the many constituents of essential oils has advanced greatly in recent years, allowing producers to tailor synthetic products to capture many of the subtleties of natural materials." The cost savings associated with these synthetic alternatives drove producers of natural flavoring and aromatic agents like the A. M. Todd Company to appeal to processors of natural foods. The article concluded that "consumer preference for natural ingredients has created an onslaught of products boasting that they contain plant-derived chemicals." In the mid-1990s, the company formed A. M. Todd Botanical Therapeutics, which the CEO at the time, Henry Todd Sr., said "applies our expertise in botanical science and extraction techniques to natural nutraceutical ingredients."[43] Todd explained, "Mint includes more than 300 chemical compounds, and our state-of-the-art flavor research and blending facility in Kalamazoo can isolate specific molecules that deliver just the flavor components that a customer needs for a proprietary application." In 2005 the director of research and development and the chief flavorist of the Todd Company wrote an article for *Perfumer and Flavorist* magazine discussing the business and technical challenges of their industry. The authors observed, "While peppermint remains one of the flavor industry's most perennially popular ingredients, businesses that traditionally rely on peppermint oils are under pressure to reduce raw material costs."[44] They suggested their company's value lay in its ability to navigate the complexity of producing a consistent product using variable natural inputs. For example, they said, "the ideal time to harvest mint is when oil yield and oil quality are at their peak. Because these two criteria rarely coincide, compromise is necessary. This is especially true for peppermint, whose oil quality varies considerably more than spearmint as harvest time approaches."[45]

While the A. M. Todd Company's approach continued to rely on harnessing the subtle flavor differences of peppermint oils from different regions, blending oils, and reducing or eliminating chemical compounds associated with unwanted flavors in the manufacturing process, others have attempted brute-force solutions to the problems of yield and oil quality. For example, frustrated over the difficulty presented by peppermint's sterility, some scientists have explored metabolic engineering as a technique for improving both peppermint oil yield and oil composition. In 2011 a team of scientists wrote in the *Proceedings of the National Academy of Sciences,* "Encouraged by the results obtained with greenhouse-grown transgenics, we performed field trials to evaluate the performance of these lines under commercial growth conditions in the Yakima River Valley growing area of Washington State."[46] The team reported, "Our transgenic plants did not show any obvious physical phenotypic differences (leaf and stem morphology) compared to wild-type controls," but "highly significant yield enhancements over wild-type controls were determined" for several genetically modified varieties. The authors also stated that because regulatory agencies in several countries require the labeling of transgenic products, they planned to add a flavorless chemical marker to make the oil produced from their transgenic plants easily recognizable. To date, experiments of this type have not produced marketable products.

In the same way that the subtle approach of the A. M. Todd Company to flavor production has been bypassed by impatient scientists with a new arsenal of biochemical tools, the industry the family company existed in has been swallowed up by billion-dollar global conglomerates. A 2016 "Fragrance and Flavor Leaderboard" listed a handful of multinational corporations that dominate a $26.5 billion market. Businesses such as the A. M. Todd Company that despite operating internationally occupied relatively narrow niches in that market have mostly been swallowed by the global conglomerates.[47] WILD Flavors, which acquired the A. M. Todd Company in 2011, was itself acquired by Archer Daniels Midland in October 2014. A.D.M. is a global producer of food ingredients, animal feeds and feed ingredients, biofuels, and other agriculture-related products with a market capitalization of $25.61 billion. The WILD website declared that with the acquisition of the A. M. Todd Company, WILD became "the most vertically-integrated natural mint ingredient and flavor provider to the chewing gum, confection, and oral care industries."[48] WILD also highlighted its new role as "a technological leader in the development of new, natural, non-GMO mint cultivars used to create a wide variety of flavor solutions." Building on the A. M. Todd Company legacy, WILD pledged to provide a sustainable supply of high-quality natural mint ingredients and highlighted sustainability and eco-efficiency as corporate goals. It will be interesting to see if the company can achieve those ideals as a subsidiary of one of the world's largest agri-business conglomerates.

The legacies of the peppermint kings in the regions where they lived and worked are varied. In Ashfield, where the Ranneys first grew and distilled peppermint oil in significant commercial quantities, the story of peppermint is the most remote in time. Peppermint plants still grow wild in Ashfield, however, and residents transplant the aromatic plants into their gardens. Some remember there was once a thriving business in the town's distant past. The house George Ranney built with the help of his sons who then moved to western New York and Michigan still stands, as does the large, rambling farmhouse Samuel Ranney built. George's house is now home to a regional theater company that in 2017 produced an original show about the Ranneys, Dr. Knowlton, peppermint, and peddlers.

In Phelps, New York, where Hiram and Leman Hotchkiss began their peppermint oil business and where Leman remained, stories of the peppermint business have faded. The local historical society has a file on Leman Hotchkiss, which includes a set of very colorful labels from Leman's peppermint oil and other essential oil bottles. Leman is regarded as a solid, wealthy citizen who is better remembered for owning the downtown hotel than for his peppermint oil business—although there are vaguely recalled stories of a fire in his home, where he occasionally stored peppermint oil. Dimly remembered images of blue flames shooting into night air and of the lingering smell of peppermint following the incident are all that remain.

In Lyons, New York, where Hiram Hotchkiss cut a decidedly large figure, the peppermint oil business is remembered in exaggerated terms. Following the outline of the propaganda Hiram put out in his own lifetime, which his descendants amplified, the history of the peppermint oil business focuses on his heroic achievements in single-handedly creating an industry. Lyons still hosts an annual Peppermint Days Festival, and a group of dedicated Hotchkiss fans have placed Hiram's old headquarters on the National Register of Historic Places. A campaign to turn the building into a museum seems always on the verge of raising enough money.

The fictitious account of Hiram's exploits is still available in a brochure reprinted for the part-time museum and is repeated on websites, Facebook pages, and murals painted in the neighborhood of the old Peppermint Depot along the Erie Canal. The claim that there was no domestic market for peppermint oil and that the quality of American peppermint oil was too poor to compete in a large international market dominated by oil from Mitcham is countered by the fact of a thriving domestic industry centered in Ashfield prior to Hotchkiss's entrance. But even in the absence of the Ranneys and their peddlers, without a market the area farmers would never have gone to the trouble and expense of growing and distilling the thousand pounds of peppermint oil they purportedly traded to Hotchkiss. Although clearly illogical, however, this story is strictly adhered to by peppermint enthusiasts in the region today. When graduate student Jenny Ann Mikulski interviewed Anne Hotchkiss, the last surviving executive of the family-owned H. G. Hotchkiss Essential Oil Company, in 2005 for her Master's Thesis in Cornell University's Landscape Architecture program, Anne Hotchkiss retold the same story.[49] When pressed by Mikulski regarding "complications with the authorship of cultural landscapes," the great-granddaughter of Hiram Hotchkiss and sole inheritor of the business insisted that "her stories and decisions have ensured that the Hotchkiss company and, by extension, the peppermint industry of Lyons, will be remembered," and she expressed determination that those would be the only stories preserved. Alarmed by the possibility the myth might be undermined, Hotchkiss ultimately refused to give Mikulski permission to publish or share the interview.[50] The Hotchkiss brand name is still used by Essex Labs, which claims to have acquired "the formulation and rights to Hotchkiss from Wm. Leman Company."[51] It is a mystery what the formulation could mean beyond a trade name, when none of the Wayne County or even Michigan peppermint oil that went into Hotchkiss's product is now available and when there is no remaining original Hotchkiss peppermint oil to provide a flavor profile.

In Kalamazoo, where a subsidiary of Archer Daniels Midland called the A. M. Todd Company still employs people who process and market peppermint oil, history blends with the present. The headquarters built in 1928 still stands, and the rich aroma of nearly a century of peppermint oil hangs in every room. Old men remember their service as managers and executives of the company that was once run exclusively by Todd family members. They tell stories of fighting to ensure the purity of their peppermint oil against the inroads of inexpensive but hated *arvensis* oil and reminisce about contract meetings with Wrigley executives in Chicago, after which they would drive into the city's western suburbs on their way home before calling in from a payphone, to prevent being overheard, and announce they had closed the deal and disclose quantities, prices, and terms. But many of the company's records were lost or destroyed after the traumatic lawsuit precipitated by the history the Todd Foundation had sponsored. And many of the images of Albert Todd and his early business photographed from the remaining records are impossible to display, since the legal department of the conglomerate that now owns the company can't be bothered to grant permission to use them.

Albert Todd's legacy, however, persists in the art that still hangs for the inspiration of students at Kalamazoo College and Western Michigan University. And Todd's voice might even be faintly heard in contemporary American politics. Todd, who castigated his congressional colleagues over the fact that "*every railroad company investigated knowingly falsified its accounts*" would surely have something similarly acerbic to say about the scandals and concentration of wealth plaguing America today.

Epilogue

The peppermint oil industry developed under the leadership of three families of peppermint kings that were each prominent during three very distinct moments in the economic history of the United States. The Ranney family dominated the peppermint oil business during the age of peddlers that corresponded with the period typically known as the market transition. The Hotchkiss brothers operated in a changing marketplace where they were pioneers of wholesale distribution and branding, challenged by the changing world of business finance triggered by the recession following the Panic of 1857 and the Civil War. Albert May Todd became peppermint king at a time when historians have described American agriculture as reaching a critical juncture when farmers' undifferentiated products lacked market power, especially relative to highly capitalized food processors, prompting a Populist reaction. The experiences of each of these families adds valuable texture and nuance to commonly held historical interpretations of rural life during these times.

To review the story briefly, we began with the earliest commerce in peppermint oil in Colonial America and peppermint's culture and distilling in the early republic. From its earliest introduction, peppermint was an inherently commercial crop. There was no gradual evolution from a subsistence-surplus phase of production to a peppermint oil

business, because peppermint had no food or fodder value in a subsistence economy. From its earliest days, peppermint oil has always been
an item of commerce. The farmers who grew and distilled peppermint
deliberately involved themselves in markets, usually distant markets.
Rural people involved with peppermint farming and distilling did not
live in a pre-commercial state of grace until affected by a market transition imposed from without. The first peppermint growers like the Ranneys, Burnetts, and Vandermarks were deeply embedded in widespread
commercial networks. Their commercial activities supplying peddlers
and transporting peppermint oil from producing areas to centers of distribution or consumption were more widespread and happened much
earlier than many historians have realized.

Although advertising is often depicted as a phenomenon of the
late nineteenth and early twentieth centuries, peppermint oil and essence were advertised heavily in newspapers throughout the British
North American colonies and the early United States. The earliest advertisements were for imported peppermint preparations, but very
quickly domestic peppermint producers began to compete with their
British counterparts. Because peppermint oil was an important component of the materia medica used in many medical preparations, it was
ubiquitous, indeed required, at any well-stocked apothecary shop. In
regions such as the American South where peppermint could not be
grown effectively, peppermint oil was imported first from England and
later from domestic sources of supply such as western Massachusetts
and later western New York. Rural consumers of peppermint oil in non-
producing regions were drawn into networks of commerce and medical
information, especially when peppermint essence became widely prescribed not only by physicians but also in popular home-health manuals
and among alternative medicine practitioners like the followers of herbalist Samuel Thomson.

The social and religious struggles of rural people in remote Ashfield,
Massachusetts, became regionally and nationally important when controversy between the town's established church and its Baptist minority
escalated all the way to the Privy Council of King George III. The use of
church membership and taxation as a weapon of class-based battles between poor local Baptists and their prosperous (and often out-of-town)

opponents suggests that religious histories of the period might consider both class and urban-rural differences in their interpretations. The resumption of Ashfield's social-religious strife in the 1830s illustrates that the distribution of secular ideology during the Second Great Awakening was more complicated than is generally understood. Although historians have depicted the evangelical movements of the 1830s as being largely attempts at social control, the "infidel" or secularist challenge is usually considered an urban intellectual phenomenon. Ashfield's physician, Dr. Charles Knowlton, was a rural intellectual. Samuel Ranney, who both introduced peppermint to Ashfield and helped end its culture there, was a remarkably insightful farmer who had absorbed many of the main ideas explored by Ashfield's materialist doctor. Neither of Ashfield's notorious infidels were urban intellectuals. And yet Knowlton wrote America's first birth control manual, and Ranney changed the fortunes of the entire region when he helped shift peppermint production to western New York.

And even after Samuel Ranney's departure rural Ashfield remained relevant on a much wider scale. Essence peddlers from Ashfield brought news, ideas, and consumer culture to the remotest farms and villages, connecting rural Americans both to commerce and to American culture and politics in ways that have not been fully appreciated. Hundreds of local men carried trunks of goods and baskets of essences not only to remote farmsteads in their region but south into the slaveholding states and west onto the frontier as well. Social and economic historians have often gauged the transition to capitalism in rural areas by the extent of their production for the urban market. Peddlers made rural populations consumers as well as producers, and in the most remote areas with the least cash-based economies even a small amount of trade with itinerant peddlers was of great cultural significance. And in addition to bringing goods, peddlers connected their customers with networks of news and ideas in an interactive, face-to-face way that could not be achieved by newspapers, pamphlets, and books. Ashfield peddler William Sanderson carried *Slavery as It Is* with his wares and discussed its contents with his customers. The peddlers' supplier, Jasper Bement, took time out of a business trip to attend rallies and speak on behalf of the Liberty Party on his way to Detroit. Ashfield's Yankee peddlers carried both commerce and their politics with them wherever they went. And the men who supplied them, Henry

Ranney and Jasper Bement, both represented their town in the state legislature in Boston.

Although historians of western migration have largely put aside the idea first proposed by Frederick Jackson Turner that the frontier experience reshaped society by erasing people's ties with home and family, the degree to which families such as the Ranneys maintained their connection has not been adequately appreciated. The Ranney brothers kept up a vigorous correspondence from Massachusetts to western New York, Michigan, Arkansas, Oklahoma, and the goldfields of the West that spanned six decades. They visited each other regularly, and their aged mother traveled extensively to divide her time between the homes of her children. And they supported each other financially as well as emotionally, loaning money and doing business across the miles. Historians often characterize this period as one when (especially urban) business transitioned to impersonal association and anonymous, one-off, transactional exchanges, but the Ranneys built their rural business on kinship networks featuring obligation, morality, and long-term commitment. The Ranney migration into the Yankee West suggests not only the cultural continuity asserted by recent historians but also a degree of connectedness even these historians have not depicted. But the Ranneys were not a uniquely close family. The story of the settlement of Phelps, New York, shows that migrants from Conway and Ashfield, Massachusetts, migrated serially and often revisited their old homes. One migrant walked back to Massachusetts to get married, and when his wife died went back again for another. And when peddler Archibald Burnett decided to live in Phelps and marry a local girl, his brother called him back to Ashfield to share the secret of peppermint.

While some rural businessmen such as Ira Cary moved to New York City in order to become successful, even Dows and Cary's success was based on transporting rural products to city consumers. This is consistent with the standard historical depiction of relatively undifferentiated agricultural goods and raw materials flowing into processing and consuming centers, frequently enriching the centers at the expense of the peripheries. The story of Hiram and Leman Hotchkiss's rise to peppermint kings challenges the standard trajectory. Peppermint oil was processed on the farm and was highly differentiated based on quality, and the Hotchkiss brothers managed to identify themselves as reliable judges of quality, create brands, and prevent the concentration of market power in the center. After their initial success showing their oil at international expositions, the Hotchkisses shifted from growing and distilling their own peppermint oil to promoting their brand. Although histories of branding tend to focus on modernity and even postmodernity, the campaign of the Hotchkiss brothers to brand their products was one of the earliest in America. Rather than raising their product above a generic mass market that barely existed yet, Hiram aimed at making his peppermint oil the rival of English oil from Mitcham. A merchant's son from a rural village in western New York, he rightly considered himself a formidable competitor in an international market.

In spite of his rural origin in the commercial and financial periphery, Hiram conducted business by his own rules. He expected his commission agents in New York City to advance money on his peppermint oil shipments, even though the oil market was substantially different from the flour market to which they were accustomed. Hiram expected foreign buyers to consider his peppermint oil equivalent to Mitcham oil because he said so. He expected his creditors to renew his notes indefinitely. He expected people to use his elaborately engraved banknotes and even his promissory notes as money. And in an ironic perversion of the kinship networks the Ranney family business had been based on, he expected his relatives to prostrate themselves on his behalf.

Hiram's relationship with finance and banking offers a rural perspective that is lacking in histories of banking and business finance. Early in his career, Hiram took advantage of his local bank's failure by speculating in mortgages and promissory notes he purchased from the bankruptcy receiver for pennies on the dollar. Contrary to the conclusions of historians who describe a growing moralism in public attitudes toward debt and credit after the Panic of 1837, Hiram learned that both value and obligation were subjective and open to negotiation. And contrary to prevailing contemporary belief that New York City was the center of finance, he believed he was the center. Once his flour or peppermint oil was loaded onto canal flatboats, he considered the transaction complete. He had created value—it was someone else's job to make sure the flour or peppermint oil was sold when it arrived in the city.

The history of American banking is largely told from an urban perspective, partly because after the Civil War control of the U.S. banking system shifted to New York City. But the Hotchkiss brothers' experiences as bankers under New York's antebellum state banking laws suggest that the dominance of central banks was not inevitable and that rural bankers had interests and objectives that were not identical to those of the urban bankers who would dominate national banking. Hiram used his Peppermint Bank irresponsibly, primarily as a source of funds for his peppermint oil business. His brother Leman ran his bank on much sounder financial principles and focused on exchange and other business services that survived the elimination of state banknotes in 1866. Thaddeus Hotchkiss succeeded his father at the bank in 1869, and William B. Hotchkiss ran it until the late 1870s. We can only speculate how our present financial system would be different had rural regional bankers retained the ability to issue currency backed by the economic activity of their regions and write mortgages on real estate, but it is clear that the interests of those rural bankers were not considered when the banking legislation of the 1860s was passed. Historians might find that rural bankers' reactions to the changes enacted during the Civil War shed light on subsequent rural movements for free silver and subtreasuries, and resistance to the money power later in the nineteenth century.

Although historians have stressed the importance of social networks in regulating business behavior, especially in the mid-nineteenth century in western New York's burned-over district, Hiram was a strong counterexample to the portrayal of an orderly, self-regulating community of entrepreneurs. He was a monomaniacal autocrat who put his own desires before the interests of business partners, friends, and family. He regularly defaulted on debts, often leaving close relatives, including his brother, his wife, and his children, to suffer the consequences. He fled to New York City to avoid his creditors, spending entire seasons living in posh hotels and speculating in the stock market rather than paying his business and family bills. Although he tried to portray himself as a jovial country gentleman (which is how his descendants too tried to present him), Hiram illustrated the capacity of rural people to operate in business with an amorality considered shocking even by city standards.

Like the Hotchkiss brothers, Albert May Todd built a brand for his peppermint oil and festooned his labels with images of the awards his products won in national and international expositions. Unlike the Hotchkisses, however, Todd approached peppermint growing and distilling with the rigor of a scientist. After reading classics at a rural union school, he attended Northwestern University to study chemistry. When he began his peppermint oil business, he identified himself as a manufacturing chemist. He corresponded with other scientists about the chemical properties of peppermint oil and published technical letters to his customers describing the tests they could use to determine the purity and quality of his (and others') peppermint oil. He was also keenly interested in agricultural improvement. He built extensive company farms complete with their own experiment stations and concerned himself with the welfare of his rural employees decades before urban Progressives developed an interest in country life. And although Progressive reformers ultimately failed to resist the dehumanizing tendency of corporate agriculture, he remained firmly focused on the social and cultural quality of life he provided for workers at his large farms.

Culture and art were a significant priority from Albert Todd's earliest days. Introduced to the classics by his well-educated mother, Todd left college after a year to travel in England and Europe. During this trip he began an art collection and a library that he expanded throughout his life and shared with his employees and with his neighbors by loaning and donating artworks for public display. He believed that art uplifted rural people and gave them hope. And unlike famous urban industrialists and bankers who became art patrons and public benefactors after death, he did not keep his collection private for his own enjoyment but gave away hundreds of artworks during his lifetime.

Todd entered politics at a time when many rural people were Populists. He organized a fusion of Democrats, Populists, Free Silverites, and Prohibitionists to win a congressional seat in a Michigan district that had not elected a Democrat since before the Civil War. He promoted policies identical with the People's Party platform, far from the South and West, usually considered the stronghold of Populism. In Congress, he drew on his experience as a rural businessman when he opposed railroads, plutocracy, and the control of the economy by autocratic Wall

Street bankers. He also drew on observations of European political economy made on several research trips. He advocated national ownership of natural monopolies such as railroads and telecommunications and expanded his focus to municipal ownership of public utilities when he founded the Public Ownership League of America. He gave generously to support radical causes such as the Rand School of Social Science in New York City. And he built a network of allies that included local and regional activists as well as national figures like Jane Addams, Caroline Rand, and Eugene V. Debs. Unlike rural Populists who are often remembered as being traumatized by modernity, Todd was a successful businessman who was comfortable with technical and financial complexity. And unlike urban Progressives, often depicted as technocrats who approached issues from the top down, he advocated democratic reforms that would put more power in the hands of regular people.

It is possible that Albert Todd was entirely unique in developing a perspective that did not fit easily into the mold of a Midwestern agricultural businessman. It is similarly possible that the interests and concerns of the Hotchkiss brothers and the activities of the Ranneys were so far from typical that they contribute little to our understanding of their times and regions. But perhaps the history of these peppermint kings shines a light on less well-known countercurrents in the general flow of history: eddies in the stream that give the river its distinct character. The peppermint oil industry itself contrasted with most agricultural businesses described by historians, in the highly differentiated nature of its product and the decentralization that resulted when control was maintained near the point of production. The personalities and stories of the industry's principal actors seem to suggest a richer and more complicated rural history than is currently appreciated. If historians look more closely at the stories of rural Americans, they may well be rewarded with a more nuanced and comprehensive view of American history. They may also discover a new treasury of interesting and compelling stories to tell.

Finally, the common element informing the attitudes and actions of the peppermint kings was their rurality. Although their individual responses to rural life and rural business differed, the peppermint kings are connected by their rurality in ways they are not unified by traditional categories such as politics, culture, ideology, and religion. Although they

sometimes battled urban powers, they did not consider themselves characters in a grand narrative organized around urban centers. The agency
they displayed as agricultural businessmen pursuing their own goals for
their own reasons confutes the widely accepted depiction of peripheral
agriculturalists increasingly dominated by centralized economic power.

American rural history has undergone somewhat of a renaissance
since Robert Swierenga described the field in 1981 as an "orphan child" of
the new social history.[1] Rural histories such as David Danbom's *Born in
the Country* have taken issue with the dismissal of rural people and their
concerns by consensus historians who had little interest in the countryside once America "moved to the city."[2] As Danbom noted in a 2010 article, "Nowadays, rural people are not much different from the rest of
us."[3] While the accuracy of Danbom's assessment is evident in the many
similarities of contemporary rural and urban life caused by technology
and social change, these very similarities hide wide differences in experience of Americans of earlier generations. The story of the peppermint
kings contributes to a more detailed, nuanced understanding of the life
experiences, interests, and attitudes of rural people and their communities. The Ranneys, the Hotchkiss brothers, and Albert May Todd exhibited a degree of agency that is not present in many histories of rural
America. The view into their lives afforded by this book helps establish
rural entrepreneurs as significant figures in business history, and the
peppermint kings' other interests and activities incorporate elements of
economic, political, and cultural history for a more complete picture
of these complex rural characters.

While their activities as peppermint kings illustrate the agency and
initiative of rural people, the subjects of this book contribute most to our
understanding of rural America in the ways they resisted mainstream
American trends. The Ranneys were secularists in a very religious society.
Samuel Ranney wrote eloquently about his rejection of organized religion, and his relatives kept up a half-century-long correspondence without once mentioning religious ideas. The Hotchkisses explored banking
and regional credit during a period when finance was being nationalized.
Their activities shed light on rarely considered elements of rural Americans' response to the consolidation of the banking industry—a perspective that has generally escaped the view of historians for whom central

banks and a national currency are often an unquestioned norm. And Albert May Todd showed how a rural entrepreneur could run a thriving, competitive business and still be a socialist. Populist and progressive opponents of monopoly are depicted in most histories as either poor farmers or academics. Todd enriches the story of resistance to economic concentration because he was a successful businessman himself. He objected to the money power not because he was antibusiness but because he believed the special privileges enjoyed by the financial elite had been attained unfairly and that large corporations behaved unjustly in society. Each of the elements of this book contribute to a more complete view of the issues, and each perspective has escaped the notice of most historians precisely because these characters lived their lives far from the cities that received the majority of attention from contemporary commentators and from historians basing their studies on sources produced by those largely urban contemporaries. In addition to exploring the differences between rural and urban life and its change over time, a new rural history could offer insights into how rural people responded to broader social changes that have often been viewed from a predominantly urban perspective. These insights might make the world we currently inhabit seem a bit less inevitable.

Notes

Abbreviated Names of Archives

Ashfield: Ashfield Historical Society Museum, 457 Main Street, Ashfield, Mass. 01330

Cornell: H. G. Hotchkiss Essential Oil Company Records, 1822–1982, Collection Number: 673, Division of Rare and Manuscript Collections, Cornell University Library

Harvard: R. G. Dun and Co./Dun and Bradstreet Collections, Baker Library, Harvard Business School

Todd: Albert May Todd papers and ledger books, A. M. Todd Company, Kalamazoo, Mich.

ONE Introduction

1. Percy Wells Bidwell, *Rural Economy in New England at the Beginning of the 19th Century* (Clifton: A. M. Kelley, 1916); Percy W. Bidwell, "The Agricultural Revolution in New England," *American Historical Review* 26, no. 4 (1921).

2. George Rogers Taylor, *The Transportation Revolution, 1815–1860* (New York: Rinehart, 1951); Paul W. Gates, *The Farmer's Age: Agriculture, 1815–1860* (New York: Holt, Rinehart and Winston, 1960).

3. Roberta Balstad Miller, *City and Hinterland: A Case Study of Urban Growth and Regional Development* (Westport, Conn.: Greenwood Press, 1979); Donald Hugh Parkerson, *The Agricultural Transition in New York State: Markets and Migration in Mid-Nineteenth-Century America* (Ames: Iowa State University Press, 1995); Carol Sheriff, *The Artificial River: The Erie Canal and the Paradox of Progress, 1817–1862* (New York: Hill and Wang, 1996).

4. Stewart Hall Holbrook, *The Yankee Exodus: An Account of Migration from New England* (New York: Macmillan, 1950); Harold F. Wilson, *The Hill Country of Northern New England: Its Social and Economic History, 1790–1930* (New York: AMS Press, 1967); Hal S. Barron, *Those Who Stayed Behind: Rural Society in Nineteenth-Century New England* (New York: Cambridge University Press, 1984).

5. Brian Donahue, "Another Look from Sanderson's Farm: A Perspective on New England Environmental History and Conservation," *Environmental History* 12, no. 1 (2007). William J. Gilmore-Lehne, *Reading Becomes a Necessity of Life: Material and Cultural Life in Rural New England, 1780–1835* (Knoxville: University of Tennessee Press, 1989).

6. Frederick Jackson Turner, *The Frontier in American History* (New York: Holt, Rinehart and Winston, 1962).

7. William Cronon, "Revisiting the Vanishing Frontier: The Legacy of Frederick Jackson Turner," *Western Historical Quarterly* 18, no. 2 (1987).

8. Fred A. Shannon, *The Farmer's Last Frontier, Agriculture, 1860–1897* (New York: Farrar and Rinehart, 1945); Robert P. Swierenga, *Pioneers and Profits: Land Speculation on the Iowa Frontier* (Ames: Iowa State University Press, 1968); Howard Roberts Lamar, *The Trader on the American Frontier: Myth's Victim* (College Station: Texas A & M University Press, 1977); Alan Trachtenberg, *The Incorporation of America: Culture and Society in the Gilded Age* (New York: Hill and Wang, 1982); John Thompson, *Closing the Frontier: Radical Response in Oklahoma, 1889–1923* (Norman: University of Oklahoma Press, 1986); William Wyckoff, *The Developer's Frontier: The Making of the Western New York Landscape* (New Haven: Yale University Press, 1988).

9. Ray Allen Billington, *Westward Expansion: A History of the American Frontier* (New York: Macmillan, 1967); Richard Slotkin, *Regeneration through Violence: The Mythology of the American Frontier, 1600–1860* (Middletown, Conn.: Wesleyan University Press, 1973); Andrew R. L. Cayton, *The Frontier Republic: Ideology and Politics in the Ohio Country, 1780–1825* (Kent, Ohio: Kent State University Press, 1986); Stephen Aron, "Pioneers and Profiteers: Land Speculation and the Homestead Ethic in Frontier Kentucky," *Western Historical Quarterly* 23, no. 2 (1992); Carville Earle and Changyong Cao, "Frontier Closure and the Involution of American Society, 1840–1890," *Journal of the Early Republic* 13, no. 2 (1993).

10. Oscar Handlin, *The Uprooted: The Epic Story of the Great Migrations That Made the American People* (Boston: Little, Brown, 1951); Richard L. Ehrlich, *Immigrants in Industrial America, 1850–1920: Proceedings of a Conference Sponsored by the Balch Institute and the Eleutherian Mills-Hagley Foundation, November 1–3, 1973* (Charlottesville: University Press of Virginia, 1973); Thomas J. Archdeacon, *Becoming American: An Ethnic History* (New York: Collier Macmillan, 1983).

11. Stephan Thernstrom and Peter R. Knights, "Men in Motion: Some Data and Speculations about Urban Population Mobility in Nineteenth-Century America," *Journal of Interdisciplinary History* 1, no. 1 (1970); Bruce Laurie, *Artisans into Workers: Labor in Nineteenth-Century America* (New York: Hill and Wang, 1989).

12. Barron; Susan E. Gray, *The Yankee West: Community Life on the Michigan Frontier* (Chapel Hill: University of North Carolina Press, 1996).

13. Charles A. Beard, *An Economic Interpretation of the Constitution of the United States* (New York: Macmillan, 1935); Louis Hartz, *The Liberal Tradition in America: An Interpretation of American Political Thought since the Revolution* (New York: Harcourt, Brace, 1955); Richard Hofstadter, *The Age of Reform: From Bryan to F.D.R.* (New York: Knopf, 1955).

14. Clarence H. Danhof, "Farm-Making Costs and the 'Safety Valve': 1850–60," *Journal of Political Economy* 49, no. 3 (1941); Gates; E. P. Thompson, *The Making of the English Working Class* (New York: Pantheon Books, 1964); Gilbert Courtland Fite, *The Farmers' Frontier, 1865–1900* (New York: Holt, Rinehart and Winston, 1966); E. P. Thompson, "The Moral Economy of the English Crowd in the Eighteenth Century," *Past and Present* 50, no. 1 (1971); James A. Henretta, "Families and Farms: Mentalite in Pre-Industrial America," *William and Mary Quarterly* 35, no. 1 (1978); Christopher Clark, "Economics and Culture: Opening up the Rural History of the Early American Northeast," *American Quarterly* 43, no. 2 (1991).

15. Christopher Clark, "Household Economy, Market Exchange and the Rise of Capitalism in the Connecticut Valley, 1800–1860," *Journal of Social History* 13, no. 2 (1979); Jeremy Atack, "Farm and Farm-Making Costs Revisited," *Agricultural History* 56, no. 4 (1982); Carole Shammas, "How Self-Sufficient Was Early America?" *Journal of Interdisciplinary History* 13, no. 2 (1982); Jeremy Atack and Fred Bateman, *To Their Own Soil: Agriculture in the Antebellum North* (Ames: Iowa State University Press, 1987); Carole Shammas, *The Pre-Industrial Consumer in England and America* (New York: Oxford University Press, 1990); Andrew H. Baker and Holly V. Izard, "New England Farmers and the Marketplace, 1780–1865: A Case Study," *Agricultural History* 65, no. 3 (1991); Clark, "Economics and Culture"; Carole Shammas, "A New Look at Long-Term Trends in Wealth Inequality in the United States," *American Historical Review* 98, no. 2 (1993); Christopher Clark, *The Communitarian Moment: The Radical Challenge of the Northampton Association* (Ithaca: Cornell University Press, 1995); Christopher Clark, "The View from the Farmhouse: Rural Lives in the Early Republic," *Journal of the Early Republic* 24, no. 2 (2004); Christopher Clark, *Social Change in America: From the Revolution through the Civil War* (Chicago: Ivan R. Dee, 2006).

16. Allan Kulikoff, "The Transition to Capitalism in Rural America," *William and Mary Quarterly* 46, no. 1 (1989); Michael Merrill, "The Anticapitalist Origins of the United States," *Review (Fernand Braudel Center)* 13, no. 4 (1990); Charles Sellers, *The Market Revolution: Jacksonian America, 1815–1846* (New York: Oxford University Press, 1991); Allan Kulikoff, *The Agrarian Origins of American Capitalism* (Charlottesville: University Press of Virginia, 1992).

17. Winifred B. Rothenberg, "A Price Index for Rural Massachusetts, 1750–1855," *Journal of Economic History* 39, no. 4 (1979); Joyce Appleby, "Commercial Farming and the 'Agrarian Myth' in the Early Republic," *Journal of American History* 68, no. 4 (1982); Joyce Oldham Appleby, *Capitalism and a New Social Order: The Republican Vision of the 1790s* (New York: New York University Press, 1984); Joyce Appleby, "Republicanism in Old and New Contexts," *William and Mary Quarterly* 43, no. 1 (1986); Winifred Barr Rothenberg, *From Market-Places to a Market Economy: The Transformation of Rural Massachusetts, 1750–1850* (Chicago: University of Chicago Press, 1992).

18. Winifred B. Rothenberg, "The Bound Prometheus," *Reviews in American History* 15, no. 4 (1987); Michael Merrill, "Putting 'Capitalism' in Its Place: A Review of Recent Literature," *William and Mary Quarterly* 52, no. 2 (1995); Joyce Oldham Appleby, "The Vexed Story of Capitalism Told by American Historians," *Journal of the Early Republic* 21, no. 1 (2001).

19. Joyce Oldham Appleby, *Inheriting the Revolution: The First Generation of Americans* (Cambridge, Mass.: Belknap Press of Harvard University Press, 2000); Allan Kulikoff, *From British Peasants to Colonial American Farmers* (Chapel Hill: University of North Carolina Press, 2000); John Lauritz Larson, *The Market Revolution in America: Liberty, Ambition, and the Eclipse of the Common Good* (New York: Cambridge University Press, 2010).

20. Sven Beckert, *The Monied Metropolis: New York City and the Consolidation of the American Bourgeoisie, 1850–1896* (New York: Cambridge University Press, 2001); Allan Nevins, *The Emergence of Modern America, 1865–1878* (New York: Macmillan, 1927).

21. Rolla M. Tryon, *Household Manufactures in the United States, 1640–1860* (New York: A. M. Kelley, 1917); James Weinstein, *The Corporate Ideal in the Liberal State, 1900–1918* (Boston: Beacon Press, 1968); Margaret Walsh, *The Manufacturing Frontier: Pioneer Industry in Antebellum Wisconsin, 1830–1860* (Madison: State Historical Society of Wisconsin, 1972); John D. Haeger, *The Investment Frontier: New York Businessmen and the Economic Development of the Old Northwest* (Albany: State University of New York Press, 1981).

22. R. Malcolm Keir, "The Unappreciated Tin-Peddler: His Services to Early Manufacturers," *Annals of the American Academy of Political and Social Science* 46 (1913); Richardson Little Wright, *Hawkers and Walkers in Early America: Strolling Peddlers, Preachers, Lawyers, Doctors, Players, and Others, from the Beginning to the Civil War* (Philadelphia: J. B. Lippincott, 1927).

23. Margaret Walsh, *The Rise of the Midwestern Meat Packing Industry* (Lexington: University Press of Kentucky, 1982); William Cronon, *Nature's Metropolis: Chicago and the Great West* (New York: W. W. Norton, 1991).

24. John Jay Knox, *United States Notes: A History of the Various Issues of Paper Money by the Government of the United States* (New York: C. Scribner's, 1892); John Jay Knox, *A History of Banking in the United States* (New York: August M. Kelley, 1900); A. Barton Hepburn, *History of Coinage and Currency in the United States and the Perennial Contest for Sound Money* (New York: Macmillan, 1903); Wesley C. Mitchell, *A History of the Greenbacks: With Special Reference to the Economic Consequences of Their Issue: 1862–65* (Chicago: University of Chicago Press, 1903).

25. Wesley C. Mitchell, "Greenbacks and the Cost of the Civil War," *Journal of Political Economy* 5, no. 2 (1897); Bray Hammond, *Banks and Politics in America: From the Revolution to the Civil War* (Princeton: Princeton University Press, 1957); Fritz Redlich, *The Molding of American Banking: Men and Ideas* (New York: Johnson Reprint, 1968).

26. Hugh T. Rockoff, "Varieties of Banking and Regional Economic Development in the United States, 1840–1860," *Journal of Economic History* 35, no. 1 (1975); Naomi R. Lamoreaux, "Banks, Kinship, and Economic Development: The New England Case," *Journal of Economic History* 46, no. 3 (1986); Larry Schweikart, "U.S. Commercial Banking: A Historiographical Survey," *Business History Review* 65, no. 3 (1991); Gretchen Ritter, *Goldbugs and Greenbacks: The Antimonopoly Tradition and the Politics of Finance in America* (New York: Cambridge University Press, 1997); Howard Bodenhorn, *A History of Banking in Antebellum America: Financial Markets and Economic Development in an Era of Nation-Building* (New York: Cambridge University Press, 2000); Edward J. Bal-

leisen, *Navigating Failure: Bankruptcy and Commercial Society in Antebellum America* (Chapel Hill: University of North Carolina Press, 2001); Howard Bodenhorn, *State Banking in Early America: A New Economic History* (New York: Oxford University Press, 2003); Stephen Mihm, *A Nation of Counterfeiters: Capitalists, Con Men, and the Making of the United States* (Cambridge, Mass.: Harvard University Press, 2007).

TWO Peppermint in America

1. Some of the newspapers held by the American Antiquarian Society featuring advertisements for peppermint products include Massachusetts: *Boston Chronicle* 1768, 1770; *Boston Evening Post* 1769; *Boston News Letter* 1769, 1773; *Boston Post Boy* 1773; *Columbian Centinel* 1790, 1798; *Daily Advertiser* 1789; *American Herald* 1784, 1785; *Hampshire Gazette* 1788, 1800; *Hampshire Chronicle* 1790, 1791; *Hampshire Herald* 1784; *Herald of Freedom* 1789; *Independent Chronicle* 1783, 1784, 1786; *Independent Ledger* 1784; *Massachusetts Gazette* 1787; *Massachusetts Mercury* 1798; *Massachusetts Sentinel* 1789; *Massachusetts Spy* 1774; *Moral and Political Telegraph* 1796; *Salem Gazette* 1784, 1785, 1795; *Salem Mercury* 1788; *Western Star* (Stockbridge) 1795; Connecticut: *Connecticut Journal* 1774, 1783, 1785, 1791; *Connecticut Gazette* 1788, 1796; *Connecticut Courant* 1791; *Bee* (New London) 1798; *Litchfield Monitor* 1791; *Norwich Courier* 1797; *American Mercury* 1784, 1785, 1797; *New Haven Gazette* 1784, 1785; Delaware: *Delaware Gazette* 1790; Georgia: *Georgia Gazette* 1769, 1790; *Augusta Chronicle* 1796; *Columbian Museum* 1796; Maryland: *Maryland Journal* 1784, 1785, 1786, 1787, 1790; *Maryland Gazette* 1790; *Baltimore Evening Post* 1792; *Federal Gazette* 1796; New Hampshire: *New Hampshire Gazette* 1784, 1789, 1795; *New Hampshire Spy* 1791; New Jersey: *New Jersey Journal* 1790; *New Jersey Political Intelligencer* 1784; *Burlington Advertiser* 1790; New York: *New York Mercury* 1763, 1771; *New York Gazette* 1764, 1765, 1776, 1777, 1778, 1779, 1782, 1783, 1790, 1791, 1792; *New York Journal* 1768, 1772, 1773, 1785; *New York Morning Post* 1784, 1785, 1786, 1788, 1789, 1790; *New York Packet* 1784, 1791; *Albany Gazette* 1791, 1798; *American Spy* (Lansingburgh) 1792; *Daily Advertiser* 1786, 1791, 1792, 1796; *Diary* 1792; *Independent Journal* 1784; *Royal American Gazette* 1777, 1778, 1779, 1781; *Royal Gazette* 1778, 1781, 1782; North Carolina: *North Carolina Journal* 1792; Pennsylvania: *Carlisle Gazette* 1787, 1792; *Pennsylvania Chronicle* 1768, 1772; *Pennsylvania Gazette* 1768, 1770, 1771, 1772, 1787; *Pennsylvania Packet* 1772, 1773, 1774, 1778, 1783, 1784, 1785, 1787, 1788.

2. "Just Imported from London," *New York Mercury*, 12/19/1763.

3. John Ray, *Synopsis Methodica Stirpium Britannicarum in Qua Tum Notae Generum Characteristicae Traduntur, Tum Species Singulae Breviter Describuntur: Ducentae Quinquaginta Plus Minus Novae Species Partim Suis Locis Inferuntur, Partim in Appendice Seorsim Exhibentur: Cum Indice & Virium Epitome* (London: Sam. Smith, 1696), 124.

4. Ibid., 126.

5. Ibid., 126.

6. Robert Harris, *Pennsylvania Chronicle and Universal Advertiser*, 5/30/1768.

7. Richard Speaight, *Royal American Gazette*, 9/24/1778.

8. Atwood, *New York Gazette and Weekly Mercury*, 12/28/1778.

9. John Joy, *Independent Chronicle and Universal Advertiser*, 6/17/1784.

10. *Hampshire Herald*, 10/19/1784.

11. George B. Griffenhagen and James Harvey Young, *Old English Patent Medicines in America* (Washington, D.C.: Smithsonian Institution, 1959).

12. *United States Chronicle: Political, Commercial, and Historical*, 5/4/1797.

13. *Eastern Argus*, 10/23/1806.

14. Dr. Hayward, *Pittsfield Sun*, 9/21/1811.

15. Olive R. Jones, "Essense of Peppermint: History of the Medicine and Its Bottle," *Historical Archaeology* 15, no. 2 (1981).

16. Loosely affiliated medical lectures were often associated with established institutions but conducted off campus and held at arm's length by conservative college presidents like Timothy Dwight at Yale and the trustees of Harvard and Dartmouth. William Henry Welch, "The Relation of Yale to Medicine," *Science* 14, no. 361 (1901); Oliver S. Hayward and Constance E. Putnam, *Improve, Perfect and Perpetuate: Dr. Nathan Smith and Early American Medical Education* (Hanover, N.H.: University Press of New England, 1998).

17. Oliver Wendell Holmes, *Medical Essays, 1842–1882* (Boston: Houghton, Mifflin, 1893; Dan Allosso, *An Infidel Body-Snatcher and the Fruits of His Philosophy: The Life of Dr. Charles Knowlton* (Minneapolis: SOTB, 2013).

18. John Duffy, *From Humors to Medical Science: A History of American Medicine* (Urbana: University of Illinois Press, 1993).

19. William Buchan, *Domestic Medicine; or, the Family Physician: Being an Attempt to Render the Medical Art More Generally Useful, by Shewing People What Is in Their Own Power Both with Respect to the Prevention and Cure of Diseases. Chiefly Calculated to Recommend a Proper Attention to Regimen and Simple Medicines. By William Buchan, M.D. To Which Is Added, Dr. Cadogan's Dissertation on the Gout* (New York: John Dunlap, 1772).

20. William Currie, "Of the Cholera," 1798.

21. William Goddard, *The Pennsylvania, Delaware, Maryland, and Virginia Almanack and Ephemeris, for the Year of Our Lord, 1788* (Philadelphia: Goddard, 1787).

22. William Cullen, *A Treatise of the Materia Medica by William Cullen . . . In Two Volumes* (Philadelphia: Joseph Crukshank, 1789).

23. Alexander Hamilton, *The Family Female Physician: Or, a Treatise on the Management of Female Complaints, and of Children in Early Infancy* (Worcester: Isaiah Thomas, 1793), 335, 347.

24. William Currie and Thomas Mifflin, *A Treatise on the Synochus Icteroides, or Yellow Fever as It Lately Appeared in the City of Philadelphia: Exhibiting a Concise View of Its Rise, Progress and Symptoms, Together with the Method of Treatment Found Most Successful: Also Remarks on the Nature of Its Contagion, and Directions for Preventing the Introduction of the Same Malady, in Future* (Philadelphia: Thomas Dobson, 1794).

25. Benjamin Rush, *An Account of the Bilious Remitting Yellow Fever, as It Appeared in the City of Philadelphia, in the Year 1793* (Philadelphia: Thomas Dobson, 1794), 220.

26. Samuel Hemenway, *Medicine Chests, with Suitable Directions: Prepared by Samuel Hemenway, at His Shop in Essex Street, Opposite Union Street, Salem* (Salem, Mass.: W. Carlton, 1796).

27. Samuel Stearns, *The American Herbal, or Materia Medica: Wherein the Virtues of the Mineral, Vegetable, and Animal Productions of North and South America Are Laid Open, So Far as They Are Known; and Their Uses in the Practice of Physic and Surgery Exhibited; Comprehending an Account of a Large Number of New Medical Discoveries and Improvements, Which Are Compiled from the Best Authorities* (Walpole, Mass.: David Carlisle, 1801), 9.

28. *Bee*, 12/28/1802.

29. Abraham Shoemaker, *Oram's New-York Almanac, for the Year of Our Lord, 1807* (New York: James Oram, 1806).

30. Howell Rogers, *On Essences and Their Use and, on the Method of Preparing and Taking a Variety of Tinctures and Syrups* (Colchester, Conn.: T. M. Skinner, 1814), 18.

31. Samuel Thomson, *A Narrative of the Life and Medical Discoveries of Samuel Thomson* (Columbus, Ohio: Jarvis, Pike, 1833), 77.

32. Sidney Mintz, *Sweetness and Power: The Place of Sugar in Modern History* (New York: Penguin Books, 1985), 116.

33. W. J. Rorabaugh, *The Alcoholic Republic: An American Tradition* (New York: Oxford University Press, 1979).

34. Charles Collard Adams, *Middletown Upper Houses: A History of the North Society of Middletown, Connecticut, from 1650 to 1800, with Genealogical and Biographical Chapters on Early Families and a Full Genealogy of the Ranney Family* (New York: Grafton Press, 1908), 16.

35. Ibid.

36. Mark Williams, *The Brittle Thread of Life: Backcountry People Make a Place for Themselves in Early America* (New Haven: Yale University Press, 2009), 209.

37. Adams, 261.

38. Ashfield: Richard V. Happel, "Peppermint Oil."

39. Phinehas Allen, *Sun*, 12/9/1800.

40. Ellen M. Raynor, Emma L. Petitclerc, and James Madison Barker, *History of the Town of Cheshire, Berkshire County, Mass* (Holyoke, Mass.: C. W. Bryan, 1885), 75.

41. Williams, 218.

42. L. H. Everts and Co., *History of the Connecticut Valley in Massachusetts: With Illustrations and Biographical Sketches of Some of Its Prominent Men and Pioneers* (Philadelphia: L. H. Everts, 1879).

43. Ashfield: H. S. Ranney's Centenary Address, 1893.

44. Williams, 249; William G. McLoughlin, "Ebenezer Smith's Ballad of the Ashfield Baptists, 1772," *New England Quarterly* 47, no. 1 (1974), 140.

45. Williams, 272, 287.

46. Ibid., 295.

47. Ibid., 297, 304; Frederick G. Howes, *History of the Town of Ashfield, Mass.* Volume 1. (West Cummington, Mass.: Wm. G. Atkins, printer, 1910), 75ff.

48. Howes, 10.

49. Isaac Backus, *Church History of New England, from 1620 to 1804: Containing a View of the Principles and Practice, Declensions and Revivals, Oppression and Liberty of the Churches, and a Chronological Table* (Philadelphia: Baptist Tract Depository, 1839), 101, 193.

50. Williams, 304.

51. Ibid., 303.

52. Ibid., 320, 330, 335.

53. David P. Szatmary, *Shays' Rebellion: The Making of an Agrarian Insurrection* (Amherst: University of Massachusetts Press, 1980); Leonard L. Richards, *Shays's Rebellion: The American Revolution's Final Battle* (Philadelphia: University of Pennsylvania Press, 2002); Williams, 342, 349–50.

54. The 1800 U.S. Census page for the township of Middle Hero on Grand Isle includes Lamberton Allen, Lamberton Allen Jr., Samuel Allen, Ebenezer H. Allen, and Enoch Allen, as well as Samuel Belden, a member of the Belden/Belding family of Deerfield and Ashfield that was also prominent in the peppermint oil business. Both Lamberton Allen and his brother Enoch were married to Beldings. Howes.

THREE   Essence and Peddlers

1. Everts and Co., 740.

2. Howes, 115–16.

3. David D. Field and Chester Dewey, *A History of the County of Berkshire, Massachusetts, in Two Parts. The First Being a General View of the County; the Second, an Account of the Several Towns* (Pittsfield: S. W. Bush, 1829), 86–87, 92, 177.

4. Clark, *The Roots of Rural Capitalism.*

5. 1826 Town Valuation of Ashfield; 1826 Town Tax Documents.

6. Williams, 70; Ashfield and New England Historic Genealogical Society, *Vital Records of Ashfield, Massachusetts to the Year 1850* (Boston: New England Historic Genealogical Society, 1942), 249.

7. Town Valuation for 1830, 6/12/1830; 1830 Tax Records; Howes.

8. J. R. Dolan, *The Yankee Peddlers of Early America* (New York: C. N. Potter, 1964).

9. Wright. Paul J. Uselding, "Peddling in the Antebellum Economy: Precursor of Mass-Marketing or a Start in Life?" *American Journal of Economics and Sociology* 34, no. 1 (1975); David Jaffee, "Peddlers of Progress and the Transformation of the Rural North, 1760–1860," *Journal of American History* 78, no. 2 (1991).

10. David Jaffee, *A New Nation of Goods: The Material Culture of Early America* (Philadelphia: University of Pennsylvania Press, 2010); Hasia R. Diner, *Roads Taken: The Great Jewish Migrations to the New World and the Peddlers Who Forged the Way* (New Haven: Yale University Press, 2015).

11. C. Merton Babcock, "The Social Significance of the Language of the American Frontier," *American Speech* 24, no. 4 (1949).

12. E. R. Ellis, *Biographical Sketches of Richard Ellis, the First Settler of Ashfield, Mass., and His Descendants* (Detroit: W. Graham, 1888).

13. Wright, 25, 26, 56–57.

14. *Gazette of the United States*, 6/12/1802.

15. It should be noted that even Allan Kulikoff, one of the most vocal proponents of the "escape" thesis, acknowledged: "The rural economy of early America was clearly commercial." Kulikoff, *The Agrarian Origins of American Capitalism*, 17.

16. Jaffee, "Peddlers of Progress."

17. Walsh, *The Rise of the Midwestern Meat Packing Industry*; Martin Bruegel, *Farm, Shop, Landing: The Rise of a Market Society in the Hudson Valley, 1780–1860* (Durham, N.C.: Duke University Press, 2002).

18. Nathaniel Hawthorne, *The American Notebooks by Nathaniel Hawthorne* (New Haven: Yale University Press, 1838), 60.

19. Michele P. Barker, *Peddlers in New England, 1790–1860* (Sturbridge, Mass.: Old Sturbridge Village, 1992); Henry S. Ranney, "Peppermint in Phelps," *Phelps Citizen*, 1893.

20. For example, "Why is the dust in such a rage? / It is he yearly caravan / Of peddlers, on their pilgrimage / To southern marts; full of japan, / And tin, and wooden furniture, / That try to charm the passing eye; / And spices which, I'm very sure, / Ne'er saw the shores of Araby." Connecticut poet Joseph H. Nichols, quoted in Wright, 29.

21. Ibid., 28.

22. Dolan, 231.

23. Priscilla Carrington Kline, "New Light on the Yankee Peddler," *New England Quarterly* 12, no. 1 (1939), 85ff.

24. Jasper Bement Account Books, 1832–40.

25. Harvard: R. G. Dun reports, 1831.

26. Ashfield: H. S. Ranney to Phelps Citizen, "Peppermint in Phelps," 1893.

27. Kline, 92–93.

28. Wright, 89.

29. Kline, 93; Barker.

30. Barker; Ashfield: Jasper Bement Account Books.

31. Ashfield: Jasper Bement Account Books.

32. Ashfield: Letter from William Sanderson to H. S. Ranney, 1845.

33. Ibid.

34. Howes, 217.

35. Ashfield: Letter from William Sanderson to H. S. Ranney, 1845.

36. Ibid.

37. James Robinson and Abraham Shoemaker, *The Philadelphia Directory, City and County Register, for 1802 Containing, the Names, Trades, and Residence of the Inhabitants of the City, Southwark, Northern Liberties, and Kensington: With Other Useful Tables and Lists* (Philadelphia: William W. Woodward, 1802). James Robinson, *The Philadelphia Directory for 1804 Containing the Names, Trades, and Residence of the Inhabitants of the City, Southwark, Northern Liberties, and Kensington: To Which Is Prefixed, a Brief Sketch of the Origin and Present State of the City of Philadelphia* (Philadelphia: John H. Oswald, 1804).

38. Rorabaugh.

39. *Daily Advertiser*, 11/4/1803.

40. Michael Krafft, *The American Distiller, or, the Theory and Practice of Distilling, According to the Latest Discoveries and Improvements, Including the Most Improved Methods of Constructing Stills, and of Rectification* (Philadelphia: Thomas Dobson, 1804).

41. *Boston Gazette,* 11/18/1805.

42. "Drugs and Medicine," *Columbian Gazette,* 2/9/1808.

43. "Opium, &c.," *New York Gazette and General Advertiser,* 2/17/1809.

44. Paul Spear, *Washingtonian,* 4/25/1814.

45. "Drugs and Chemicals," *New York Gazette and General Advertiser,* 10/9/1818; Phinehas Allen, *The Pittsfield Sun,* 1818.

46. *Pittsfield Sun,* 7/10/1823; Joan E. Kaiser, *The Glass Industry in South Boston* (Lebanon, N.H.: University Press of New England, 2009), 20, 58

47. "New Article of Domestic Manufacture," *Boston Commercial Gazette,* 1824.

48. "Peppermint," *Rhode-Island American,* 1825.

49. I have not been able to locate the source document for this quote, and it has occurred to me that the number might be exaggerated or the result of a transcription error. But the other statistics and values cited in the discussion surrounding this quote are all very accurate, which lends credibility to the data. Howes, 126.

50. Louis McLane, *Documents Relative to the Manufactures in the United States Collected and Transmitted to the House of Representatives, in Compliance with a Resolution of Jan. 19, 1832, 22d Cong., 1st Sess. House. Doc; 308* (Washington, D.C.: D. Green, 1833).

51. Ibid.

52. Although he focused primarily on urban, immigrant labor, Bruce Laurie noted: "As late as 1860, more wage earners worked in farmhouses and in small workshops than in factories, and most used hand tools, not power-driven equipment." Laurie, 16.

53. "Wholesale Prices," 1836.

54. "Summary," *Pittsfield Sun,* 12/21/1837.

55. Town Valuation for 1838, 1838 Ashfield Tax Records. Jasper Bement Account Books. Town Valuation for 1838.

56. Chester Sanderson, Town Valuation for 1835, 7/15/1835, 1835 Ashfield Tax Records.

57. Ashfield Town Valuation for 1838.

58. "Essence Peddling," *Boston Courier,* 12/10/1833.

59. Howes, 41–42.

60. Ibid., 45.

61. Ibid., 103–4.

62. Clark, *Social Change in America;* Appleby, "The Vexed Story of Capitalism Told by American Historians."

63. Parkerson.

64. Cronon, *Nature's Metropolis.*

65. Bruegel, 42.

66. In addition to Euro-Americans, there were Africans, Asians, and South Americans who were instrumental in importing crops such as rice and alfalfa to North America. Edward D. Melillo, *Strangers on Familiar Soil: Rediscovering the Chile-California*

Connection (New Haven: Yale University Press, 2015); Judith Ann Carney, *Black Rice: The African Origins of Rice Cultivation in the Americas* (Cambridge, Mass.: Harvard University Press, 2002); Sucheng Chan, *This Bittersweet Soil: The Chinese in California Agriculture, 1860–1910* (Berkeley: University of California Press, 1986).

67. Geo P. Burnham, *The History of the Hen Fever: A Humorous Record* (Philadelphia: James French, 1855); Virginia DeJohn Anderson, *Creatures of Empire: How Domestic Animals Transformed Early America* (New York: Oxford University Press, 2004).

68. Town Valuation for 1830; Ashfield *Vital Records,* 258.

69. Ontario County indentures (land sales), 1838.

70. These events are described in great detail in my biography of Knowlton. Allosso.

71. Ashfield: Mason Grosvenor, Congregational Church Records, 1834.

72. Ibid.

73. Spelling errors—including the possibly deliberate misspelling of the pastor's name—are original. Ashfield: Samuel Ranney Letter, 5/20/1834.

74. Charles Knowlton, *Elements of Modern Materialism Inculcating the Idea of a Future State, in Which All Will Be More Happy, under Whatever Circumstances They May Be Placed Than If They Experienced No Misery in This Life* (Adams, Mass.: A. Oakey, 1829).

75. U.S. Land Office records, April 15, 1837.

76. Ashfield: H. S. Ranney to Phelps Citizen, "Peppermint in Phelps," 1893

77. Samuel Ranney, Last Will and Testament, 1837.

78. Ashfield: Letter from L. G. Ranney to H. S. Ranney, 5/19/1839

79. Ashfield: H. S. Ranney to Phelps Citizen, "Peppermint in Phelps," 1893

80. Cornell: Letter from L. B. Hotchkiss to H. G. Hotchkiss, 9/15/1845

81. Cornell: Letter from L. B. Hotchkiss to H. G. Hotchkiss, 9/17/1845

82. Roswell Ranney Estate Inventory, 1848.

FOUR　Migration

1. Kulikoff, *From British Peasants to Colonial American Farmers,* 285.

2. Ibid., 287.

3. Holbrook, 17.

4. O. Turner, *History of the Pioneer Settlement of Phelps and Gorham's Purchase, and Morris Reserve* (Rochester: William Alling, 1851), 79.

5. Ibid., 127.

6. Kenneth E. Lewis, *West to Far Michigan: Settling the Lower Peninsula, 1815–1860* (East Lansing: Michigan State University Press, 2002).

7. Turner, 135ff.

8. Ibid., 224ff.

9. Helen Post Ridley, *When Phelps Was Young* (Phelps, N.Y.: Phelps Echo, 1939), 10, 90.

10. Ibid., 90ff.

11. Hal S. Barron, *Those Who Stayed Behind: Rural Society in Nineteenth-Century New England* (New York: Cambridge University Press, 1984), 2.

12. Ridley, 123.

13. O. Turner, 227.

14. George S. Conover, *History of Ontario County, New York* (Syracuse: D. Mason, 1893), 59, 353.

15. Archibald Burnett's name was also included on a list of early physicians who were members of the Ontario County Medical Society, established in 1806. Ibid., 182; Henry S. Ranney, "Peppermint in Phelps," *Phelps Citizen*, 1893.

16. Quoted in Taylor.

17. Haeger, 67.

18. Ellis, 389.

19. Michigan Land Office Records.

20. Ashfield: Letter from L. G. Ranney to H. S. Ranney, 5/19/1839.

21. Phelps Assessments; W. R. Cutter and W. F. Adams, *Genealogical and Personal Memoirs Relating to the Families of the State of Massachusetts* (Boston: Lewis Historical, 1910).

22. Ashfield: Jasper Bement Account Books.

23. Harvard: R. G. Dun credit assessment of H. S. Ranney, 1852.

24. *Boston Daily Courier*, 1/24/1842, 1.

25. Ashfield: Letter from John Bement to Moses Cook, 4/15/1842.

26. Ashfield: Letter from Lucius Ranney to H. S. Ranney, 5/15/1842.

27. Silas Farmer, *The History of the Detroit and Michigan: Or, The Metropolis Illustrated* (Detroit: Silas Farmer, 1884). 902

28. Ashfield: Letter from Lucius Ranney to H. S. Ranney, 4/30/1843.

29. Ashfield: Letter from L. G. Ranney to H. S. Ranney, 11/13/1843.

30. Ashfield: Letter from L. G. Ranney to H. S. Ranney, 2/15/1844.

31. Ashfield: Letter from Charles Sanderson to H. S. Ranney, 5/24/1844.

32. Ashfield: Letter from Augustus Graves to H. S. Ranney, 1/8/1844.

33. Ashfield: Letter from Jasper Bement to H. S. Ranney, 8/23/1844.

34. Ashfield: Letter from Jasper Bement to H. S. Ranney, 8/29/1844.

35. Harvard: R. G. Dun credit assessment of H. S. Ranney, May 1847.

36. Preston Salts were ammonia-based smelling salts. Ashfield: Letter from Augustus Graves to H. S. Ranney, 5/8/1847.

37. Clark, *Social Change in America.*

38. Ashfield: Letter from Frederick T. Ranney to H. S. Ranney, 8/28/1847.

39. Ashfield: Letter from Jasper Bement to H. S. Ranney, 5/30/1845.

40. Ashfield: Letter from George C. Goodwin to H. S. Ranney, 6/14/1850.

41. Paul E. Johnson, *A Shopkeeper's Millennium: Society and Revivals in Rochester, New York, 1815–1837* (New York: Hill and Wang, 1978).

42. Ashfield: Letter from Lucius Ranney to H. S. Ranney, 2/2/1851.

43. Ashfield newspaper article, "Death of Henry Ranney," 1899.

44. Ashfield: Letter from Lucius Ranney to H. S. Ranney, 10/12/1851.

45. Ashfield: Letter from L.G. Ranney to H. S. Ranney, 9/11/1853.

46. Ashfield: Letter from Lucius Ranney to H. S. Ranney, 10/4/1853.

47. Ashfield: Letter from Lucius Ranney to H. S. Ranney, 6/18/1854.

48. Ashfield: Letter from Harrison Ranney to Anson B. Ranney, 8/25/1855.

49. Ashfield: Letter from Lucius Ranney to H. S. Ranney, 9/24/1855.

50. Ironically, Harrison's letters are among the most legible of all the brothers' letters. Ashfield: Letter from Harrison Ranney to H. S. Ranney, 11/18/1855.

51. Ashfield: Letter from Lucius Ranney to H. S. Ranney, 7/19/1857.

52. Ashfield: Letter from Lucius Ranney to H. S. Ranney, 12/27/1857.

53. Ashfield: Letter from Lemuel Ranney to H. S. Ranney, 2/9/1858.

54. Christopher Clark has written extensively on this shift. The words are Naomi Lamoreaux's, quoted in *Social Change in America*, p. 119. Christopher Clark, *Social Change in America: From the Revolution through the Civil War* (Chicago: Ivan R. Dee, 2006).

55. Clark said, "The 'local' ethic valued the longer-term reciprocity between dealers embedded in a network of social connections; morality lay in accepting obligations and discharging them over time. The 'market' ethic emphasized quick payment and assumed a formal equality between individual dealers at the point of exchange." The Ranneys, and later the Hotchkisses, tried to remain in a system oriented toward long-term obligations and preference of some partners over others, by staying focused on the kinship network rather than the impersonal ethics of markets. As we will see later, this focus did not always lead to the best possible results. Clark, *The Roots of Rural Capitalism*, 196.

56. In a later letter, Lawrence mentions that his wife, Mary, has been away visiting and has stayed overnight with Harrison Ranney's family and seen Lucius and Lewis. Ashfield: Letter from H. H. Lawrence to H. S. Ranney, 8/15/1863.

57. Ashfield: Letter from H. H. Lawrence to H. S. Ranney, 10/11/1858.

58. *Emigration: Practical Advice to Emigrants: On All Points Connected with Their Comfort and Economy, from Making Choice of a Ship to Settling on and Cropping a Farm*, Earl Grey Pamphlets Collection (1834), 90; "Notes and Queries," *American Journal of Numismatics, and Bulletin of the American Numismatic and Archaeological Society* 24, no. 2 (1889).

59. Ashfield: Letter from George C. Goodwin to H. S. Ranney, 10/22/1858.

60. Ashfield: Letter from H. H. Lawrence to H. S. Ranney, 10/25/1858.

61. Ashfield: Letter from H. S. Ranney to George C. Goodwin, 10/29/1858.

62. This mention of a family visit to Hillsdale further supports my suspicion that Lawrence's wife, Mary, and Harrison's wife, Helen, likely were sisters. Although I have not been able to ascertain Mary's maiden name, both women were born in New York and moved to Michigan as young girls. They were either sisters or close friends who had grown up together. Ashfield: Letter from H. H. Lawrence to H. S. Ranney, 11/25/1858.

63. Ashfield: Letter from George C. Goodwin to H. S. Ranney, 1/21/1859.

64. Ashfield: Letter from Harrison Ranney to Anson B. Ranney, 1/16/1859.

65. Ashfield: Letter from Lemuel Ranney to H. S. Ranney, 4/10/1859.

66. Ashfield: Letter from H. H. Lawrence to H. S. Ranney, 10/13/1859.

67. Ashfield: Letter from George C. Goodwin to H. S. Ranney, 10/31/1859.

68. Ashfield: Letter from H. H. Lawrence to H. S. Ranney, 10/20/1860.

69. Ashfield: Letter from H. S. Ranney to George C. Goodwin, 11/9/1860.

70. Ashfield: Letters from George C. Goodwin to H. S. Ranney, 11/21/1860, 5/29/1861.

71. Ashfield: Letter from H. H. Lawrence to H. S. Ranney, 9/2/1861.

72. Ashfield: Letter from H. H. Lawrence to H. S. Ranney, 9/23/1861.

73. Ashfield: Letter from H. S. Ranney to George C. Goodwin, 9/7/1861.

74. Ashfield: Letter from George C. Goodwin to H. S. Ranney, 10/21/1861.

75. Ashfield: Letter from H. H. Lawrence to H. S. Ranney, 11/11/1861.

76. Ashfield: Letter from H. H. Lawrence to H. S. Ranney, 12/4/1861.

77. Ashfield: Letter from Lucius Ranney to H. S. Ranney, 11/17/1861.

78. Gray, 3.

79. Ashfield: Letter from H. H. Lawrence to H. S. Ranney, 9/8/1862.

80. Ashfield: Letter from H. S. Ranney to George C. Goodwin, 9/13/1862.

81. Ashfield: Letter from H. H. Lawrence to H. S. Ranney, 10/22/1862.

82. Ashfield: Letter from George C. Goodwin to H. S. Ranney, 8/31/1863.

83. Ashfield: Letter from H. H. Lawrence to H. S. Ranney, 9/16/1864.

84. Ashfield: Letter from H. H. Lawrence to H. S. Ranney, 8/18/1864.

85. Ashfield: Letter from H. H. Lawrence to H. S. Ranney, 9/9/1867.

86. Ashfield: Letter from H. H. Lawrence to H. S. Ranney, 9/10/1868.

87. Ashfield: Letter from H. S. Ranney to H.H. Lawrence, 10/15/1862.

88. Ashfield: Letter from Ralph Ranney to H. S. Ranney, 9/13/1868.

89. Ashfield: Letter from Ralph Ranney to H. S. Ranney, 10/4/1868.

90. Ranney was elected to represent Ashfield in 1852 and 1868. Ashfield: newspaper article, "Death of Henry Ranney," 1899.

91. Ashfield: Letter from H. H. Lawrence to H. S. Ranney, 10/25/1868.

92. Ashfield: Letter from H. H. Lawrence to H. S. Ranney, 11/20/1868; Letter from George C. Goodwin to H. S. Ranney, 1/11/1869.

93. Ashfield: Letter from Lemuel Ranney to H. S. Ranney, 8/16/1869.

94. Ashfield: Letter from A. F. Ranney to H. S. Ranney, 6/24/1877.

95. Ashfield: Letter from Anson B. Ranney to H. S. Ranney, 4/24/1881.

96. Ashfield: Letter from Harrison Ranney to H. S. Ranney, 9/8/1885.

97. Ashfield: H. S. Ranney to Phelps Citizen, "Peppermint in Phelps," 1893.

98. Ashfield: newspaper article, "Death of Henry Ranney," 1899.

FIVE Prize Medal Oil of Peppermint

1. "Due to Yankee Shrewdness. Start of the Peppermint Crop That Has Given Wayne County $20,000,000," *Macon Weekly Telegraph,* 1903.

2. Mabel E. Oaks, *Phelpstown Footprints* (Phelps, N.Y.: Phelps Historical Society, 1962), 54.

3. 1833, "Chloe Hotchkiss," Lyons, N.Y., *Western Argus.*

4. George W. Cowles, *Landmarks of Wayne County* (Syracuse: D. Mason, 1895), 29.

5. James Emmitt and M. J. Carrigan, *Life and Reminiscences of Hon. James Emmitt as Revised by Himself* (Chillicothe, Ohio: Peerless Print, 1888), 241.

6. Edwin Williams, *The New York Annual Register* (New York: J. Leavitt, 1830), 129.

7. *Harper's Weekly, a Journal of Civilization Collection—1890* (1890), 283; *Memorial. David Dows* (Chicago: Rock Island Chicago and Co. Pacific Rail Road, 1890), 9.

8. U. P. Hedrick, *A History of Agriculture in the State of New York* (Albany: New York State Agriculture Society, 1933), 248.

9. Cornell: Letter from Dows and Cary to H. G. Hotchkiss, 12/3/1842.

10. Cornell: Letter from Dows and Cary to H. G. Hotchkiss, 12/10/1842.

11. Cornell: Letter from Dows and Cary to H. G. Hotchkiss, 12/12/1842.

12. Cornell: Letters from Dows and Cary to H. G. Hotchkiss, 3/21/1844, 4/26/1844.

13. H. G. Hotchkiss Essential Oil Co., *History of Hotchkiss Essential Oil of Peppermint* (Lyons, N.Y.: The Company, 1980).

14. James E. Landing, *American Essence: A History of the Peppermint and Spearmint Industry in the United States* (Kalamazoo: Kalamazoo Public Museum, 1969), 27.

15. Cronon, *Nature's Metropolis: Chicago and the Great West* (New York: W. W. Norton, 2009).

16. Landing, 61.

17. Cornell: Letter from Dows and Cary to H. G. Hotchkiss, 2/22/1843.

18. Cornell: Contract between Dows and Cary and H. G. Hotchkiss, 8/8/1843.

19. Cornell: Letter from Dows and Cary to H. G. Hotchkiss, 2/8/1844.

20. Cornell: Letter from Dows and Cary to H. G. Hotchkiss, 11/4/1844.

21. Cornell: Letter from H. G. Hotchkiss to Dows and Cary, 11/14/1844.

22. Cornell: Letter from L. B. Hotchkiss to Dows and Cary, 12/9/1844.

23. Cornell: Letter from Dows and Cary to H. G. Hotchkiss, 12/16/1844.

24. Cornell: Letter from H. G. Hotchkiss to Dows and Cary, 3/4/1845.

25. Cornell: Letter from Dows and Cary to H. G. Hotchkiss, 3/19/1845.

26. Cornell: Letter from H. G. Hotchkiss to Morewood, 3/15/1845.

27. Cornell: Letter from H. G. Hotchkiss to Dows and Cary, 5/25/1845.

28. Cornell: Letter from Dows and Cary to H. G. Hotchkiss, 5/24/1845.

29. Cornell: Letter from Dows and Cary to H. G. Hotchkiss, 7/3/1845.

30. Cornell: Letter from L. B. Hotchkiss to H. G. Hotchkiss, 9/4/1845.

31. Cornell: Letter from L. B. Hotchkiss to H. G. Hotchkiss, 9/15/1845.

32. W. H. McIntosh, *History of Wayne County, New York; with Illustrations Descriptive of Its Scenery, Palatial Residences, Public Buildings, Fine Blocks, and Important Manufactories* (Philadelphia: Everts, Ensign and Everts, 1877).

33. Cornell: Letter from Morewood to H. G. Hotchkiss, 7/23/1845.

34. Cornell: Letter from H. G. Hotchkiss to Morewood, 7/28/1845.

35. Cornell: Letter from Morewood to H. G. Hotchkiss, 9/15/1845.

36. Mark Tungate, *Adland: A Global History of Advertising* (Philadelphia: Kogan Page, 2007), 9.

37. Cornell: Letter from L. B. Hotchkiss to H. G. Hotchkiss, 10/23/1845; *Northwestern Miller* magazine (Miller Publishing Company, 1882), 11.

38. Cornell: Letter from L. B. Hotchkiss to H. G. Hotchkiss, 11/23/1845.

39. Cornell: Letter from Morewood to H. G. Hotchkiss, 11/7/1845.

40. Cornell: Letter from H. G. Hotchkiss to Morewood, 9/26/1846.

41. Cornell: Letter from Morewood to H. G. Hotchkiss, 10/1/1846.

42. Cornell: Letter from H. G. Hotchkiss to Morewood, 1/18/1847.

43. Landing, 45.

44. Because peppermint requires long day lengths to thrive, it is generally grown in latitudes with long summer photoperiods. Landing, 27, 181.

45. Ibid. 28.

46. Cornell: Letter from H. G. Hotchkiss to Morewood, 3/26/1847.

47. Cornell: Contract between E. C. Patterson and H. G. Hotchkiss, 1847.

48. Cornell: Letter from E. C. Patterson to H. G. Hotchkiss, 6/15/1847.

49. Cornell: Letter from L. B. Hotchkiss to H. G. Hotchkiss, 6/16/1847.

50. Cornell: Letter from H. G. Hotchkiss to Stevens Trott, 7/7/1847.

51. Cornell: Letter from Stevens Trott to H. G. Hotchkiss, 7/12/1847.

52. Cornell: Letter from H. G. Hotchkiss to Stevens Trott, 7/30/1847.

53. Cornell: Letter from E. C. Patterson to H. G. Hotchkiss, 8/9/1847.

54. Ashfield: Letter from Frederick T. Ranney to H. S. Ranney, 8/28/1847.

55. Cornell: Letter from L. B. Hotchkiss to H. G. Hotchkiss, 9/9/1847.

56. Cornell: Letter from L. B. Hotchkiss to H. G. Hotchkiss, 10/14/1847.

57. Cornell: Letter from L. B. Hotchkiss to H. G. Hotchkiss, 12/15/1847.

58. Cornell: Letter from H. G. Hotchkiss to E. C. Patterson, 2/11/1848.

59. Cornell: Letter from Morewood to H. G. Hotchkiss, 2/15/1848.

60. Cornell: Letter from Morewood to H. G. Hotchkiss, 3/3/1848.

61. Cornell: Letter from Morewood to H. G. Hotchkiss, 3/20/1848.

62. Cornell: Letter from H. G. Hotchkiss to Morewood, 3/27/1848.

63. Cornell: Letter from Morewood to H. G. Hotchkiss, 3/31/1848.

64. Cornell: Letter from John Bement to H. G. Hotchkiss, 6/3/1848.

65. Cornell: Letter from Miller to H. G. Hotchkiss, 3/31/1851

66. Cornell: Letter from Miller to H. G. Hotchkiss, 9/17/1850.

67. Ursula Lehmkuhl and Gustav Schmidt, *From Enmity to Friendship: Anglo-American Relations in the 19th and 20th Century* (Augsburg: Wissner, 2005), 31, 48.

68. Cornell: Letter from H. G. Hotchkiss to Miller, 7/2/1851.

69. B. P. Johnson, *Report on International Exhibition of Industry and Art, London, 1862* (London: C. Van Benthuysen, 1863), 30.

70. Andrew Bevan and D. Wengrow, *Cultures of Commodity Branding* (London: Taylor and Francis, 2016), 22.

71. Cornell: Letter from H. G. Hotchkiss to Morewood, 12/27/1855; Mark Pendergrast, *For God, Country, and Coca-Cola: The Definitive History of the Great American Soft Drink and the Company That Makes It* (New York: Basic Books, 2000); "A Look Back on 150 Years," *History of General Mills,* https://history.generalmills.com/the-story.html.

72. James Harvey Young, *The Toadstool Millionaires: A Social History of Patent Medicines in America before Federal Regulation (*Princeton: Princeton University Press, 1961).

73. Cornell: Hotchkiss Certificate Advertisement, 1851.

74. James Carrier, "The Rituals of Christmas Giving." Daniel Miller, *Unwrapping Christmas* (New York: Clarendon Press, 1993), 55ff.

75. T. J. Jackson Lears, *Fables of Abundance: A Cultural History of Advertising in America* (New York: Basic Books, 1994).

76. Cornell: L. B. Hotchkiss Warning Label, 1857.

77. Cornell: L. B. Hotchkiss Warning Label, 1876.

SIX Peppermint Bank

1. Historical arguments mobilized to support political positions regarding a Federal Reserve included: Horace White, *An Elastic Currency, "George Smith's Money" in the Early Northwest: An Address to the American Bankers' Association at Chicago, October 19, 1893*; Wesley C. Mitchell, "The Value of the 'Greenbacks' during the Civil War," *Journal of Political Economy* 6, no. 2 (1898); Knox, *A History of Banking in the United States*; Mitchell, *A History of the Greenbacks*; J. P. Huston, "The Use of Credit Currency by Country Banks," *Annals of the American Academy of Political and Social Science* 36, no. 3 (1910); J. Laurence Laughlin, "Banknotes and Lending Power," *Journal of Political Economy* 18, no. 10 (1910); Willford I. King, "Circulating Credit: Its Nature and Relation to the Public Welfare," *American Economic Review* 10, no. 4 (1920).

2. See, for example, the account of Civil War financial legislation in the third chapter of Heather Cox Richardson's 1997 book, in which the historian is either unaware of or unconcerned with the overwhelmingly urban focus of her account and sources. Heather Cox Richardson, *The Greatest Nation of the Earth: Republican Economic Policies during the Civil War* (Cambridge, Mass.: Harvard University Press, 1997).

3. Utica *Daily Gazette*, 2/3/1843; Schenectady *Cabinet*, 9/20/1842.

4. Auburn *Cayuga Republican*, 2/15/1832; Lyons *Western Argus*, 5/9/1838.

5. Lyons *Western Argus*, 4/6/1842.

6. Cornell: H. G. Hotchkiss notes on Lyons Bank Assets, 12/18/1842.

7. Cornell: H. G. Hotchkiss notes on Lyons Bank Failure, 9/14/1843.

8. Cornell: H. G. Hotchkiss notes on Receiver Sale, 1843.

9. Cornell: Letter from H. G. Hotchkiss to Doctor, 10/12/1843.

10. Cornell: Letter from H. G. Hotchkiss to Morrison, 6/14/1844.

11. Clark, *The Roots of Rural Capitalism*, 215ff.

12. Cornell: Letter from L. B. Hotchkiss to H. G. Hotchkiss, 4/28/1845.

13. Quoted in Hammond, 699.

14. Ibid., 700.

15. Cornell: Letter from L. B. Hotchkiss to H. G. Hotchkiss, 10/24/1845.

16. Cornell: Letter from L. B. Hotchkiss to H. G. Hotchkiss, 11/7/1845.

17. Cornell: Letter from L. B. Hotchkiss to H. G. Hotchkiss, 11/15/1845.

18. Cornell: Letter from H. G. Hotchkiss to Calvin Hotchkiss, 11/2/1855.

19. Writing in 1893, White was using the example of George Smith's money to argue for an elastic currency not controlled by the government. White, 4.

20. Cornell: Letter from Calvin Hotchkiss to H. G. Hotchkiss, 11/27/1855.

21. Cornell: Letter from Bank to Calvin Hotchkiss, 1/2/1856.

22. Cornell: Letter from L. B. Hotchkiss to H. G. Hotchkiss, 1/8/1856.

23. Cornell: Letter from Calvin Hotchkiss, to H. G. Hotchkiss, 1/14/1856.

24. Cornell: Letter from Calvin Hotchkiss, to H. G. Hotchkiss, 1/28/1856.

25. Rockoff.

26. Fritz Redlich, "On the Origin of Created Deposits in the Commonwealth of Massachusetts," *Business History Review* 43, no. 2 (1969), 204.

27. Bodenhorn, *State Banking in Early America*, 192.

28. Charles M. Kahn and William Roberds, "Demandable Debts as a Means of Payment: Banknotes Versus Checks," *Journal of Money, Credit, and Banking* 31, no. 302 (1999), 500–501.

29. Cornell: Letter from H. G. Hotchkiss to P. C. Wells, 9/5/1860.

30. Bodenhorn, *A History of Banking in Antebellum America*, 62–64.

31. Richardson, 73.

32. Cornell: Letter from Calvin Hotchkiss to H. G. Hotchkiss, 3/14/1856.

33. Ibid., Cornell: Letter from L. B. Hotchkiss to H. G. Hotchkiss, 1/8/1856.

34. Cornell: Letter from H. G. Hotchkiss to A. Bell, 5/20/1856.

35. Cornell: Letter from A. Bell to H. G. Hotchkiss, 5/22/1856.

36. Cornell: Letter from H. G. Hotchkiss to A. Bell, 5/24/1856.

37. Cornell: Letter from A. Bell to H. G. Hotchkiss, 5/26/1856.

38. Hammond, 700.

39. Ibid., 702.

40. Ibid., 704.

41. Ibid., 716.

42. Herman Melville, Hershel Parker, and Mark Niemeyer, *The Confidence-Man: His Masquerade: An Authoritative Text, Contemporary Reviews, Biographical Overviews, Sources, Backgrounds, and Criticism* (New York: Norton, 2006).

43. White.

44. Ibid., 1.

45. Ibid., 2.

46. Cornell: Letter from L. B. Hotchkiss to H. G. Hotchkiss, 1/30/1846.

47. Cornell: Letter from Calvin Hotchkiss to H. G. Hotchkiss, 11/17/1856.

48. Cornell: Letter from Calvin Hotchkiss to H. G. Hotchkiss, 12/29/1856.

49. Cornell: Letter from L. B. Hotchkiss to H. G. Hotchkiss, 2/27/2857.

50. Cornell: Letter from Calvin Hotchkiss to H. G. Hotchkiss, 4/25/1857.

51. Cornell: Letter from L. B. Hotchkiss to H. G. Hotchkiss, 5/29/1857.

52. Cornell: Letter from L. B. Hotchkiss to H. G. Hotchkiss, 6/12/1857.

53. Ibid., Cornell: Letter from Calvin Hotchkiss to H. G. Hotchkiss, 7/13/1857.

54. Cornell: Letter from Calvin Hotchkiss to H. G. Hotchkiss, 1/8/1858.

55. Harvard: R. G. Dun credit report. Calvin and L. B. Hotchkiss, 1858–59.

56. Cornell: Letter from L. B. Hotchkiss to H. G. Hotchkiss, 5/20/1858.

57. Cornell: Letter from Calvin Hotchkiss to H. G. Hotchkiss, 9/12/1859.

58. Cornell: Letter from Calvin Hotchkiss to H. G. Hotchkiss, 4/20/1860.

59. Cornell: Letter from Calvin Hotchkiss to H. G. Hotchkiss, 8/11/1860.

60. Cornell: Letter from Calvin Hotchkiss to H. G. Hotchkiss, 8/17/1860.

61. Cornell: Letter from Cook to H. G. Hotchkiss, 9/1/1860.

62. Stephen Mihm, *A Nation of Counterfeiters: Capitalists, Con Men, and the Making of the United States* (Cambridge, Mass.: Harvard University Press, 2007), 223ff.

63. Quoted in Daniel S. Mevis, *Pioneer Recollections: Semi-Historic Side Lights on the Early Days of Lansing* (Lansing, Mich.: MARULA, 2017), 33–34.

64. Mihm, 10.

65. Cornell: Letter from William Hotchkiss to H. G. Hotchkiss, 1/12/1862.

66. Richardson, 66.

67. Ibid., 67.

68. David M. Gische, "The New York City Banks and the Development of the National Banking System, 1860–1870," *American Journal of Legal History* 23, no. 1 (1979), 59.

69. Ibid., 22.

70. Ibid., 40.

71. Mitchell, "The Value of the 'Greenbacks' during the Civil War," 139, 154.

72. Salmon Chase, quoted in ibid., 140.

73. Ibid., 141.

74. Jane Knodell, "Interregional Financial Integration and the Banknote Market: The Old Northwest, 1815–1845," *Journal of Economic History* 48, no. 2 (1988), 291.

75. Hammond, 724.

76. Gary Gorton, "Reputation Formation in Early Bank Note Markets," *Journal of Political Economy* 104, no. 2 (1996), 347.

77. Ibid., 353.

78. King, 742.

79. Richardson, 87.

80. Ibid., 89.

81. Ibid., 91.

82. Ibid., 92.

83. Ibid., 101.

84. Ibid., 95.

85. Ibid., 97, 99.

86. Ibid., 100–101.

87. Cornell: Letter from George C. Hotchkiss to H. G. Hotchkiss, 11/1/1864.

88. Cornell: Letter from H. G. Hotchkiss to George C. Hotchkiss, 11/9/1864.

89. Cornell: Letter from George C. Hotchkiss to H. G. Hotchkiss, 11/9/1864.

90. Cornell: Letter from H. G. Hotchkiss to George C. Hotchkiss, 11/16/1864.

91. Cornell: Letter from H. G. Hotchkiss to George C. Hotchkiss, 11/17/1864.

92. Cornell: Letter from Calvin Hotchkiss to H. G. Hotchkiss, 3/9/1864.

93. Cornell: Letter from Calvin Hotchkiss to H. G. Hotchkiss, 12/21/1864.

94. Cornell: Letter from Calvin Hotchkiss to H. G. Hotchkiss, 3/24/1865.

95. Cornell: Letter from Calvin Hotchkiss to H. G. Hotchkiss, 10/26/1865.

96. Cornell: Letter from Calvin Hotchkiss to H. G. Hotchkiss, 10–16–1865.

97. *Syracuse Journal*, 1/22/1867, 8.

98. Eugene Nelson White, "The Political Economy of Banking Regulation, 1864–1933," *Journal of Economic History* 42, no. 1 (1982), 35.

99. Ibid., 34.

100. B. G. Carruthers and S. Babb, "The Color of Money and the Nature of Value: Greenbacks and Gold in Postbellum America," *American Journal of Sociology* 101, no. 6 (1996), 1556.

101. Bodenhorn, *A History of Banking in Antebellum America*, 214.

102. Hammond, 733.

103. Harvard: R. G. Dun credit report, 9/8/1858.

104. Harvard: R. G. Dun credit report, 4/1860.

105. Harvard: R. G. Dun credit report, 1/17/1869.

106. Harvard: R. G. Dun credit report, 7/10/1873.

107. Harvard: R. G. Dun credit report, 10/12/1877.

108. Harvard: R. G. Dun credit report, 12/7/1889.

109. Harvard: R. G. Dun credit report, 9/20/1867.

110. Harvard: R. G. Dun credit report, 5/19/1869.

111. Harvard: R. G. Dun credit report, 5/2/1879.

112. Warren Susman, *Culture as History: The Transformation of American Society in the Twentieth Century* (New York: Pantheon Books, 1984). Kindle locations 5468, 5605.

SEVEN The Dark Side of Family Business

1. Clyde, N.Y., *Democratic Herald*, 10/28/1897.

2. Ibid.

3. Paul Edward Johnson, *A Shopkeeper's Millennium: Society and Revivals in Rochester, New York, 1815–1837* (New York: Hill and Wang, 2004), 22.

4. Cornell: Letter from H. G. Hotchkiss to Mary Hotchkiss, 5/21/1845.

5. Cornell: Letter from H. G. Hotchkiss to Mary Hotchkiss, 8/16/1845.

6. Cornell: Letter from L. B. Hotchkiss to H. G. Hotchkiss, 8/16/1845.

7. Cornell: Letter from L. B. Hotchkiss to H. G. Hotchkiss, 8/30/1845.

8. Cornell: Letter from L. B. Hotchkiss to H. G. Hotchkiss, 12/13/1845.

9. Cornell: Undated draft letter from H. G. Hotchkiss to David Dows, 5/1845.

10. Cornell: Legal Complaint between H. G. Hotchkiss and David Dows, 5/1846.

11. Cornell: New York Supreme Court judgment, 1846.

12. Cornell: Letter from L. B. Hotchkiss to H. G. Hotchkiss, 11/27/1845.

13. Cornell: Settlement between L. B. Hotchkiss and H. G. Hotchkiss, 11/6/1855.

14. Ibid., Cornell: Letter from L. B. Hotchkiss to H. G. Hotchkiss, 2/27/1856.

15. Ibid., Cornell: Letter from L. B. Hotchkiss to H. G. Hotchkiss, 2/28/1856.

16. Cornell: Letter from L. B. Hotchkiss to H. G. Hotchkiss, 3/17/1856.

17. Cornell: Letter from Calvin Hotchkiss to H. G. Hotchkiss, 3/17/1856.

18. Cornell: Letter from L. B. Hotchkiss to H. G. Hotchkiss, 3/27/1856.

19. Cornell: Letter from L. B. Hotchkiss to H. G. Hotchkiss, 3/30/1856.

20. Cornell: Letter from H. G. Hotchkiss to L. B. Hotchkiss, 3/31/1856.

21. Cornell: Letter from William T. Hotchkiss to H. G. Hotchkiss, 4/13/1856.

22. Cornell: Letter from Calvin Hotchkiss to H. G. Hotchkiss, 4/14/1856.

23. Cornell: Letter from L. B. Hotchkiss to H. G. Hotchkiss, 6/23/1856

24. Cornell: Letter from L. B. Hotchkiss to H. G. Hotchkiss, 7/8/1856.

25. Cornell: Letter from L. B. Hotchkiss to H. G. Hotchkiss, 7/19/1856.

26. Cornell: Letter from Chapman to L. B. Hotchkiss, 7/25/1856; Letter from L. B. Hotchkiss to H. G. Hotchkiss, 7/29/1856.

27. Cornell: Letter from L. B. Hotchkiss to H. G. Hotchkiss, 9/18/1856.

28. Cornell: Letter from H. G. Hotchkiss to L. B. Hotchkiss, 9/22/1856.

29. Cornell: Letter from L. B. Hotchkiss to H. G. Hotchkiss, 9/7/1857.

30. Cornell: Letter from William Hotchkiss to H. G. Hotchkiss, 5/9/1857.

31. Cornell: Letter from L. B. Hotchkiss to H. G. Hotchkiss, 3/26/1858.

32. Cornell: Letter from L. B. Hotchkiss to H. G. Hotchkiss, 5/15/1585.

33. Cornell: Letter from L. B. Hotchkiss to H. G. Hotchkiss, 5/17/1858.

34. Cornell: Letter from L. B. Hotchkiss to H. G. Hotchkiss, 7/16/1858.

35. Cornell: Letter from L. B. Hotchkiss to H. G. Hotchkiss, 8/17/1858.

36. Cornell: Letter from Calvin Hotchkiss to H. G. Hotchkiss, 9/27/1858.

37. Cornell: Letter from H. G. Hotchkiss to L. B. Hotchkiss, 11/3/1858.

38. Cornell: Letter from L. B. Hotchkiss to H. G. Hotchkiss, 11/5/1858.

39. Cornell: Letter from L. B. Hotchkiss to H. G. Hotchkiss, 11/22/1858.

40. Cornell: Letter from H. G. Hotchkiss to L. B. Hotchkiss, 11/24/1858.

41. Cornell: Letter from L. B. Hotchkiss to H. G. Hotchkiss, 12/21/1858.

42. Cornell: Letter from H. G. Hotchkiss to L. B. Hotchkiss, 12/25/1858.

43. Cornell: Letter from L. B. Hotchkiss to H. G. Hotchkiss, 2/5/1859.

44. Cornell: Letter from L. B. Hotchkiss to H. G. Hotchkiss, 2/9/1859.

45. Cornell: Letter from Calvin Hotchkiss to H. G. Hotchkiss, 2/21/1859.

46. Cornell: Letter from H. G. Hotchkiss to L. B. Hotchkiss, 2/24/1859.

47. Cornell: Letter from L. B. Hotchkiss to H. G. Hotchkiss, 3/2/1859.

48. Cornell: Letter from Calvin Hotchkiss to H. G. Hotchkiss, 3/7/1859.

49. Cornell: Letter from L. B. Hotchkiss to H. G. Hotchkiss, 3/16/1859.

50. Cornell: Letter from L. B. Hotchkiss to H. G. Hotchkiss, 4/6/1859.

51. Cornell: Letter from L. B. Hotchkiss to H. G. Hotchkiss, 6/16/1859.

52. Cornell: Letter from H. G. Hotchkiss to L. B. Hotchkiss, 11/2/1859.

53. Cornell: Letter from H. G. Hotchkiss to L. B. Hotchkiss, 11/28/1859.

54. Cornell: Letter from H. G. Hotchkiss to L. B. Hotchkiss, 11/29/1859.

55. Cornell: Letter from L. B. Hotchkiss to H. G. Hotchkiss, 1/9/1860.

56. Cornell: Letter from L. B. Hotchkiss to H. G. Hotchkiss, 7/6/1860.

57. Cornell: Letter from H. G. Hotchkiss to L. B. Hotchkiss, 7/7/1860.

58. Cornell: Letter from P. C. Wells to H. G. Hotchkiss, 8/16/1860.

59. Cornell: Letter from P. C. Wells to H. G. Hotchkiss, 8/21/1860.

60. Cornell: Letter from P. C. Wells to H. G. Hotchkiss, 8/22/1860.

61. Cornell: Letter from H. G. Hotchkiss to L. B. Hotchkiss, 8/27/1860.

62. Cornell: Letter from L. B. Hotchkiss to H. G. Hotchkiss, 8/29/1860.

63. Cornell: Letter from H. G. Hotchkiss to L. B. Hotchkiss, 8/30/1860.

64. Cornell: Letter from P. C. Wells to H. G. Hotchkiss, 8/30/1860.

65. Cornell: Letter from H. G. Hotchkiss to P. C. Wells, 9/1/1860.

66. Cornell: Letter from H. G. Hotchkiss to P. C. Wells, 9/13/1860.

67. Cornell: Letter from Calvin Hotchkiss to H. G. Hotchkiss, 9/27/1858.

68. Cornell: Letter from H. G. Hotchkiss to P. C. Wells, 9/15/1860.

69. Cornell: Letter from P. C. Wells to H. G. Hotchkiss, 9/16/1860.

70. Cornell: Letter from P. C. Wells to H. G. Hotchkiss, 9/17/1860.

71. Cornell: Letter from P. C. Wells to H. G. Hotchkiss, 9/20/1860.

72. Cornell: Letter from H. G. Hotchkiss to P. C. Wells, 9/27/1860.

73. Cornell: Letter from H. G. Hotchkiss to P. C. Wells, 10/2/1860.

74. Cornell: Agreement between L. B. Hotchkiss and H. G. Hotchkiss, 10/3/1860.

75. Cornell: Letter from H. G. Hotchkiss to L. B. Hotchkiss, 8/27/1860.

76. Cornell: Letter from L. B. Hotchkiss to H. G. Hotchkiss, 1/9/1860.

77. Cornell: Letter from L. B. Hotchkiss to H. G. Hotchkiss, 1/9/1860.

78. Cornell: Letter from L. B. Hotchkiss to H. G. Hotchkiss, 1/9/1860.

79. Cornell: Letter from H. G. Hotchkiss to L. B. Hotchkiss, 8/27/1860.

80. Cornell: Letter from L. B. Hotchkiss to H. G. Hotchkiss, 1/9/1860.

81. Cornell: Agreement between L. B. Hotchkiss and H. G. Hotchkiss, 10/3/1860.

82. Cornell: Letter from Calvin Hotchkiss, to H. G. Hotchkiss, 4/24/1862.

83. Cornell: Letter from H. G. Hotchkiss to George C. Hotchkiss, 11/12/1864.

84. Cornell: Letter from George C. Hotchkiss to H. G. Hotchkiss, 11/19/1864.

85. Cornell: Letter from H. G. Hotchkiss to George C. Hotchkiss, 11/21/1864.

86. Cornell: Letter from Mary Hotchkiss to H. G. Hotchkiss, undated, regarding "Outrage."

87. Cornell: Letter from H. G. Hotchkiss to George C. Hotchkiss, 11/24/1864.

88. Cornell: Letter from P. C. Wells to H. G. Hotchkiss, 12/2/1864.

89. Cornell: Letter from H. G. Hotchkiss to P. C. Wells, 12/7/1864.

90. Cornell: Letter from L. B. Hotchkiss to H. G. Hotchkiss, 5/29/1865.

91. Cornell: Letter from L. B. Hotchkiss to Chad Hotchkiss, 7/12/1866.

92. Cornell: Letter from Mary Hotchkiss to H. G. Hotchkiss, undated, regarding "Breakfasts."

93. Cornell: Letter from Mary Hotchkiss to H. G. Hotchkiss, undated, regarding "Money for Leman."

94. Cornell: Letter from Mary Hotchkiss to H. G. Hotchkiss, undated, regarding "Treat Chad Better."

95. Cornell: Letter from Mary Hotchkiss to H. G. Hotchkiss, undated, regarding "Vexed."

96. Cornell: Letter from Horner and Quetting to H. G. Hotchkiss, 2/24/1874.

97. Cornell: Letter from L. B. Hotchkiss to H. G. Hotchkiss, 4/11/1874.

98. Cornell: Letter from L. B. Hotchkiss to H. G. Hotchkiss, 4/16/1874.

99. Cornell: Letter from L. B. Hotchkiss to H. G. Hotchkiss, 4/23/1874.

100. Cornell: Letter from Cal Hotchkiss to H. G. Hotchkiss, 4/25/1874.

101. Cornell: Letter from Leman Hotchkiss to H. G. Hotchkiss, 1/9/1860.

102. Cornell: Letter from Leman Hotchkiss to H. G. Hotchkiss, 1/9/1860.

103. Cornell: Letter from Leman Hotchkiss to H. G. Hotchkiss, 1/9/1860.

104. Cornell: Letter from Mary Hotchkiss to H. G. Hotchkiss, 7/1/1874.

105. Cornell: Letter from Cal Hotchkiss to H. G. Hotchkiss, 7/20/1874.

106. Cornell: Letter from Leman Hotchkiss to H. G. Hotchkiss, 7/22/1874.

107. Cornell: Letter from Mary Hotchkiss to H. G. Hotchkiss, 7/26/1874.

108. Cornell: Letter from George C. Hotchkiss to H. G. Hotchkiss, 9/29/1874.

109. Cornell: Letter from H. G. Hotchkiss to George C. Hotchkiss, 10/5/1874.

110. Cornell: Letter from George C. Hotchkiss to H. G. Hotchkiss, 11/6/1874.

111. Harvard: R. G. Dun credit report, 10/12/1877.

112. Cornell: Letter from George C. Hotchkiss to H. G. Hotchkiss, 3/12/1877.

113. Cornell: Letter from H. G. Hotchkiss to George C. Hotchkiss, 4/11/1877.

114. Harvard: R. G. Dun credit report, 12/7/1887.

115. Cornell: Letter from H. G. Hotchkiss to George C. Hotchkiss, 7/17/1888.

116. Harvard: R. G. Dun credit report, 2/9/1889.

117. Cornell: Letter from Cal Hotchkiss to H. G. Hotchkiss, 4/1/1895.

118. Wayne *Democratic Press*, 11/3/1897.

119. http://essexlabs.com/products.html, accessed 3/15/2019.

EIGHT Crystal White

1. Landing, 36–37.

2. Ibid., 45.

3. Rochester *Daily Union and Advertiser*, 11/18/1862, 2.

4. Oral history provided by Winship Todd and Ian Blair in conversation with the author.

5. A. M. Todd, "Copy of Some Rough Notes Hastily Written at the Request of the Ladies Club of Mendon Describing Some of the Objects in my Art Museum and Library," undated.

6. Sturgis, *Journal*, 3/8/1875.

7. Todd: Letter from A. M. Todd to Oliver Todd, 1/18/1877.

8. Cornell: Letter from H. G. Hotchkiss to Sons, 12/2/1876.

9. Cornell: Letter from H. G. Hotchkiss to Sons, 12/4/1876.

10. Todd: Letter from A. M. Todd to Oliver Todd, 1/18/1877.

11. Todd: Letter from A. M. Todd to H. G. Hotchkiss's Sons, 1/17/1877.

12. Cornell: Letter from H. G. Hotchkiss to Sons, 1/27/1877.

13. Todd: Letter from A. M. Todd to H. G. Hotchkiss's Sons, 12/18/1876.

14. Todd: Letter from A. M. Todd to I. W. re: Cushman, 10/1/1878.

15. Todd: 1920 Peppermint Oil label.

16. Todd: newspaper article, 10/18/1925.

17. Landing, 61.

18. Todd: Patent, 1884.

19. Todd: Trademark, 1884.

20. American Pharmaceutical Association, *General Index to Volumes One to Fifty of the Proceedings of the American Pharmaceutical Association from 1852 to 1902, Inclusive* (Baltimore: The Association, 1886).

21. Todd: Letter regarding election to Congress, 1897.

22. Landing, 59.

23. Todd: Company Statement, 1897.

24. Cornell: Letter from A. P. Emery to H. G. Hutchkiss, 10/18/1894

25. Western Michigan University local history archives. Blotter book of Letters by F. D. Garrison.

26. Todd: Letter from A. M. Todd to James Todd, 1899.

27. "Lost 2,000 Acres of Mint. Crop Will Be Short Says Ex-Congressman Todd," *Grand Rapids Herald,* 1899.

28. Daniel T. Rodgers, *Atlantic Crossings: Social Politics in a Progressive Age* (Cambridge, Mass.: Harvard University Press, 1998), 9, 10.

29. Landing, 59.

30. Todd: Incorporation paperwork, 1901.

31. Todd: Profit Sharing, 1902.

32. Todd: Farm Workers notice, 1901.

33. Conference on Research in Income, *Trends in the American Economy in the Nineteenth Century: A Report of the National Bureau of Economic Research, New York* (Princeton: Princeton University Press, 1960), 462.

34. "Has a Corner in Peppermint," *Charlotte Observer,* 1902.

35. Todd: Outlook, 1901.

36. Ibid.

37. Personal conversation with Winship Todd and Ian Blair, June 15, 2010.

38. Todd: Adulteration, 1902.

39. Todd: Price List, 1902.

40. Todd: Adulteration, 1903.

41. Todd: Outlook, 1903.

42. Todd: Letter from A. M. Todd to James Todd, 1903.

43. Todd: Spring Outlook, 1904.

44. Todd: Fall Outlook, 1904.

45. Todd: Patent, 1906.

46. Todd: newspaper article, 10/5/1908.

47. Todd: Letter from A. M. Todd to Paul Todd, 6/14/1909.

48. Todd: Company Statement, 1908.

49. Todd: Company Statement, 1909.

50. "History of Toothbrushes and Toothpaste," Colgate-Palmolive Company. http://www.colgate.com/en/us/oc/oral-health/basics/brushing-and-flossing/article/history-of-toothbrushes-and-toothpastes, last accessed 9/9/2019.

51. Landing, 77.

52. Kerry Segrave, *Chewing Gum in America, 1850–1920: The Rise of an Industry* (Jefferson, N.C.: McFarland, 2015), 4.

53. Ibid., 22.

54. Ibid., 126.

55. Todd: Note about American Chicle, 1910.

56. Todd: Letter from Bert Todd to Mother, 1913.

57. Todd: Letter from A. M. Todd to Bert regarding Mentha, 1913.

58. Todd: Letter from A. M. Todd to Bert regarding Mentha, 1913.

59. Todd: Letter denying trademark, 1917.

60. Todd: Letter from Chemist re: USP, 1915.

61. Landing, 78–79.

62. Todd: Company Statement, 1917.

63. "Oregon Ships Peppermint Willamette Valley Growers Get $1.55 on 4000 Pounds of Oil," *Oregonian*, 1916.

64. Todd: 1920 Peppermint Oil label.

65. Ibid.

66. Todd: Undated note to Norris.

67. Todd: Letter from A. M. Todd to Children, 3/9/1920.

68. Todd: Letter from A. M. Todd to Children, 3/15/1920.

69. Todd: Note on Stroud, 1930.

70. Todd: Wrigley Agreement, 1920.

71. Todd: Wrigley Agreement, 1921.

72. Todd: Company Statement, 1921.

73. Todd: Wrigley Spearmint Contract, 1923.

74. Todd: Wattles Agreement, 1923.

75. Todd: George Wattles, 1906.

76. Todd: "Mint in the US" article, 1927.

77. Ibid.

NINE Socialist Capitalist

1. Lewis, 100.

2. Roy Strickland, *An Honor and an Ornament: Public School Buildings in Michigan* (Lansing: Michigan Department of History, Arts and Libraries, 2003).

3. Todd told the story of "The Advent of the Republican Party" in a congressional speech in 1899. Congress, *Congressional Record: Vols. 30–32, Proceedings and Debates of the 55th Congress, Session/United States of America, Congress* (Washington, D.C.: Government Printing Office, 1897), 2482; Carl C. Taylor, *The Farmers' Movement, 1620–1920* (Westport, Conn.: Greenwood Press, 1971), 187.

4. *History of St. Joseph County, Michigan: With Illustrations Descriptive of Its Scenery, Palatial Residences, Public Buildings, Fine Blocks and Important Manufactories, from Original Sketches by Artists of the Highest Ability* (La Crosse, Wis.: Brookhaven Press, 1999), 76.

5. Rodgers, 319.

6. Ibid., 148.

7. *Congressional Record*, 2482.

8. Peter H. Argersinger, ' "A Place on the Ballot': Fusion Politics and Antifusion Laws," *American Historical Review* 85, no. 2 (1980), 288.

9. Ibid., 296.

10. Lewis, 371; Heather Cox Richardson, *Wounded Knee: Party Politics and the Road to an American Massacre* (New York: Basic Books, 2010), 301.

11. *New York Times*, 3/25/1895.

12. Todd: Letter to Friends and Patrons, 1896.

13. *Congressional Record*, 154.

14. Ibid., 841.

15. Ibid., 339, 343.

16. M. Elizabeth Sanders, *Roots of Reform: Farmers, Workers, and the American State, 1877–1917* (Chicago: University of Chicago Press, 1999), 219.

17. *Congressional Record*, appendix, 330.

18. Ibid., appendix, 325.

19. Landing, 93–94.

20. *Congressional Record*, 328.

21. Ibid., 169.

22. Ibid., 172.

23. Ibid., 2301.

24. A. M. Todd papers. List of organizations receiving regular membership dues, Todd ledger book.

25. *Congressional Record*, 2991.

26. Ibid., 3401.

27. Ibid., 4503–4.

28. Ibid., 4524.

29. Ibid., 4821–24.

30. Ibid. 4883.

31. Quoted in *Chicago Tribune*, 12/8/1898, 12.

32. *Ticket Brokerage Hearings Had on December 16, 1897, January 6 and 7, 1898, and January 15, 1898, before the Committee on Interstate Commerce of the United States Senate on the Bill (S. 1575) to Amend an Act Entitled "an Act to Regulate Commerce."* 382 P. O (U.S.A. 55th Congress, 2d Session, Senate. Document No. 128, 1898), 218.

33. *Congressional Record*, appendix, 3–17.

34. A. J. Halford, *Official Congressional Directory for the Use of the United States Congress, . . . Compiled . . . By A. J. Halford. 56th Congress, 2d Session, 2d Edition* (Washington, D.C.: Government Printing Office, 1901), 50.

35. *Congressional Record*, 6184.

36. Ibid., 1216.

37. Ibid., 2840.

38. "Against the Trusts Temporary Organization Is Effected at Chicago," *Duluth News-Tribune*, 1899; "Will Be Largely Attended Conference at Chicago to Discuss Questions of Trusts," *Omaha World Herald*, 1899.

39. "Mr. Todd Will Not Run," *Grand Rapids Herald,* 1900.

40. "Socialists to Start a College. Leader, It Is Said, Will Organize a School of Appiled Christianity," *New Haven Register,* 1900.

41. Edward T. James et al., *Notable American Women, 1607–1950: A Biographical Dictionary* (Cambridge, Mass.: Harvard University Press, 1971), 112–13, 482.

42. Todd: *Chemist and Druggist* article, 1903.

43. "Todd's Little Ticket," *Wilkes-Barre Times,* 1913.

44. Albert May Todd, *Municipal Ownership, with a Special Survey of Municipal Gas Plants in America and Europe; Comprising a View of the General Principles of Public Ownership; Its Relation to the Public Welfare: With a Special Study of Gas Works in American and European Cities under Both Public and Private Ownership; a Comparison of Efficiency, Costs, and Rates of Charge; and the Influence of Public Ownership on General Prosperity, Good Government and Democracy* (Chicago: Public Ownership League of America, 1918), 64–6, 73.

45. Todd: Account Book of investments, 1914.

46. Todd, *Municipal Ownership.*

47. Carl D. Thompson, "The Public Ownership League of America," *Washington Times,* 10/8/1918.

48. Alfred M. Todd, *Public Ownership of Railroads,* 65th Congress, 3rd Session, ed. Interstate Commerce Committee (Washington, D.C.: Government Printing Office, 1919), 4.

49. Ibid., 6.

50. Todd, *Municipal Ownership,* 43.

51. Science Rand School of Social, *The Case of the Rand School* (New York City: The School, 1919), 1.

52. Albert M. Todd, "Relation of Public Ownership to Democracy and Social Justice," *Proceedings of the Academy of Political Science in the City of New York* 8, no. 4 (1920), 731.

53. Ibid., 732–33.

54. Original italics, ibid., 735.

55. Ibid., 738.

56. Original italics, ibid., 750.

57. Ibid., 751–52.

58. Ibid., 759.

59. Todd: Letter from A. M. Todd to Jane Addams, 5/7/1921.

60. Todd: Letter from A. M. Todd to Jane Addams, 5/27/1921.

61. Morgan admitted in his will that he had neglected to make these arrangements. Quoted in Rachel Cohen, "J. P. Morgan: The Man Who Bought the World," *Apollo: The International Art Magazine* (September 5, 2015).

62. Todd: Norris notes.

63. Todd: Letter from A. M. Todd to Oliver Todd, 1/18/1877.

64. Todd: Ian Blair article on A. M. Todd art collection.

65. Charles Postel, *The Populist Vision* (Oxford: New York, 2007), vii.

66. Ibid., 288.

67. Sanders, 56.

TEN Global Peppermint

1. "Woman Farmer's Success. Miss Mary Clark of Michigan Does All the Work on 80 Acres," *Kansas City Star*, 1905.

2. "Girl Runs Peppermint Farm," *Kansas City Star*, 1906.

3. "Wealth for Women on Peppermint Farms," *Philadelphia Inquirer*, 1912.

4. Horace Curzon Plunkett, *The Rural Life Problem of the United States: Notes of an Irish Observer* (New York: Macmillan, 1910).

5. Ibid., 111.

6. Ibid., 115.

7. Ibid., 123.

8. Ibid., 125.

9. Todd: Notes from 1936 FTC Investigation.

10. Landing, 126.

11. Ibid., 127.

12. "Peppermint Fields Offer Jobs," *New York Times*, 10/10/1937.

13. Todd: Notes on Britain, 1938.

14. N. K. Ellis and E. C. Stevenson, "Domestic Production of the Essential Oils of Peppermint and Spearmint," *Economic Botany* 4, no. 2 (1950), 148.

15. "Peppermint Oil Prices Jump $1 a Pound Here," *Wall Street Journal*, 12/17/1941.

16. "Vick Chemical Orders Peppermint Extract Menthol," *Wall Street Journal*, 3/26/1942.

17. "Oil of Peppermint Prices," *Wall Street Journal*, 1/6/1942.

18. Landing, 139.

19. Ibid., 141.

20. Ellis and Stevenson, 139.

21. Ibid., 141.

22. Landing, 178.

23. Ralph; Cheri Janssen; Fred Whitford; Steve Weller Green, *Mint Production and Pest Management in Indiana* (West Lafayette, Ind.: Purdue University Cooperative Extension Service, 2004).

24. Landing, 150.

25. Ibid., 184.

26. Ibid., 175.

27. N. K. Ellis, "Peppermint and Spearmint Production," *Economic Botany* 14, no. 4 (1960), http://www.jstor.org/stable/4252193, last accessed 9/9/2019, 284.

28. Landing, 179.

29. Gordon Enoch Patty, *U.S. Mint Oil in the European Market* (Washington, D.C.: Foreign Agricultural Service, 1972), 4.

30. Landing, 151.

31. Ellis, 280.

32. Landing, 178.

33. Ellis, 281.

34. Landing, 183.

35. Xiaohuan Wang et al., "Highly Efficient in Vitro Adventitious Shoot Regeneration of Peppermint (Mentha X Piperita L.) Using Internodal Explants," *In Vitro Cellular and Developmental Biology: Plant* 45, no. 4 (2009), http://www.jstor.org/stable/20541049.435, last accessed 9/9/2019.

36. Patty, 4.

37. Ibid., 6.

38. Ibid., 14.

39. Ibid., 7.

40. Winship Todd, personal conversation, June 15, 2010.

41. M. Morris and E. Robbins, "Mint Landscape: From Field to Flavor," *Perfumer and Flavorist* 30, no. 4 (2005), 47

42. Wendy F. Marley and Edward G. Thomas, "The Plant-Derived Chemicals Marketplace," *Business Economics* 34, no. 4 (1999), http://www.jstor.org/stable/23488143, 63–66, last accessed 9/9/2019.

43. "Happy Anniversary—a Matter of Taste: From Pepprmint King to Beyond," *Perfumer and Flavorist*, May 2005, 29.

44. Morris and Robbins. 50.

45. Ibid. 49.

46. Bernd Markus Lange et al., "Improving Peppermint Essential Oil Yield and Composition by Metabolic Engineering," *Proceedings of the National Academy of Sciences of the United States of America* 108, no. 41 (2011), http://www.jstor.org/stable/41321813. 16947–8.

47. "2016 Flavor & Fragrance Leaderboard an Exclusive Look at the Top Companies' Financial Reports, Sustainability Strategies, R&D Initiatives, M&A Activity and More," *Perfumer and Flavorist* 41, no. 7 (2016).

48. 2017 WILD Flavors and Specialty Ingredients, https://www.wildflavors.com/NA-EN/products/mint-oils-extracts/, last accessed 9/9/2019.

49. Jenny Ann Mikulski, "Mint in the Mucklands: Imagining the 19th Century Peppermint Industry in Lyons, NY," master's thesis, Cornell University, 2007, 40ff.

50. Ibid., 29; personal correspondence with Jenny Mikulski.

51. http://www.essexlabs.com/products.html, accessed 3/13/2019.

ELEVEN Epilogue

1. Robert P. Swierenga, "The New Rural History: Defining the Parameters," *Great Plains Quarterly* 1, no. 4 (Fall 1981), 211.

2. David B. Danbom, *Born in the Country: A History of Rural America* (Baltimore: Johns Hopkins University Press, 1995), xiii.

3. David B. Danbom, "Reflections: Whither Agricultural History?" *Agricultural History* 84, no. 2 (Spring 2010), 173.

Index